DATE DUE			

Insect Juvenile Hormones

Chemistry and Action

Proceedings of a Symposium on
The Chemistry and Action of Insect Juvenile Hormones
Held in Washington, D. C., September 12-17, 1971
Sponsored by The Division of Pesticide Chemistry
of The American Chemical Society

Insect Juvenile Hormones

Chemistry and Action

EDITED BY

Julius J. Menn

Stauffer Chemical Company
Agricultural Research Center
Mountain View, California

Morton Beroza

Entomology Research Division
Agricultural Research Service
USDA
Beltsville, Maryland

ACADEMIC PRESS 1972 New York and London

ACADEMIC PRESS, INC.
111 Fifth Avenue, New York, New York 10003

United Kingdom Edition published by
ACADEMIC PRESS, INC. (LONDON) LTD.
24/28 Oval Road, London NW1

LIBRARY OF CONGRESS CATALOG CARD NUMBER: 72-77363

PRINTED IN THE UNITED STATES OF AMERICA

CONTENTS

Part I. BIOLOGICAL ASPECTS

Part II. BIOCHEMICAL ASPECTS

CONTENTS

vi

CONTRIBUTORS

R. W. Bagley, Chemical Research Department, Hoffmann-La Roche Inc., Nutley, New Jersey 07110

J. C. Bauernfeind, Chemical Research Department, Hoffmann-La Roche Inc., Nutley, New Jersey 07110

M. Beroza, Agricultural Research Service, U. S. Department of Agriculture, Beltsville, Maryland 20705

D. L. Bull, Agricultural Research Service, U. S. Department of Agriculture, College Station, Texas 77840

H. R. Bullock, Agricultural Research Service, U. S. Department of Agriculture, Baton Rouge, Louisiana 70803

John E. Casida, Division of Entomology, University of California, Berkeley, California 94720

W. F. Chamberlain, Agricultural Research Service, U. S. Department of Agriculture, Kerrville, Texas 78028

Sarjeet S. Gill, Division of Entomology, University of California, Berkeley, California 94720

Bruce D. Hammock, Division of Entomology, University of California, Berkeley, California 94720

Joseph Ilan, Department of Anatomy and Developmental Biology Center, Case Western Reserve University, School of Medicine, Cleveland, Ohio 44106

Judith Ilan, Department of Anatomy and Developmental Biology Center, Case Western Reserve University, School of Medicine, Cleveland, Ohio 44106

M. Jacobson, Agricultural Research Service, U. S. Department of Agriculture, Beltsville, Maryland 20705

CONTRIBUTORS

Fotis C. Kafatos, The Biological Laboratories, Harvard University,
Cambridge, Massachusetts 02138

Patrick M. McCurry, Jr., Department of Chemistry, Carnegie-Mellon
University, Pittsburgh, Pennsylvania 15213

T. P. McGovern, Agricultural Research Service, U. S. Department of
Agriculture, Beltsville, Maryland 20705

Julius J. Menn, Agricultural Research Center, Stauffer Chemical Company,
Mountain View, California 94040

Andre S. Meyer, Department of Biology, Case Western Reserve University,
Cleveland, Ohio 44106

Ferenc M. Pallos, Western Research Center, Stauffer Chemical Company,
Richmond, California 94804

Narayan G. Patel, Central Research Department, Experimental Station,
E. I. duPont de Nemours and Co., Wilmington, Delaware 19898

B. A. Pawson, Hoffman-La Roche Inc., Nutley, New Jersey 07110

R. E. Redfern, Agricultural Research Service, U. S. Department of
Agriculture, Beltsville, Maryland 20705

Lynn M. Riddiford, The Biological Laboratories, Harvard University,
Cambridge, Massachusetts 02138

R. Sarmiento, Agricultural Research Service, U. S. Department of
Agriculture, Beltsville, Maryland 20705

F. Scheidl, Hoffmann-La Roche Inc., Nutley, New Jersey 07110

Howard A. Schneiderman, Center for Pathobiology and Developmental
Biology Laboratory, University of California, Irvine, California 92664

M. Schwarz, Agricultural Research Service, U. S. Department of
Agriculture, Beltsville, Maryland 20705

*Michael Slade,** Zoëcon Corporation, Research Laboratories, Palo Alto,
California 94304

P. E. Sonnet, Agricultural Research Service, U. S. Department of
Agriculture, Beltsville, Maryland 20705

*Present Address: 127-20th Ave., San Francisco, California 94121

Gerardus B. Staal, Zoëcon Corporation, Research Laboratories, Palo Alto, California 94304

Barry M. Trost, Department of Chemistry, University of Wisconsin, Madison, Wisconsin 53706

F. Vane, Hoffmann-La Roche Inc., Nutley, New Jersey 07110

N. Wakabayashi, Agricultural Research Service, U. S. Department of Agriculture, Beltsville, Maryland 20705

R. M. Waters, Agricultural Research Service, U. S. Department of Agriculture, Beltsville, Maryland 20705

Carroll M. Williams, The Biological Laboratories, Harvard University, Cambridge, Massachusetts 02138

J. E. Wright, Agricultural Research Service, U. S. Department of Agriculture, College Station, Texas 77840

*Izuru Yamamoto,** Division of Entomology, University of California, Berkeley, California 94720

Charles H. Zibitt, Zoëcon Corporation, Research Laboratories, Palo Alto, California 94304

*Present Address: Department of Agricultural Chemistry, Tokyo University of Agriculture, Setagaya, Tokyo, Japan

PREFACE

Although insecticides are invaluable in suppressing damage to our agricultural products and to the health of man and animals, they are not without side effects on the environment and its biota. Pressure to find alternatives that do not depend on toxic agents have spurred scientists to delve into the biological and biochemical transformations within the insect system in search of an "Achilles heel." The discovery of the juvenile hormone, a vital growth-regulating chemical in insect metamorphosis, and of chemicals with similar properties has raised hopes, originally advanced by Professor Carroll Williams in 1956, that the normal growth patterns of insects could be upset with these chemicals, thereby preventing their survival. The approach has considerable appeal because the hormones (and synthetic analogs), while having a powerful effect on insect development, do not appear to have adverse effects on most other life forms. The environmental impact of the use of chemicals of this kind is therefore expected to be negligible.

This book attests to the intense vigor and interdisciplinary activity with which juvenile hormone chemistry, biochemistry, and biology are currently being pursued. It brings together in one volume the latest and most complete survey of knowledge on juvenile hormones and analogs to date. Subject matter ranges from theoretical discussions contributed by some of our most distinguished scientists and thinkers to down-to-earth laboratory and field trials of insect development regulating chemicals found active by empirical laboratory tests. Its contents will interest chemists, biochemists, biologists, endocrinologists, entomologists, insect physiologists, and others concerned with insect development and control.

To speed publication contributors furnished camera copy of their manuscripts for direct reproduction. This procedure has led to some overlap in the presentations and some variations in format. The reader may also note some differences in opinion, apparent contradictions, and inconsistencies in nomenclature among the presentations, but such discrepancies may be considered normal at this early stage of knowledge. Indeed, it is hoped that such divergence will pinpoint problem areas requiring attention in the future.

The book is not meant to be exhaustive, but one that will brief scientists on current thinking and methodology in the field, as well as provide references to prior work. Hopefully it will acquaint scientists with studies outside their own areas of specialization and catalyze interdisciplinary joint ventures which are necessary to achieve maximum progress toward the development of safer means for suppression of undesirable insects.

Julius J. Menn
Morton Beroza

INTRODUCTION

A major objective in recent efforts to improve the quality of our environment has been the development of means of insect control more selective in action than the broad-spectrum insecticides, which in some instances have been implicated in detrimental side effects on nontarget organisms and on the ecosystem. Among the approaches being explored are biological control with parasites and predators, microbial and viral insecticides, chemosterilants, resistant varieties of crops and breeds of animals, improved tillage practices, crop rotation, electromagnetic energy, repellents, attractants, and antifeedants.

One approach that has captured the imagination of many scientists is the possibility of controlling insect pests by causing derangement of their growth processes with their own hormones or related compounds, more specifically with the juvenile hormones (JH), their analogs (JHA), and other JH-active chemicals (also referred to as JHA).

At the Symposium on the Chemistry and Action of Insect Juvenile Hormones, sponsored by the Division of Pesticide Chemistry of the American Chemical Society at the 162nd National Meeting of the Society in Washington, D. C., September 12-17, 1971, eminent scientists drawn from a variety of disciplines and representing universities, government, and industry were invited to present and discuss their latest findings in the field of JH and JHA chemistry and biology. This volume is the outgrowth of their presentations and deliberations; it summarizes what is known about JH and their analogs, their chemistry, their biological effects and mode of action, their biochemical fate in target and nontarget organisms, and their stability. Although divided into three general areas for convenience—biological, biochemical, and chemical—the book in its entirety is a multidisciplinary discourse, a foundation upon which our understanding of the action or inaction of JH and JHA may be based which hopefully will provide a springboard for future direction and research.

Insect endocrinology, which includes JH research, has fascinated researchers since the pioneering studies of Sir Vincent Wigglesworth in the mid-1930's showed that the molting and metamorphosis of *Rhodnius prolixus* nymphs were regulated by hormones. The possibility that juvenile hormones and synthetic analogs had practical potential in managing insect populations was first recognized by Professor Carroll Williams in 1956. Following his discovery that the abdomen of the adult male of *Hyalophora cecropia* was a rich source of JH, he proposed JH-active substances as powerful "third generation" insect control agents.

In subsequent years, a remarkable proliferation of scientific discoveries occurred in this field. In 1967, Professor H. Röller and his co-workers at the University of Wisconsin scored a major breakthrough in their identification of the major JH in *H. cecropia* as methyl *trans, trans, cis*-10,11-epoxy-7-ethyl-3,11-dimethyl-2,6-tridecadienoate. This discovery was followed by the identification of the 7-methyl analog as another natural juvenile hormone. Many synthetic terpenoid derivatives were synthesized and shown to exert on insects varying degrees of morphogenetic, gametogenic, and diapause-disrupting activity.

Two events greatly stimulated these synthetic efforts. The first was the discovery of the extraordinary morphogenetic activity of the "paper factor" on the linden bug, *Pyrrhocoris apterus,* by Drs. Karel Slama and Carroll Williams in 1965, leading to the subsequent identification of this factor as the methyl ester of todomatuic acid or "juvabione" by Dr. W. S. Bowers and his co-workers. The second breakthrough occurred when Dr. Bowers found simple terpene derivatives other than those of farnesol to be highly active JHA. The significance of the latter discovery was augmented by the fact that these JHA had activity on a variety of insect species. These discoveries provided many new leads for synthesis of additional JHA.

The growing interest in recent years in insect juvenile hormones is well documented by the proliferation of literature on this subject. The number of papers cited in five reviews appearing between 1968 and 1971 on the subject of JH and JHA were 52 (1968), 50 (1969), 96 (1970), 134 (1970), and 172 (1971). At this rate, publications dealing with JH research could number over 1000 by 1975.

While great strides have been made in elucidating the chemistry and biological activity of JH and JHA, our understanding of the mode of action of JH at the subcellular level is still embryonic. The status of our knowledge in this field and the best current theories on the mode of action are presented here.

Metabolic studies with JH and JHA, another previously unexplored area of research, receive detailed treatment in this volume. Knowledge and information in this area are vital prerequisites to the launching of extensive development programs in which large amounts of JH or JHA are to be released into the environment. Understanding of the biotransformation steps and identification of products of JH and JHA metabolism in target and non-target organisms will help predict the impact and ultimate disposition of these products in the total environment.

Finally, pilot field trials with JHA have been promising enough to consider the practical use of JHA as selective, nonpersistent, and effective chemical agents for the safe management of at least some insect species that destroy food and fiber crops or threaten the health and well-being of man and animals. Prospects for the application of JHA as part of integrated control programs are also encouraging.

Julius J. Menn
Morton Beroza

PART I
BIOLOGICAL ASPECTS

INSECT HORMONES AND INSECT CONTROL

Howard A. Schneiderman

Center for Pathobiology and
Developmental Biology Laboratory
University of California
Irvine, California 92664

Introduction

For each human being on earth there are 300,000,000 insects. Along with their marine relatives, the crustaceans, they constitute most of the animal biomass of our planet. Fortunately most insects are benign or beneficial and only a small minority--fewer than 1 per cent of the species--are in direct competition with human beings for food or are vectors of human disease. But because of the vastness of their numbers and their devastating efficiency, tempered by 400,000,000 years of natural selection, they are mankind's greatest competitors. Without continued vigilance against insect pests, man faces world famine and disease. Indeed even with our present efforts at food production, more than half of our fellow men are hungry most of the time.

In recent years many well-established methods of insect control have come under increasing assault because of their undesirable effects on the environment. A new approach which has captured world-wide attention is the use of analogues and antagonists of insect growth regulators such as juvenile hormones and ecdysones to control pest populations. Should this approach prove feasible, then insect growth regulators may replace some of the compounds now used for pest control which have unwanted ecological side effects or high toxicity to mammals. Hopefully they could become key parts of the network of integrated controls we are establishing to aid us in our never-ending competition with other species for food.

This chapter introduces the principal hormones that insects use to regulate their development and it considers the effects, biological assays and mechanism of action of these hormones. It also explores certain features of insect hormone action which must be understood if insect growth regulators are to be used as agents of pest and vector control, such as: when in the life history of an insect these agents should be applied to kill or sterilize insects; whether one can expect them to have a broad or narrow spectrum of insect targets; what organisms besides insects may be affected by insect hormones; and whether the development of resistance is to be expected.

1. Three major insect hormones.

The growth and molting of immature insects is regulated by three main groups of hormones (1, 2). The brain hormones (which are probably polypeptides (3, 4) are secreted by neurosecretory cells in the protocerebrum and activate the prothoracic glands. It has been generally assumed that the activated prothoracic glands secrete one or several closely related steroids, the ecdysones (1, 5, 6, 7), although this has not yet been proven (8). But it is known with certainty that the prothoracic glands secrete either ecdysones or something necessary for the production of ecdysones, perhaps an ecdysone glycoside (9). Soon after the prothoracic glands are activated, ecdysones appear in the insect's body and these ecdysones or their metabolic products cause the insect to molt.

The kind of cuticle secreted by the epidermal cells at each molt is affected by a third group of hormones secreted by the corpora allata (10), the juvenile hormones (which are almost, but not quite sesquiterpenoids). As long as juvenile hormones are secreted, larvae molt into larvae. However at the end of the last larval instar, internal physiological mechanisms (both neural and humoral) turn off the corpora allata and juvenile hormone concentration falls rapidly. In the absence of juvenile hormones, the larvae of exopterygote insects such as Rhodnius metamorphose into adults, and the larvae of endopterygote insects such as the Cecropia moth, Tenebrio and Drosophila, molt into pupae and then into adults. When larval epidermal cells are stimulated by ecdysone, in the presence of high concentrations of juvenile hormone, they secrete a larval cuticle, whereas in the presence of low concentrations of juvenile hormones or in the absence of juvenile hormones, they secrete a pupal or adult cuticle. Molting is controlled by regulating the release of brain hormone. Maturation and metamorphosis are controlled by regulating the release of juvenile hormones. In simplest terms, the ecdysones stimulate the synthetic activities necessary for molting, whereas juvenile hormones influence the kinds of synthetic activities that occur in response to the ecdysones.

From this account it becomes clear that juvenile hormones are the handmaidens to the ecdysones. In their effects on morphogenesis, juvenile hormones act only in concert with the ecdysones. There is a common misconception that juvenile hormones and ecdysones act antagonistically. This idea probably arose from the fact that metamorphosis requires ecdysones and can be blocked by juvenile hormones. However, larval molting requires both juvenile hormones and ecdysones. There is no evidence that these two groups of hormones act antagonistically. Since it is necessary to understand how ecdysones act in order to analyze the effects of juvenile hormones on development, we shall examine the ecdysones first.

2. <u>Ecdysones--effects and assays.</u>

Insects use alpha ecdysone, its 20-hydroxy derivative beta ecdysone (11, 12), and perhaps other ecdysones (13) as molting hormones (Fig. 1). Alpha ecdysone is efficiently converted to beta ecdysone by certain tissues such as the fat body (14) and beta ecdysone alone can induce molting. Whether the different ecdysones play distinct biological roles in molting as first proposed by Oberlander (15, 16) is not yet clear. In the molting process the epidermal cells detach from the old cuticle by a process called apolysis, secrete a new cuticle and a molting fluid which digests the inner layers of the old cuticle, and reabsorb the products of digestion. After reabsorption, the

5

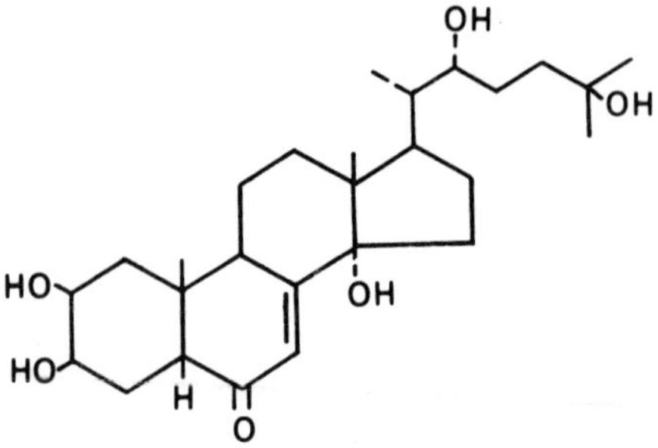

alpha-ECDYSONE

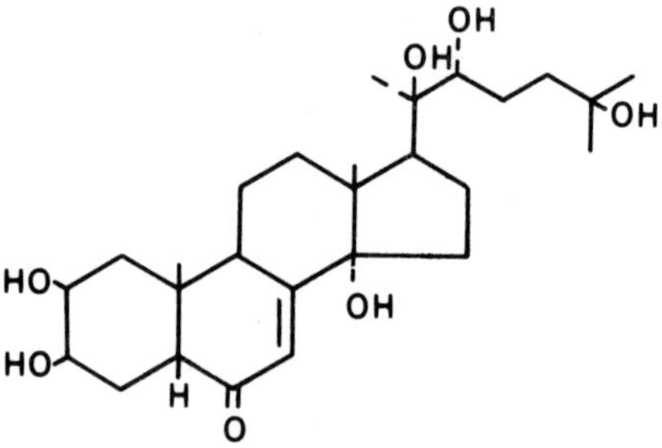

beta-ECDYSONE

Fig. 1.   Structural formulas of alpha ecdysone and beta ecdysone.

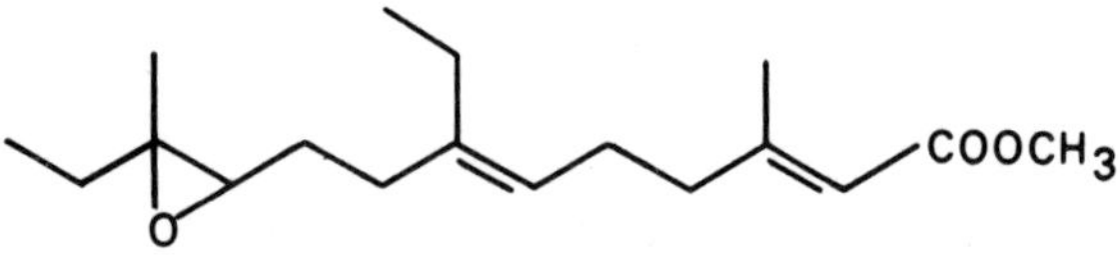

J.H.-1

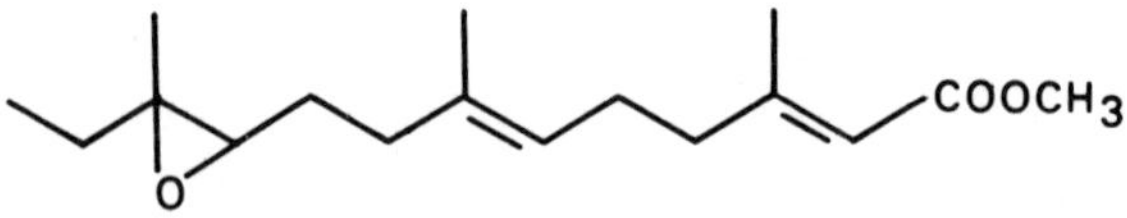

J.H.-2

Fig. 2.   Structural formulas of the two natural juvenile hormones of the Cecropia silkworm.

6

insect sheds the old cuticle by a process termed ecdysis.
After apolysis the epidermal cells may divide. These
cell divisions are essential for growth and metamorphosis
but are not necessary for molting. It has been assumed
that ecdysone functions only in post-embryonic development
(1). However the recent demonstration that ecdysones are
present in young embryos of the silkworm <u>Bombyx mori</u>
(17) suggests an essential role for ecdysones in embryonic
development.

Biological assays for ecdysone provide a useful
picture of its effects on various insects. The substance
to be tested is injected into an isolated fragment
of an insect which is devoid of major endocrine glands
(usually an isolated abdomen) (6, 18) or by dipping
the isolated fragment into a methanolic or ethanolic
solution of an ecdysone for a few seconds (19). If
the abdomen molts or forms a puparium, then the material
has ecdysone activity. The most sensitive injection
assays employ isolated larval abdomens of the blowfly
<u>Calliphora</u> and can detect about 0.01 micrograms of
ecdysone. Most insects require about 0.5 to 5 micrograms/g
to induce a molt. The dipping assays are more convenient
but usually less sensitive and commonly require solutions
containing 0.1 to 1 mg/ml of an ecdysone (i.e., about
10 to 100 micrograms/g). Excellent results with dipping
have been obtained with isolated abdomens of various
lepidopterous larvae such as the wax moth, <u>Galleria
mellonella</u> (20, 21). An even simpler assay for ecdysone
employs intact pupae of the mealworm, <u>Tenebrio molitor</u>
which are collected within four hours after the larval-
pupal molt. Control pupae dipped for five seconds
into ethanol or methanol without ecdysone, molt in
8 days at 25°C, whereas pupae dipped into a beta ecdysone
solution (5 mg per ml for 5 seconds) secrete a new
cuticle and molt precociously within 48-72 hours (22).

It is of special interest that most insects die
soon after they have been induced to molt by an injection
or topical application of an ecdysone. Alpha ecdysone
appears to be less toxic than the other ecdysones,
perhaps because the insect regulates its rate of conversion
to the active form, beta ecdysone. The cause of ecdysone
toxicity is not hard to find. During a normal molt

cycle, ecdysones are released at a precise rate, and
normal development and molting ensue. Some of the
events of normal development are initiated by low
concentrations of ecdysones and may take several days
to be completed. If the insect is experimentally
exposed to large amounts of ecdysones, or exposed
to ecdysones at an abnormal time, some of these normal
developmental events are by-passed as the epidermal
cells hastily secrete a new and often incomplete cuticle.
Such pathological effects have been termed "hyper-
ecdysonism" (23) and appear to represent the first
example of hyperhormonism in invertebrates. For instance,
when a pupa of the Cynthia silkworm, Samia cynthia,
is exposed to high concentrations of ecdysones, it
may secrete an adult cuticle before all of the cell
divisions necessary for scale formation have been
completed, and give rise to an adult which lacks most
of its scales and soon dies (23). When a lepidopterous
larva is treated with ecdysones soon after a molt,
it often fails to secrete wax and the insect starts
to make a new cuticle before the old one is completed (24).

The most striking abnormalities produced by ecdysones
are juvenile hormone-like effects. These effects
were first reported in pupae of various silkworms (23, 25)
but have since been demonstrated in many other insects.
For example, if a pupa of Tenebrio is injected with
25 micrograms of beta ecdysone it molts into a second
pupa instead of into an adult. The reasons for this
paradoxical juvenilizing effect were made clear by
Krishnakumaran in a number of recent experiments (20, 24).
An autoradiographic study of Tenebrio pupae injected
with tritiated thymidine revealed that the epidermal
cells of normal pupae engaged in extensive DNA synthesis
before they secreted an adult cuticle. In contrast,
the epidermal cells of Tenebrio pupae injected with
25 micrograms of beta ecdysone showed no detectable
DNA synthesis before they secreted a second pupal
cuticle. These data suggest that the large dose of
ecdysone stimulated the pupal epidermal cells to secrete
a second pupal cuticle before the cells had time to
"reprogram" for adult syntheses. Normally, low
concentrations of endogenous ecdysone stimulate DNA
replication and cell division, which are followed by

8

cuticle synthesis and the other events of molting. However, a single injection of a large dose of beta ecdysone stimulates the immediate secretion of a cuticle. Apparently, reprogramming of epidermal cells requires DNA replication (24, 26, 27). A cell that is making larval or pupal cuticle must "clean its genes" before it can make pupal or adult cuticle. If high concentration of ecdysones force epidermal cells to make a new cuticle before they have undergone DNA replication, they make the same old kind of cuticle again (20, 24).

These experiments with Tenebrio also showed that the inhibition of DNA synthesis by the beta ecdysone was not restricted to epidermal cells alone but also occurred in all internal tissues and organs except blood cells and connective tissues (20). A similar inhibition of DNA synthesis in internal tissues by beta ecdysone has also been demonstrated in the crayfish Procambarus (29) (also see section 9). Although the principal effect of beta ecdysone is to induce molting by the epidermis, it apparently has been "captured" during evolution by many other tissues, and coordinates their activities as well (30, 31, 32).

3. Ecdysones--potential insecticidal action.

The fact that exogenous ecdysones usually kill insects raises the question of whether ecdysones may be suitable as insecticides. They affect insects at all stages from newly-hatched larvae to adults. They can be applied topically in various solvents and penetrate the cuticle, and volatile derivatives have been synthesized so that ecdysones can be used as fumigants. Some analogues are effective when fed to insects. Moreover many ecdysones are quite stable. Thanks to the efforts of Robbins and his colleagues at the U.S.D.A. significant progress has been made to develop and test appropriate ecdysone-based compounds as potential agents for insect control. For example, they have presented evidence that certain compounds may act as anti-ecdysones and block molting (33), a result which opens up a whole new area for insecticide development. Efforts are now underway to synthesize ecdysone derivatives which will be translocated by plants. Also, various conjugated ecdysones are being synthesized in an effort to produce ecdysones which the insect cannot break down. Finally, it has been demonstrated by Robbins and his co-workers that various conventional insecticide synergists like piperonyl butoxide synergize the action of ecdysone analogues.

An attractive feature of the potential use of ecdysones and related substances for insect control is that they are already widespread in the environment. This fact emerged six years ago when it was discovered that substances with ecdysone activity are found in many vascular plants, in some cases accounting for as much as 1 per cent of the dry weight of certain plant tissues. Thus far about 40 different steroids with ecdysone activity in insects have been isolated from higher plants by Nakanishi, Takemoto, Horn, Kaplanis and their colleagues (34-38). These phytoecdysones include authentic alpha and beta ecdysone. Indeed, one of the most ubiquitous appears to be beta ecdysone. Their role in plants remains obscure. The initial view was that they may have evolved as defensive systems against insects (36, 39). However recently it has been discovered that a plant sex hormone, antheridiol, is a steroid and resembles a number of phytoecdysones (40). This has led to the suggestion that phytoecdysones may play a role in implant reproduction and their defensive properties, if any, are secondary (41).

It seems likely that the next few years will see the testing of various ecdysone-based substances for use as agents of insect control (13, 42). In addition we may anticipate a search for agents which block ecdysone synthesis, which compete with ecdysones for binding sites in tissues and which prevent brain hormone from initiating ecdysone production. For the present, these are speculative prospects. In contrast the use of juvenile hormone mimics as agents of insect control is already upon us (see for example Bagley and Bauernfeind in this volume).

4. Juvenile hormone effects.

Growth in higher vertebrates and in higher insects

is associated with the non-reproductive juvenile stage
and in both vertebrates and insects, maturation is
under hormonal control. But the control mechanisms
for maturation are very different. Maturation in
man and other higher vertebrates is promoted by the
secretion of maturation hormones, the gonadotropins
of the pituitary. The juvenile condition in man hinges
upon the absence of these maturing hormones. The
situation in insects is just the opposite. The juvenile
condition in insects depends upon the continued presence
of the juvenile hormones, which act on the cells
themselves, and prevent them from maturing.

Thus far two closely related juvenile hormones
have been isolated and identified from the Cecropia
silkworm and some of its close relatives: methyl
12, 14-dihomojuvenate or JH-1 (methyl 10,11-epoxy-7-ethyl-
3,11-dimethyl-2,6-tridecadienoate) (10, 43, 44, 45) and
methyl 12-homojuvenate or JH-2 (methyl 10,11-epoxy-
3,7,11-trimethyl-2,6-tridecadienoate) (44, 45) (Fig. 2).
These juvenile hormones affect virtually all insects
upon which they have been tested. In immature insects
they produce a variety of morphogenetic effects. The
most obvious action is on epidermal cells where these
hormones influence the kind of cuticle the epidermal
cells secrete in response to ecdysones. But they
also affect the development of internal organs including
the central nervous system, the gonads, and the midgut,
where they prevent maturation and metamorphosis (46).

Juvenile hormones also block the maturation of
imaginal discs which are the primordia of many adult
integumentary structures in endopterygote insects.
Imaginal discs occur in larvae as tiny sacs of epithelial
cells which come directly from the embryo. In Lepidoptera
for example each imaginal wing disc is set aside in
the embryo as a small nest of cells destined to form
the pupal and adult wing. These imaginal disc cells
divide during larval life but fail to secrete a cuticle
until the time of pupation. Pupation is brought about
by a falling concentration of juvenile hormone and
results in the rapid morphogenesis of the wing disc
and the secretion of a cuticle. If juvenile hormone
is applied to a lepidopterous larva prior to pupation,

it prevents both morphogenesis and cuticle synthesis in
the wing disc. When juvenile hormone disappears,
the imaginal wing disc continues its development.

Since juvenile hormone affects the development
of imaginal discs which are basically embryonic cells
that persist in the larva, it should not be too surprising
that juvenile hormone also affects the rest of the embryo.
Slama, Williams and Riddiford (47, 48, 49) have demonstrated that application of juvenile hormones to young
embryos interferes with their development. Thus juvenile
hormone blocks not only the metamorphosis of the larva
to the adult, but it also blocks the equally profound
metamorphosis of the embryo to the larva, a matter
which is discussed in detail elsewhere in this volume
by Riddiford. Although these effects on embryos result
from the experimental application of juvenile hormone,
there is evidence that juvenile hormones may play
a role in the normal embryonic development of some
insects. Thus White (50) has presented evidence that
the degree of activity of the corpora allata (and
presumably the concentration of juvenile hormone)
in female aphids influences the extent to which the
wing buds of the embryo develop and by this means
controls aphid polymorphism. (For a summary of other
effects of juvenile hormones on polymorphism, see
Wigglesworth (1).)

Juvenile hormones also exert a gonadotropic effect
and promote the synthesis of yolk proteins by the
fat body and the accumulation of these proteins by
the developing oocytes of many insects (51, 52, 53).
They also affect the activity of accessory sexual
glands in some male insects. Unlike the morphogenetic
effects of juvenile hormone, these effects on reproduction
do not require the presence of ecdysones, although
they may sometimes involve a brain hormone (54). Juvenile
hormones may also activate the prothoracic gland of
Lepidoptera and break adult reproductive diapause
in insects such as the alfalfa weevil. They may also
have conspicuous effects on behavior such as cocoon
spinning. In some adult insects they appear to be
necessary for the production of pheromones and are
involved in various sorts of sexual behavior.

It is of some interest and practical importance
that, so far as we can tell, all of the juvenile hormone
activities just described are shared by all compounds
that show juvenile hormone activity in morphogenetic
tests. Apparently, the receptor sites in diverse
target tissues affected by juvenile hormone analogues
are similar. Evidently during evolution, diverse
target organs have "captured" juvenile hormones and
used them to coordinate various activities. Such
endocrinological opportunism is common in nature and
there are many examples in vertebrates. Indeed as
a general rule the evolution of hormonal mechanisms
involves not so much the evolution of hormones as
such, but more the evolution of receptor sites which
acquire a sensitivity to specific small molecules
that may have been present from earliest times, and
the development of systems that can ensure the timely
production of appropriate amounts of these specific
molecules.

The fact that juvenile hormones have so many
different effects in insects raises the question of
what might have been the original function of juvenile
hormones in the earliest insects. Juvenile hormones
regulate the cyclic reproduction of the most primitive
contemporary insects, the Apterygota, which have almost
no metamorphosis and reproduce throughout adult life.
Presumably this type of regulation of sexual maturation
and reproduction is the basic function of juvenile
hormone in insects; regulation of the maturation of
other tissues seems to be a secondary effect that
evolved later.

5. Juvenile hormone assays.

A key feature of juvenile hormone action is that
local application produces localized epidermal or
internal effects (55, 56, 57, 58, 59). Thus juvenile
hormones act directly upon their numerous target cells
and do not require the mediation of any other specialized
organ. A second feature is that juvenile hormones
and most of their analogues readily penetrate the
cuticle of insects (55, 59). A third feature is that,
although the juvenile hormones and most juvenile hormone

analogues are readily inactivated by insects soon
after they are injected, they can be protected by
being dissolved as a dilute solution in oil from which
they gradually partition into the insect (58). These
features provide the basis for a number of bioassays.
All of these bioassays for juvenile hormone depend
upon the presence of ecdysones to stimulate cuticle
secretion and molting. Thus if juvenile hormone is
injected or topically applied to a fragment of an
insect devoid of endocrine glands, such as an isolated
abdomen, no juvenile hormone effects are evident because
formation of new cuticle does not occur. However,
if juvenile hormone is applied to an intact immature
insect by injection, by topical application or by
dipping the entire insect into a juvenile hormone
solution, the insect usually molts into some strange
creature intermediate between the immature and the
adult stages and soon dies.

These bioassays are discussed in detail in the
chapter by Staal. They are mentioned here briefly to
provide indispensible background for the arguments to
be advanced in sections 6 and 7 which follow. The
simplest assay for juvenile hormone activity is the
topical Tenebrio test (59). A microliter of an acetonic
solution of the material to be tested is applied to
the ventral surface of the abdomen of a Tenebrio pupa
less than 18 hours old. If the material has juvenile
hormone activity, many of the pupal epidermal cells
secrete a second pupal cuticle instead of an adult
cuticle. When such a pupa molts, it shows large areas
of pupal cuticle in the abdomen, whereas other structures
on the anterior of the animal are often adult. With
very active juvenile hormone compounds, the effects
cease to be localized and the entire pupa may molt
into a second pupa. An even simpler assay involves
dipping Tenebrio pupae for 30 seconds into a solution
containing the juvenile hormone compound dissolved
in 5 percent acetone and surfactants (60). With active
compounds the pupae molt into second pupae. These topical
and dipping tests for juvenile hormone activity can
detect as little as 2×10^{-4} micrograms of juvenile
hormone 1.

The most sensitive tests for juvenile hormone activity are the wax tests (57, 61, 62). Regenerating cells are extraordinarily sensitive to juvenile hormone. In the Galleria wax test, a small puncture is made on the dorsum of the thorax of a fresh Galleria pupa and sealed with a mixture of the substance to be tested in low melting point wax. If the substance has juvenile hormone activity, when the pupal-adult transformation is completed the adult moth will display a patch of pupal cuticle over the wound. The size and characteristics of this pupal patch and the frequency of its occurrence in different animals provides a measure of the juvenile hormone activity of the substance. The Galleria wax test can detect juvenile hormone activity in extracts containing as little as 5×10^{-6} micrograms of juvenile hormone (63). A similar wax test employing pupae of the Polyphemus moth, Antheraea polyphemus, is even more sensitive and can detect activity in extracts containing as little as 10^{-6} micrograms of juvenile hormone (58).

Injection assays are somewhat less sensitive than the topical assays and the wax test. The Polyphemus injection assay, in which the substance to be tested is injected in a peanut oil solution, is probably the most sensitive of the injection tests and can detect juvenile hormone activity in extracts containing about 2×10^{-3} micrograms of juvenile hormones 1 and 2 (58).

6. Juvenile hormones and the cell cycle.

The precise mechanism of juvenile hormone action remains to be determined. In this volume, Ilan and Ilan, and Williams and Kafotos present distinct hypotheses on juvenile hormone action in molecular terms. It is not the intention of this chapter to present a third hypothesis, but to direct attention to a considerable body of evidence relating to the timing of hormonal stimuli and to the changing sensitivity of cells to hormonal stimuli, which provides important clues to the mode of action of the juvenile hormone. Curiously, insects appear to be sensitive to ecdysones at all stages of their development. As we have already noted, if a sufficient amount of an ecdysone is applied to

an insect, the epidermal cells of the insect promptly
secrete a cuticle. In contrast, insect cells are
sensitive to juvenile hormones only at certain stages
in the cell cycle. This conclusion may be drawn from
experiments such as the following performed some years
ago by Krishnakumaran (20, 24).

Pupae of _Antheraea polyphemus_ were injected with
a juvenile hormone extract containing approximately
50 ng of juvenile hormones 1 and 2 on the first, second
and third days after the initiation of the pupal-
adult transformation and simultaneously injected with
tritiated thymidine. The pupae so treated molted
into pupal-adult intermediates containing patches
of pupal cuticle of varying size. Autoradiographs
of these intermediates revealed that pupal patches
occurred only in regions of the epidermis that showed
intense incorporation of the isotope, indicating that
only those cells that had not already completed DNA
replication when the juvenile hormone was injected
had responded to juvenile hormone by secreting a pupal
cuticle.

Numerous other experiments conducted by Frantisek
Sehnal over several years both in my laboratory and
at the Entomological Institute at Prague, illustrate
the same point; namely, that juvenile hormones affect
only epidermal cells which have not replicated their
DNA (2, 21, 64). Cells which have replicated their
DNA are insensitive to juvenile hormone except at
extremely high doses. These observations indicate
that juvenile hormones affect cells only during a
limited part of the cell cycle, probably the end of
the G_1-period or during the S-period. This fact accounts
for the observation that there is only a relatively
short juvenile hormone-sensitive period in insect
development, after which juvenile hormone ceases to
have effects (58).

These data provide continued support for the
hypothesis that juvenile hormone acts on cells before
transcription occurs and, in some way determines what
part of the genome will be used for new syntheses
(24, 26, 27). It seems to permit current genes to

16

operate but prevents the activation of other groups
of genes. Furthermore, it can only affect cells which
are replicating their DNA. Reprogramming by juvenile
hormones--or by any other agent for that matter--
requires DNA replication (see section 2). This observation
enables us to predict when juvenile hormones should
be applied to insects to produce morphogenetic effects,
to understand the toxicity of juvenile hormones, and
to rationally use juvenile hormones and their analogues
and mimics as control agents, as we shall now see.

7. Toxic effects of juvenile hormones--potential insecticidal action.

Immature insects which have been affected by
an exogenous juvenile hormone usually fail to ecdyse
spontaneously, die soon after ecdysis or fail to reproduce.
Examination of their integument and internal organs
reveals that these affected insects are intermediates
between larva and pupa, pupa and adult, or larva and
adult. Unlike the intermediates produced by ecdysone,
which result from hyperhormonism (an excess of ecdysone,
see section 2), intermediates produced by juvenile
hormone do not result from excessive amounts of juvenile
hormone. Rather, they occur when insects are exposed
to juvenile hormones at abnormal times in their developmental programs. The application of juvenile hormones
to larvae or pupae at a time when some cells have
ceased DNA replication and therefore lost their sensitivity
to juvenile hormone, but others have not, leads to
the production of intermediates. This fact influences
the practical application of juvenile hormones and
their analogues as control agents.

Young insect larvae are not killed by juvenile hormone
analogues. In order for these agents to kill insects
they must act during the last larval instar or during
metamorphosis where they cause the production of intermediates. Alternatively, juvenile hormone analogues must
act upon adults where they function as chemosterilants,
or upon embryos. Juvenile hormone analogues must
be applied at the proper time and must persist for
several days to be effective in producing non-viable
intermediates. This matter has recently been analyzed

17

by Frantisek Sehnal and Schneiderman (24, 65). The main argument is this: to produce maximum kill with minimum dose, juvenile hormone analogues must be applied when some parts of the insect's body are sensitive to these substances whereas other parts are not. Since juvenile hormones appear to act only at certain times in the cell cycle, one can predict these hormone-sensitive stages from the timing of DNA replication in various parts of the integument of developing insects.

For example, bugs, locusts, and other exopterygote insects usually become insensitive to juvenile hormone analogues a few days after the last larval ecdysis. Consequently, one must apply juvenile hormone analogues shortly after the last larval ecdysis, generally during the first third of the last larval instar or, much later, after adult emergence, where juvenile hormone analogues will have an ovicidal effect. Larvae of most endopterygote insects such as Lepidoptera and Coleoptera can only be deranged at the end of the last larval instar. Pupae of endopterygote insects are sensitive to juvenile hormone analogues only for several hours or at most a few days after the larval-pupal ecdysis. These sensitive periods represent the periods of DNA replication. To be effective in the field, juvenile hormone analogues must be applied at the right time and must persist long enough so that all members of the population are exposed to them for an adequate time when they enter their sensitive periods. Thus, juvenile hormone analogues must persist in the environment for several weeks if they are to be effective. This requirement for field stability of juvenile hormone analogues is extremely important if these agents are to be of practical use. This matter is discussed by Bagley and Bauernfeind elsewhere in this volume.

Although exogenous juvenile hormone is usually toxic to larvae about to pupate and to pupae about to transform into adults, this is not always the case. If juvenile hormone is applied judiciously one can obtain supernumerary larval molts which are normal. Several laboratories have produced giant Tenebrio larvae by rearing mature larvae on food containing

18

various juvenile hormone analogues. In this process, the larvae are exposed to the juvenile hormone analogue both topically from crawling about in the food and internally from feeding. When such giant larvae are removed from the juvenile hormone, they can sometimes be induced to pupate and produce giant adults. Fortunately, it is rather difficult to produce such giant insects and the experiments just described may be viewed as an endocrinological <u>tour</u> de <u>force</u>. There is little likelihood that juvenile hormone when applied in nature would prolong the larval life and produce giant larvae of some economically important pest. The production of such giant insects requires that the juvenile hormone remain effective for months and most of the juvenile hormone analogues that have been discovered to date are far less stable than that.

A final point that merits reemphasis is the insensitivity of young larvae to juvenile hormones. None of the more than 500 compounds with juvenile hormone activity which have been synthesized (66) is toxic to young larvae. This is unfortunate, for in most cases it is the larval stages which cause the damage. This circumstance has led several laboratories to consider the development of new kinds of juvenile hormone antagonists which might permit an attack on larval stages. Agents which interfere with juvenile hormone synthesis, release, transport or tissue binding should cause young larval insects to mature precociously and abnormally. For the present these agents, like the anti-ecdysones mentioned in section 3, remain speculations.

8. Can insects develop resistance to insect growth regulators?

Closely tied to the potential insecticidal action of insect growth regulators is the question of the development of resistance. The fact that juvenile hormones and ecdysones are indispensable for the normal development of insects has led to the suggestion that insect pests would not be able to develop resistance to juvenile hormone analogues and other insect growth regulators. It follows from this argument that hormonally-based insecticides would have a supreme advantage over conventional insecticides to which many populations of more than 250 insect pest species have already become resistant. An abiding faith in Charles Darwin compels me to disagree with these arguments and to believe instead that resistance to exogenously applied insect growth regulators is bound to occur. Any insecticide, hormonally based or not, is bound to act "as a powerful sieve for concentrating resistant mutants that were present in low frequencies in the original population" (67). Indeed, insects already have the ingredients necessary for the development of such resistance.

Consider for example juvenile hormone analogues. At certain stages in their development, insects normally inactivate, sequester or excrete juvenile hormone and many juvenile hormone analogues. Thus, nature has endowed insects with a built-in mechanism to resist the artificial application of juvenile hormones and their analogues at specific stages. Siddall and his colleagues have shown that the half life of juvenile hormone 1 in larvae of the tobacco horn worm, Manduca sexta, is only twenty minutes. Now, to be sure, mechanisms which inactivate juvenile hormone and juvenile hormone analogues normally function only at specific times in development. However, the existence of such mechanisms guarantees that natural selection could produce populations of insects which would be resistant to exogenous juvenile hormone analogues. Similar arguments can be made about almost any insecticide one can imagine.

Another circumstance which insures the appearance of insects resistant to juvenile hormone analogues is the fact that there are great differences in sensitivity of different families of insects to specific juvenile hormone analogues (66, 68). The evidence at hand indicates that this specificity may extend to the family level. Thus, some juvenile hormone analogues affect bugs of the family Pyrrhocoridae but are much less active on bugs of the family Lygaeidae. Other juvenile hormone analogues affect Tenebrionid beetles but not Curculionid beetles, and so forth. Group-specific sensitivity to juvenile hormone analogues does not

mean that different natural juvenile hormones exist for
each family of insects; indeed, it appears likely
that there may be only a very few different naturally-
occurring juvenile hormones. It appears more likely
that the differences in the sensitivity to juvenile
hormones among different families stems from differences
in rates of penetration, breakdown, excretion, storage
and so forth or from differences in behavior, feeding,
habits, etc. of the insects tested. For purposes
of the present arguments, the fact that insects of
one genetic constitution may respond to a particular
juvenile hormone analogue, whereas rather closely
related insects of a different genetic constitution
fail to respond, tells us that resistance to juvenile
hormone analogues could be selected for in nature.

This conclusion should not dismay us. Instead
it should encourage efforts to identify the mechanisms
of resistance to these agents so that resistance can
be anticipated and possibly minimized before it occurs
in the field. Advance knowledge of the possible counter-
measures which insects may adopt in response to synthetic
insect growth regulators should enable man to stay
several steps ahead. In any case, it seems imprudent
to wait until resistance appears in nature before attempts
are made to cope with it.

9. Effects of insect hormones on other arthropods
and on vertebrates.

It is of both theoretical and practical interest
to learn whether insect growth regulators have effects
on arthropods other than insects. Most zoologists
distinguish two major groups of arthropods whose ancestors
became distinct from each other about 500 million
years ago. These are the insects and crustaceans
on the one hand and the arachnids on the other. Recent
studies have demonstrated that alpha and beta ecdysones
and many phytoecdysones act on all of the major subphyla
and classes of arthropods (29, 69, 70, 71). Injection
of beta ecdysone into spiders, horseshoe crabs or crayfish,
for example, causes them to molt in much the same
way that insects molt when similarly treated. No
one has discovered any group-specific ecdysones which

affect only one group of arthropods. These observations
indicate that the ecdysones are ancient molecules
which have been used by arthropods for molting for
at least 500 million years.

Our knowledge of juvenile effects on various
arthropods is much less complete. It has been established
that juvenile hormones 1 and 2 affect virtually all
insects if they are applied at appropriate developmental
stages in sufficient amounts. Even in the most primitive
insects, the Apterygota, it normally controls reproduction
and under experimental conditions inhibits embryonic
development (72). This finding has raised the prospect
that juvenile hormone might also act on the embryos
of other arthropods. However, the effects of juvenile
hormones on arthropods other than insects have only
begun to be explored. Recent experiments indicate
that topical application of juvenile hormone 1 and
several juvenile hormone analogues to eggs inhibited
the embryonic development of a crustacean, the terrestrial
isopod, Armadillidium vulgare. Early embryonic stages
were the most sensitive to the hormones, as is true
for insects, but the doses required were at least ten
times higher than those required to inhibit embryonic
development of insects (73). The issue is not yet
settled but the evidence at hand leads us to suspect
that the juvenile hormones, like the ecdysones, are
also ancient molecules and may affect arthropods other
than insects.

What can be said about the effects of ecdysones
and juvenile hormones upon mammals and other vertebrates?
It is useful to recall that the fossil remains of
the ancestors of insects and of the vertebrates, the
trilobites and protochordates, are found in Cambrian
rocks. Hence, arthropods and vertebrates must have
diverged from their common ancestor before that time,
at least six hundred million years ago. During the
six hundred million years in which these two groups
of organisms have undergone divergent evolution, there
have been numerous opportunities for biochemical
innovation. Many processes such as protein and nucleic
acid synthesis, mechanisms of cellular respiration,
etc. have not changed. Other processes such as the

hormonal control of reproduction are very different
in vertebrates and arthropods. One process which is
peculiar to arthropods is cuticle synthesis and molting,
a process controlled by brain hormone, ecdysones and
juvenile hormones. Since vertebrates do not have a
comparable process, one might not expect ecdysones
and juvenile hormones to have important effects on
them. The evidence published to date indicates that
this is probably true and that neither ecdysones nor
juvenile hormones have conspicuous effects in vertebrates,
although some of the ecdysones may exert some physiological
effects on mammalian cells. For example several phytoecdysones act as anabolic steroids and stimulate protein
and RNA synthesis by mouse liver (74, 75). Also alpha
ecdysone injected into mice has a definite mineralocor-
ticoid effect (76), but no androgenic, estrogenic or
carcinogenic effects have been reported. Apparently
some ecdysones are sufficiently similar to some vertebrate
steroid hormones to mimic a few of their effects.

Thus far no effects of juvenile hormones on vertebrates have been described in the literature. Siddall
and Slade (77) have reported that high doses of juvenile
hormone 1 and an analogue are without effects on adult
rats and mice. The chapters by Pallos and Menn and
by Bagley and Bauernfeind also describe numerous other
tests of juvenile hormone analogues on vertebrates
which have failed to demonstrate toxicity. Hopefully
future research will confirm that six hundred million
years of divergent evolution have made insects and
vertebrates sufficiently different so that insect growth
regulators will not prove a serious threat to vertebrates.

Acknowledgments

I wish to thank several of my colleagues for many
useful discussions which have helped to shape the ideas
in this chapter. I am particularly indebted to Drs.
Alipati Krishnakumaran, Frantisek Sehnal, Peter J. Bryant
and Mr. R. Eugene Granger. My colleagues in the
Developmental Biology Laboratory and Center for
Pathobiology made helpful comments on the typescript,
particularly Dr. Peter J. Bryant and Mr. John Haynie.

References

1. V. B. Wigglesworth, Insect Hormones, Oliver and Boyd, Edinburgh (1970).
2. F. Sehnal, in Chemical Zoology (M. Florkin and B. T. Scheer, Eds.) Vol. 6, p. 307, Academic Press, New York (1971).
3. M. Yamazaki and M. Kobayashi, J. Insect Physiol. 15, 1981 (1969).
4. M. Yamazaki and M. Kobayashi, Bull. Sericul. Exp. Sta. 24, 523 (1971).
5. R. Huber and W. Hoppe, Chem. Ber. 98, 2403 (1965).
6. P. Karlson and C. E. Sekeris, Recent Progr. Horm. Res. 22, 473 (1966).
7. H. H. Rees, in Aspects of Terpenoid Chemistry and Biochemistry (T. W. Goodwin, ed.), Academic Press, London (1971).
8. L. I. Gilbert, Proc. Int. Cong. Endocrinol., 3rd, 340 (1969); in Physiology of Insecta (M. Rockstein, ed.) p. 149, Academic Press, New York (1964).
9. A. Willig, H. H. Rees and T. W. Goodwin, J. Insect Physiol. 17, 2317 (1971).
10. H. Röller and K. H. Dahm, Recent Progr. Horm. Res. 24, 651 (1968).
11. F. Hampshire and D. H. S. Horn, Chem. Commun., 37 (1966).
12. D. H. S. Horn, E. J. Middleton and J. A. Wunderlich, Chem. Commun., 339 (1966).
13. W. E. Robbins, J. N. Kaplanis, J. A. Svoboda and M. J. Thompson, Ann. Rev. Entomol. 16, 53 (1971).
14. H. Moriyama, K. Nakanishi, D. S. King, T. Okauchi, J. B. Siddall and W. Hafferl, Gen. Comp. Endocrinol. 15, 80 (1970).
15. H. Oberlander, J. Insect Physiol. 15, 1803 (1969).
16. H. Oberlander, J. Insect Physiol. 18, in press (1972).
17. E. Ohnishi, T. Ohtaki and S. Fukuda, Proc. Jap. Acad. 47, 413 (1971).
18. T. Ohtaki and C. M. Williams, Biol. Bull. 138, 326 (1970).
19. Y. Sato, M. Sakai, S. Imai and S. Fujioka, Appl. Entomol. Zool. 3, 49 (1968).
20. R. E. Granger, A. Krishnakumaran and H. A. Schneiderman, in preparation (1972).

21. F. Sehnal, in press (1972).
22. H. A. Schneiderman, unpublished observations.
23. C. M. Williams, Biol. Bull. 134, 344 (1968).
24. H. A. Schneiderman, A. Krishnakumaran, P. J. Bryant and F. Sehnal, Proc. Symposium on Potentials in Crop Protection, 14 (1969); Agric. Sci. Rev. 8, 13 (1970).
25. M. Kobayashi, T. Takemoto, S. Ogawa and N. Nishimoto, J. Insect Physiol. 13, 1395 (1967).
26. H. A. Schneiderman, in Ontogeny of Immunity, (R. T. Smith, ed.) p. 5, University of Florida Press (1967).
27. H. A. Schneiderman, in Biology and the Physical Sciences, (S. Devons, ed.) p. 186, Columbia University Press, New York (1969).
28. H. A. Schneiderman, Mitt. Schweiz. Entomol. Ges. 44, in press (1971).
29. A. Krishnakumaran and H. A. Schneiderman, Biol. Bull. 139, 520 (1970).
30. R. L. Pipa, J. Exp. Zool. 170, 1 (1969).
31. K. F. Judy and E. P. Marks, Gen. Comp. Endocrinol. 17, 351 (1971).
32. C. L. M. Poels, A. deLoof and H. D. Berendes, J. Insect Physiol. 17, 1717 (1971).
33. W. E. Robbins, J. N. Kaplanis, M. J. Thompson, T. J. Shortino, C. F. Cohen and S. C. Joyner, Science 161, 1158 (1968).
34. K. Nakanishi, M. Koreeda, S. Sasaki, M. L. Chang and H. Y. Hsu, Chem. Commun., 915 (1966).
35. T. Takemoto, S. Ogawa, N. Nishimoto and H. Hoffmeister, Z. Naturforsch. 22b, 681 (1967).
36. M. N. Galbraith and D. H. S. Horn, Chem. Commun., 905 (1966).
37. J. N. Kaplanis, M. J. Thompson, W. E. Robbins and B. M. Bryce, Science 157, 1436 (1967).
38. J. B. Siddall, in Chemical Ecology, (E. Sondheimer and J. B. Simeone, eds.) p. 281, Academic Press, New York (1970).
39. C. M. Williams, in Chemical Ecology, (E. Sondheimer and J. B. Simeone, eds.) p. 103, Academic Press, New York (1970).
40. G. P. Arsenault, K. Biemann, A. W. Barksdale and T. C. McMorris, J. Amer. Chem. Soc. 90, 5635 (1968).
41. C. E. Berkoff, Proc. Calif. Assoc. Chem. Teachers 48, 577 (1971).

42. W. E. Robbins, J. N. Kaplanis, M. J. Thompson, T. J. Shortino and S. C. Joyner, Steroids 16, 105 (1970).
43. H. Roller, K. H. Dahm, C. C. Sweely and B. M. Trost, Angew. Chem. Intern. Ed. English 6, 179 (1967).
44. A. S. Meyer, H. A. Schneiderman, E. Hanzmann and J. H. Ko, Proc. Nat. Acad. Sci. U. S. 60, 853 (1968).
45. A. S. Meyer, E. Hanzmann, H. A. Schneiderman, L. I. Gilbert and M. Boyette, Arch. Biochem. Biophys. 137, 190 (1970).
46. F. Sehnal, J. Insect Physiol. 14, 73 (1968).
47. K. Slama and C. M. Williams, Nature 210, 329 (1966).
48. L. M. Riddiford and C. M. Williams, Proc. Nat. Acad. Sci U. S. 57, 595 (1967).
49. L. M. Riddiford, Develop. Biol. 22, 249 (1970).
50. D. F. White, J. Insect Physiol. 17, 761 (1971).
51. F. Engelmann, Ann. Rev. Entomol. 13, 1 (1968).
52. F. Engelmann, The Physiology of Insect Reproduction, Pergamon Press, Oxford (1970).
53. F. Engelmann, L. Hill and J. L. Wilkens, J. Insect Physiol. 17, 2179 (1971).
54. P. Sroka and L. I. Gilbert, J. Insect Physiol. 17, 2409 (1971).
55. C. M. Williams, Nature 178, 212 (1956).
56. V. B. Wigglesworth, J. Insect Physiol. 2, 73 (1958).
57. H. A. Schneiderman and L. I. Gilbert, Biol. Bull. 115, 53 (1958).
58. L. I. Gilbert and H. A. Schneiderman, Trans. Amer. Microscop. Soc. 79, 38 (1960).
59. W. S. Bowers, Science 161, 895 (1968).
60. C. R. Roseland and D. J. Gallacher, unpublished observations.
61. H. A. Schneiderman and L. I. Gilbert, in Cell, Organism and Milieu, (D. Rudnick, ed.) p. 157, Ronald Press, New York (1959).
62. H. A. Schneiderman, A. Krishnakumaran, V. G. Kulkarni and L. Friedman, J. Insect Physiol. 11, 1641 (1965).
63. J. de Wilde, G. B. Staal, C. A. de Kort and G. Baard, Proc. Kon. Ned. Akad. Wetensch. Ser. C 71, 321 (1968).
64. F. Sehnal and V. J. A. Novak, Acta Entomol. Bohemoslov. 66, 137 (1969).
65. F. Sehnal and H. A. Schneiderman, submitted for publication.
66. K. Slama, Ann. Rev. Biochem. 40, 1079 (1971).

67. J. F. Crow, Ann. Rev. Entomol. 2, 227 (1957).
68. M. Suchy, K. Slama and F. Sorm, Science 162, 582 (1968).
69. A. Krishnakumaran and H. A. Schneiderman, Nature 220, 601 (1968).
70. H. Kurata, Bull. Jap. Soc. Sci. Fish. 34, 909 (1968).
71. J. E. Wright, Science 163, 390 (1969).
72. E. B. Rohdendorf, cited in (2) (1968).
73. G. Greer, unpublished observations.
74. S. Okui, T. Otaka, M. Uchiyama, T. Takemoto, H. Hikino, S. Ogawa and N. Nishimoto, Chem. Pharm. Bull. (Tokyo) 16, 384 (1968).
75. T. Otaka and M. Uchiyama, Chem. Pharm. Bull. (Tokyo) 17, 1883 (1969).
76. J. Siddall cited in C. M. Williams and W. E. Robbins, BioScience 18, 791 (1968).
77. J. B. Siddall and M. Slade, Nature New Biol. 229, 158 (1971).

THEORETICAL ASPECTS OF THE ACTION
OF JUVENILE HORMONE *

Carroll M. Williams and Fotis C. Kafatos

The Biological Laboratories, Harvard University
Cambridge, Massachusetts 02138

Abstract

We propose a model of JH action in which the hormone participates in the negative control of three hypothetical "master regulatory genes" each of which codes for a certain RNA polymerase or sigma factor. The "larval RNA polymerase" is presumed to have template specificity for the promoter sequence of all the genes in the "larval gene-set." In like manner the "pupal RNA polymerase" exercises positive control of the "pupal gene-set"; the "adult RNA polymerase," of the "adult gene-set." Therefore, the essence of the model is positive control of successive gene-sets by master regulatory genes which are themselves under JH-influenced negative control. The model can account for virtually all of the firmly established experimental findings.

The Genetic Construction Manual

The construction manual for building an holometabolous insect is subdivided into three successive chapters. The first chapter gives instructions for transforming the egg into a larva. Days, weeks, or months later, the second chapter tells how to change the larva into an essentially new organism, the pupa. Then, within the closed system of the pupa, the third and final chapter prescribes the reworking of the cells and tissues to form the adult. This analogy serves to emphasize that the more advanced forms of metamorphosis involve the turning-on and acting-out of

---

* An earlier version appeared in Mitt. Schweiz. Ent. Ges. 44, 151 (1971); reprinted here with permission of Journal.

successive batches of genetic information. One may think of the genome as being subdivided into three different "gene-sets" corresponding to the successive chapters in the construction manual.

We do not underestimate the complexity of the mechanisms which operate within each of the three gene-sets to control the orderly playback and implementation of genetic information in specific cell types. These controlling mechanisms are presumably no less complicated in insects than in human beings. Be that as it may, we suspect that juvenile hormone (JH) has little to do with specifying detailed instructions to particular differentiated cells. Virtually everything we know about this hormone suggests that it is involved in gene-switching on a massive scale such, for example, as would be required for the turning-off of one gene-set and the turning-on of another—in short, that it controls sequential polymorphism (1).

Replication and Recognition of the Gene-Sets

To provide a mechanism for this massive gene-switching, we suggest that the three gene-sets are distinguishable by information encoded in the genome and, moreover, that the members of each set are identifiable in terms of a certain nucleotide sequence which serves as their "promoters." According to this scheme, the promoters of the larval gene-set have template specificity for an RNA polymerase peculiar to the larva. In like manner, the promoters of the pupal gene-set will be recognized by a pupal RNA polymerase; the promoters of the adult gene-set, by an adult RNA polymerase.

To account for those enzymes and structural proteins which are synthesized at all stages in development, we conjecture that the corresponding genes may be represented in all three gene-sets. Alternatively, it is possible that some or all of these constitutive genes have promoters recognized by a species of RNA polymerase present at all stages. Still another possibility is that these genes possess all three promoter sequences and may therefore be recognized by all three polymerases. Similarly, specific genes may participate in any two gene-sets; the sets may be overlapping.

Since, according to these assumptions, the gene-sets and their corresponding promoters are encoded in the DNA, it

follows that they are replicated in each mitotic cycle.
Consequently, we presume that all three sets are defined
in all cells throughout embryonic and postembryonic development.

By virtue of the mysterious determinative events which
begin in the early embryo and continue on a decreasing
scale into the post-embryonic period, the cells are programmed for the specific roles which they and their progeny
will play in the future larva, pupa, and adult. We offer
no precise molecular explanation of these happenings
which, in more ways than one, constitute the central problem of developmental biology (2). Thankfully, we are not
obliged to do so since there is not the slightest evidence
that JH plays any role in the spatial programming of cells
or the pre-patterning of the insect as a whole. For our
present purpose the determinative events are nevertheless
of great interest since they prescribe on a cell-by-cell
basis those parts of each gene-set that can be read and
those parts that cannot be read.

Juvenile Hormone as a Co-Repressor of the Master
Regulatory Genes

As diagrammed in Fig. 1[*] we propose a model of JH
action in which each of the three gene-sets is presumed to
be under the control of a certain "master regulatory gene"
which we have called MG_L, MG_P, and MG_A, respectively. We
suggest that the operator (O_P) of MG_P is subject to inhibition by a repressor (R_P) which is active only in the
presence of a high titer of JH. So, also, the operator
(O_A) of MG_A is subject to inhibition by another repressor
(R_A), the important difference being that this repressor
remains active in the presence of even a low titer of JH.
Both repressors become inactive in the absence of JH. Thus,
according to this model, JH is involved in the "negative
control" of transcription of the master regulatory genes.

The most economical hypothesis is to regard JH as a
co-repressor which activates R_P and R_A by binding directly
.to them. Under this point-of-view, R_P^A would have a lower
affinity for JH than does R_A. Alternatively, JH might
affect the repressors in an indirect manner--for example,
by binding to JH receptors elsewhere in the cells and
thereby bringing into play one or more "second messengers"
which react with the repressors.   * Figures follow text.

31

Gene-Switching in Unicellular Metamorphosis

Manifestly, the model up to this point is a simple
adaptation of Jacob-Monod principles as derived from
studies of gene-switching in bacteria. Further aspects of
the model lean heavily upon recent findings of positive control, which have likewise been derived from investigations
of microbial systems. We refer in particular to the pioneering studies which Losick and his collaborators have
carried out on sporulation in B. subtilis (3).

The broad implications of these studies have already
been lucidly set forth by Watson (4). In brief, the en-
vironmentally induced transformation of the vegetative
bacillus into a spore proves to be a bona fide metamorphosis involving the shut-down of the gene-set responsible
for vegetative growth and, simultaneously, the activation
of a second gene-set which directs the new synthetic operations required for the formation of the spore. Losick and
his co-workers have evidence that the unicellular metamorphosis implicit in sporulation involves the synthesis of a
new sigma (σ) factor which differs from that used by the
vegetative cell (Losick, personal communication). The new
σ combines with the "core enzyme" of RNA polymerase to form
a new polymerase with specific template affinity for the
promoter sites of the gene-set for making the spore. Simultaneously, the core enzyme is altered so that it loses its
affinity for the old σ of the vegetative cell. In this
manner the old gene-set is turned-off and the new gene-set
is turned-on.

We do not know whether this scheme of positive control
of transcription applies to eucaryotic cells. However,
Roeder and Rutter (5) have demonstrated two RNA polymerase
activities in rat liver nuclei (apparently differing in
subunit structure; Rutter, personal communication) and a
shifting balance of three distinct RNA polymerase activities in developing sea urchin embryos. No studies have
thus far been reported as to the presence of σ factors in
insect cells, but specificity factors are attractive candi-
dates for controlling the template specificities of the
successive RNA polymerases which we postulate. In any
case, the essence of the model is positive control of gene-
sets by master regulatory genes, themselves under hormon-
ally-influenced negative control. Although we specify that
each master regulatory gene codes for one (or more)

32

specific σ factors, we would be equally happy if evidence were found that it codes for entirely new RNA polymerases, as has been shown to be the case in the T_7 bacteriophage (6).

Larval Growth without Metamorphosis

The recurrent molting of immature larval insects is known to take place when ecdysone is secreted in the presence of a high titer of JH. As we suggest in Fig. 2, JH acts in conjunction with the repressors, R_P and R_A, to repress the master regulatory genes, MG_P and MG_A. By contrast, MG_L exists in the active state and is therefore subject to transcription by RNA polymerase. As indicated in Fig. 2, we suggest that this polymerase makes use of a "constitutive σ factor" (σ_C) with template specificity for the promoters of all three master regulatory genes.

According to the scheme diagrammed in Fig. 2, MG_L continues to be transcribed as a messenger RNA which codes for the synthesis of σ Factor$_L$. The latter combines with pre-existing core enzyme to form an RNA polymerase with template specificity for the promoters of genes in the larval gene-set. Consequently, Gene-set$_L$ remains operational and continues to be transcribed as gene products (GP_L) which code for the enzymes and other proteins of the larva. Among these proteins are the repressors, R_P and R_A. So, as long as a high titer of JH is present, Gene-set$_L$ remains turned-on and Gene-set$_P$ and Gene-set$_A$ remain locked-off.

The Larval-Pupal Transformation

In the mature larva the corpora allata curtail their activity so that pupation takes place in the presence of a high titer of ecdysone and a low but finite titer of JH. That being so, the repressor, R_P, loses its affinity for MG_P and falls off (Fig. 3). The net result is that the constitutive RNA polymerase can proceed to transcribe MG_P as a mRNA coding for the new σ Factor$_P$ whose template specificity is for the promoters of Gene-set$_P$. The latter is thereby turned-on, provoking the transcription of gene products (GP_P) which code for synthetic operations of the pupal type. These operations include the continued synthesis of the repressor, R_A, and the synthesis of a new repressor (r_L). The latter differs from pre-existing repressors in that its affinity for the operator of MG_L does not depend on the presence of JH.

In summary, the declining titer of JH within the mature larva allows Gene-set$_P$ to be turned-on and MG_L and MG_A to be turned-off.

The Pupal-Adult Transformation

The corpora allata are known to be inactive in the pupa as well as throughout the first two-thirds of adult development. The latter therefore takes place when ecdysone acts in the absence of JH. The consequences are diagrammed in Fig. 4.

In the absence of JH, the repressor, R_A, loses its affinity for MG_A and falls off. This leads to the transcription of MG_A, the synthesis of σ Factor$_A$, and the activation of Gene-set$_A$. The latter codes for gene products of the adult type (GP_A), including templates of repressors r_L and r_P whose activity does not depend on JH. Thus, Gene-set$_A$ is turned-on and Gene-set$_L$ and Gene-set$_P$ are locked-off.

Tests of the Model

The model can account for nearly all of the developmental aberrations which one can induce by the administration of JH. For example, it is well known that by the injection of JH one can block the pupal-adult transformation and provoke the formation of a second pupa. Fig. 5 illustrates how the model can explain this result. The injected hormone activates the repressor, R_A, thereby blocking the transcription of MG_A. Since MG_L is repressed by a JH-independent repressor, the presumably unstable pupal repressor, R_P, cannot be replenished, and MG_P remains active regardless of how much JH is supplied. In analogous manner, injected JH could block the larval-pupal transformation by preventing the dissociation of the repressor, R_P, from MG_P. In this case the observed result is the retention of larval characters due to the sustained activity of Gene-set$_L$ as illustrated in Fig. 2.

The model can also account for the precocious metamorphosis observed in immature larvae after the excision of corpora allata. Precocious pupation, as illustrated in Fig. 3, would take place if the succeeding molt occurred in the presence of a low but finite residual titer of JH. This is the typical result observed, for example, in <u>Bombyx mori</u> (7). But if the succeeding larval molt takes place in the absence of residual JH, one would anticipate a bizarre state-of-affairs—namely, the simultaneous activation of both pupal and adult gene-sets followed by the shut-down of MG_p. This could account for the faulty metamorphosis of mature Cecropia silkworms after the excision of corpora allata (8). Thus, as illustrated in Fig. 6, the typical result is the formation of pupal-adult intermediates in which the abdomen shows pupal characters, but numerous organs, including the eyes, antennae, legs, wings, genitalia, and gonads have differentiated adult characters.

The model does not account for two developmental phenomena which have generally been attributed to JH. For example, it cannot explain the ability of JH to trigger the deposition of yolk in the eggs of certain species of adult insects. This so-called gonadotropic function of JH appears to be peculiar to species in which the adults are long-lived. Non-feeding, short-lived adults such, for example, as the Cecropia silkmoth, can mature their eggs in the absence of JH (9). For these several reasons we suspect that during evolution JH was "captured" for the ancillary gonadotropic function in certain adult insects and that its mode of action in adults may be substantially different from its primary role in controlling metamorphosis.

The model, at least in its present form, also fails to account for the "reversal of metamorphosis"—the occasional reappearance of traces of juvenile characters in pupae or adults which are caused to molt in the presence of JH. We do not doubt the validity of the experimental observations as reported in the literature [for summary, see (1)]. However, it is clear that reversal of metamorphosis is exceedingly difficult to accomplish; in silkmoths we have not substantiated this phenomenon to date. In fact, under most circumstances unidirectionality is one of the most striking aspects of metamorphosis. An attractive novel feature of the present model is that it explains unidirectionality.

Prospects

So, in summary, we have proposed what we believe to be

the most parsimonious model of JH action which can account
for all, or nearly all, of the firmly established experimental findings. The worth of the model is to be measured,
not so much by its certain inadequacies, as by its ability
to suggest new avenues of approach to the comprehension of
insect metamorphosis.

One such approach is to search among the hundreds of
presently known lethal strains of <u>Drosophila</u> (10) for aberrations in development which may qualify as mutations of
one of the hypothetical master regulatory genes. A mutation of this sort would probably be recessive and, when
homozygous, would presumably inactivate one of the postulated σ factors, thereby preventing the transcription of an
entire gene-set.

By attention to the diagrams which we have presented
in the several figures, one may predict the consequences of
such mutations. Thus, a mutation of MG_L would permit the
proliferation of embryonic cells while blocking any trace
of the formation of the first instar larva. In like manner, a mutation of MG_P would block pupation; one might
anticipate a prolongation of larval life including one or
more extra larval molts or, indeed, the precocious appearance of adult characters.

A mutation of MG_A would probably be most easily detected. MG_P would continue to be transcribed to produce one
or more extra pupal instars without any trace of the appearance of adult characters.

On the assumption that such mutants already exist or
can be produced by appropriate tactics, the task of screening for them remains formidable. Yet this obstacle can
undoubtedly be surmounted. Once presumptive mutant tissues
and organs are available, it will be necessary to show that
they cannot be "rescued" by implanting them into non-mutant
hosts.

The model also encourages a search for the site of
action of JH. This line of inquiry has now become feasible
thanks to the synthesis of   radiolabeled JH. If injected
hormone reacts directly with the hypothetical repressors
of the master regulatory genes, one would expect to re-
cover a significant portion of the label in the nuclear
fraction of homogenates. Most importantly, nuclear label
should be bound relatively tightly to a protein fraction,
and the JH-protein complex should be specifically
retained on insect-DNA columns. By contrast, a preferen-

tial binding to the non-nuclear fraction would argue in favor of an indirect action of JH.

Finally, we direct attention to a central requirement of the model--namely, that multiple RNA polymerases or σ factors be demonstrated in insects. Moreover, these polymerases or sigmas must be shown to undergo systematic change during successive phases of metamorphosis. This aspect of the model appears to be immediately accessible to direct experimental attack by methods worked out on previously-mentioned systems. That being so, a detailed study of insect RNA polymerases and a search for σ factors have already been initiated at the Harvard laboratory.

* * *

We wish to thank the members of the Harvard Laboratories of Insect and Developmental Physiologies for helpful discussions during the evolution of the model as here proposed. We are particularly indebted to Prof. Lynn M. Riddiford, to Drs. Lucy Cherbas, John W. Postlethwait, and James Truman, and to Mr. Peter Cherbas. Our studies have been supported, in part, by grants from The Rockefeller Foundation, the National Science Foundation, and the National Institutes of Health.

References

1. V. B. Wigglesworth, Insect Hormones. Oliver and Boyd Ltd. (1970).
2. R. Geigy, Arch. Entwicklungsmech. Organ. 125, 406 (1931); M. Lüscher, Rev. Suisse Zool. 51, 532 (1944); D. Bodenstein, In: Insect Physiology, R. D. Roeder, edit. John Wiley Co., 780 (1953); A. S. Goldman and R. B. Setlow, Exp. Cell Res. 11, 146 (1956); C. M. Williams, In: A Symposium on the Chemical Basis of Development. W. D. McElroy and B. Glass edit., Johns Hopkins Press, 794 (1958); W. J. Gehring, In: Problems in Biology: RNA in Development. E. W. Hanly edit. Univ. Utah Press, 231 (1970); P. A. Lawrence, Advances Insect Physiol. 7, 197 (1970); H. Wildermuth, Sci. Prog., Oxf. 58, 329 (1970); M. Ashburner, Advances Insect Physiol. 7, 2 (1970); L. N. Chan and W. Gehring, Proc. Nat. Acad. Sci. U.S. 68, 2217 (1971).
3. R. Losick and A. L. Sonenshein, Nature 224, 35 (1969);

A. L. Sonenshein and R. Losick, Nature 227, 906 (1970); R. Losick, R. G. Shorenstein, and A. L. Sonenshein, Nature 227, 910 (1970); R. Losick, A. L. Sonenshein, R. G. Shorenstein, and C. Hussey, Cold Spring Harbor Symp. Quant. Biol. 35, 443 (1970); R. Losick, In vitro transcription. Ann. Rev. Biochem. (In press)

4. J. D. Watson, Molecular Biology of the Gene. 2nd Edit. W. A. Benjamin, Inc. (1970).

5. R. G. Roeder and W. J. Rutter, Nature 224, 234 (1969); Proc. Nat. Acad. Sci. U.S. 65, 675 (1970); Biochem. 9, 2543 (1970).

6. M. Chamberlin, J. McGrath, and L. Waskell, Nature 228, 227 (1970).

7. S. Fukuda, J. Fac. Sci., Tokyo Imp. Univ., Sec. 4, 6, 477 (1944).

8. C. M. Williams, Biol. Bull. 121, 572 (1961).

9. C. M. Williams, Biol. Bull. 116, 323 (1959).

10. E. Hadorn, Developmental Genetics and Lethal Factors. (English translation). John Wiley and Sons (1961).

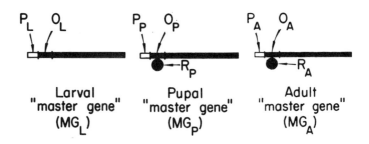

Larval "master gene" (MG_L)

Pupal "master gene" (MG_P)

Adult "master gene" (MG_A)

R_P *(the repressor of the "pupal master gene") is active only in the presence of a high titer of JH.*

R_A *(the repressor of the "adult master gene") remains active in the presence of a low titer of JH.*

1

Both repressors are inactive in the total absence of JH.

$$LARVA_n \longrightarrow LARVA_{n+1}$$

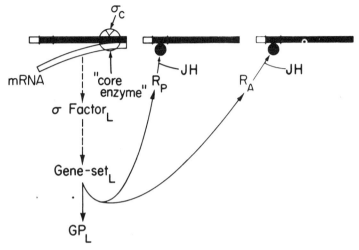

2

$$LARVA \longrightarrow PUPA$$

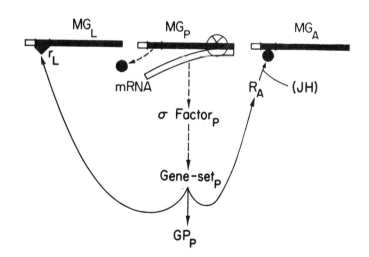

3

PUPA → ADULT

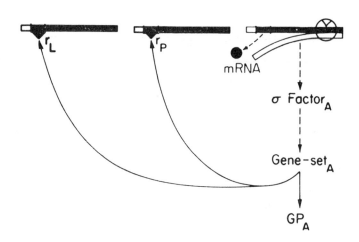

4

PUPA$_1$ → PUPA$_2$

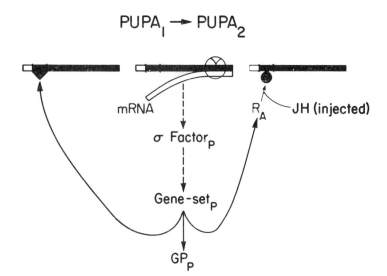

5

Figures 1-5. Diagrammatic representation of a hypothetical scheme of gene control during insect growth and metamorphosis. The genome of each cell is viewed as subdivis-
ible into three gene-sets, each controlled by its own
master regulatory gene. Juvenile hormone (JH) is depicted
as a co-repressor which participates in the negative control of the master regulatory genes of the pupal and adult
gene-sets. Abbreviations not defined in the diagrams are
as follows: P_L, P_P, and P_A are the promoters of the corresponding master genes; O_L, O_P, and O_A are the operators.
σ_C is the sigma factor of a constitutive RNA polymerase
which recognizes the promoter sequences of all three master
genes. mRNA is depicted as a messenger ribonucleic acid
transcribed from a master gene and coding for the sigma
factor(s) of the corresponding gene-set. r_L and r_P are
repressors which bind to the operators of the larval and
pupal master genes irrespective of the titer of JH. GP_L,
GP_P, and GP_A are gene products which code for the proteins
of the larval, pupal, and adult gene-sets, respectively.
For further details, see text.

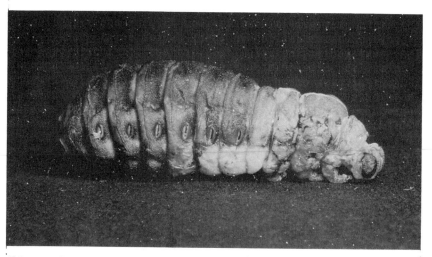

Figure 6. By excision of the corpora allata during the final larval instar, this Cecropia silkworm was caused to
undergo pupation in the absence of JH. A large number of
larval tissues and organs have undergone precocious adult
differentiation without traversing the pupal stage. (From
Williams, 1961).

REGULATION OF MESSENGER RNA
TRANSLATION MEDIATED BY JUVENILE HORMONE*

Joseph Ilan and Judith Ilan

Department of Anatomy and Developmental
Biology Center, Case Western Reserve
.   University, School of Medicine,
Cleveland, Ohio

Narayan G. Patel

Central Research Department, Experimental Station,
E.I. duPont de Nemours and Co.,
Wilmington, Delaware

Introduction

In insects growth and differentiation are regulated by several hormones. In larvae the brain hormone stimulates the prothoracic gland to secrete ecdysone. The latter in the presence of juvenile hormone which is secreted from the corpora allata, causes another larval molt. The number of larval instars varies within and among species. At the end of larval life the corpora allata cease to secrete juvenile hormone and the mature larva is left with a low concentration of hormone. Under these conditions the response to high titre of ecdysone will bring about a pupal molt. At the end of pupation, when almost no juvenile hormone remains, epidermal cells respond to high titre of ecdysone by secreting adult cuticle (Schneiderman and Gilbert, 1964).

The development of pupa into adult can be regulated by juvenile hormone. Topical application of juvenile hormone or juvenile hormone mimics on first day pupae of Tenebrio molitor brings about a second pupal molt eight days later. Therefore this system is most suitable for the study of gene expression mediated by hormone. The epidermis is one

*Supported by NSF Grant GB 30906

of the target tissues of juvenile hormone. Normally the
pupa develops into an adult and the epidermis secretes a
new adult cuticle which contains protein with a high
content of tyrosine (20%). When juvenile hormone is
topically applied on first day pupae it brings about a
second pupal molt and the epidermis secretes pupal cuticular protein which differs from the adult cuticular protein
in its tyrosine content (low tyrosine) and its amino acid
sequence. Therefore such a system provides a useful tool
for the study of involvement of juvenile hormone in morphogenesis and development and is useful in the study of
molecular events which are under the influence of juvenile
hormone. Thus the use of juvenile hormone serves the
purpose of studying mechanisms of gene expression. We have
found that the major influence of juvenile hormone in
promoting the synthesis of the two classes of cuticular
protein--adult and pupal--is at the translational level.
This is facilitated by controlling the translation of
cuticular messenger RNA. The translational control is
mediated by the appearance of new rate limiting aminoacyl-
tRNA.

Stable Messenger RNA for Cuticular Protein in Tenebrio.

When actinomycin D is injected into Tenebrio pupae
in doses which are sufficient to inhibit RNA synthesis
almost completely, it causes abnormal development. The
animal molts into a modified adult. However, most of the
adult cuticular protein is synthesized. Since actinomycin
D is known to inhibit DNA dependent RNA synthesis, the
synthesis of adult cuticular protein in the presence of the
drug and in the absence of RNA synthesis indicates the
presence of a stable template for this protein (Ilan, Ilan
and Quastel, 1966). This kind of behavior follows
inhibition of RNA synthesis. The inhibition of DNA
synthesis will bring about complete developmental arrest
(Ilan and Quastel, 1966).

Stable mRNA is not peculiar to Tenebrio. It was shown
for the cocoonase protein in the differentiated zymogen
cells of a silk moth (Kafatos and Reich, 1968). Indeed
stable messenger RNA is not unique to insects. To mention
a few examples, reticulocytes synthesize hemoglobin, lack
DNA and are incapable of RNA synthesis (Marks et al.,
1968). In sea-urchin eggs there is stable messenger RNA

which supports protein synthesis during the period of fertilization up through the blastula stage (Gross and Cousineau, 1963). During the development of slime mold, messenger RNA for the enzyme UDP-galactose polysaccharide transferase is very stable (Sussman, 1966). Induction of glutamine synthetase in chick embryo retina cells leads to accumulation of stable messenger RNA (Moscona et al., 1968). Stable messenger RNA is characteristic of differentiated cells engaged in the synthesis of specific protein such as hemoglobin, thyroglobulin and lens protein (Seed and Goldberg, 1963, 1965).

The observation that the messenger RNA for cuticular protein is stable and that it is not translated under the influence of juvenile hormone may suggest that the hormone effects synthesis through translational control. Such an influence must be mediated by a rate limiting reaction. Therefore attention was focussed on the preparation of a cell free system for protein synthesis from Tenebrio pupae and the identification of a rate limiting step in the reaction leading to the final product.

Cell Free System for Protein Synthesis from Tenebrio Pupae.

A cell free system which is capable of incorporating amino acids into protein utilizing microsomes or ribosomes containing the endogenous messenger RNA was developed (Ilan and Lipmann, 1966; Ilan, 1968). A typical microsomal amino acid incorporating system is given in Table I.

It can be seen that the system has an absolute requirement for microsomal particles, for ATP and its regenerating system, for GTP and for magnesium ions. Insect supernatant fluid does not stimulate, but supernatant fractions from E. coli or rabbit liver stimulate the system about three fold. There are at least two possible interpretations for the above stimulation a) that the supernatant fluid provides tRNA and amino acid activating enzymes which are both limiting. The amino acid is then transferred from tRNA into protein, since as observed by Nathans and Lipmann (1960) once tRNA is aminoacylated the source of aminoacyl tRNA is not important. b) that the insect microsomes might contain a limiting amount of transfer factors which are supplied by the supernatant fraction of E. coli or rat liver. The second possibility proved to be incorrect by the following experiment.

45

tRNA charged with 19 C^{12}-amino acids and C^{14}-leucine was
incubated with insect microsomes. Under such conditions the
transfer reaction is studied separately and is uncoupled
from the activation and charging of tRNA. Table II shows
that the transfer reaction was neither stimulated by rabbit
liver supernatant fluïd nor by insect supernatant fluid.
E. coli supernatant fluid was inhibitory probably because
of the presence of nucleases.

Table I
Properties of microsomal system

Incubation system	Incorporation of ^{14}C-leucine
	cpm/mg RNA
Complete..................................	4,260
Without ATP and its regenerating system.	102
Without GTP..............................	150
Without amino acids......................	1,685
With supernatant fluid...................	4,350
With RNase, 25 µg per ml................	50
With puromycin (4 X 10^{-4} M).............	406
With E. coli supernatant fluid..........	12,750
With rabbit liver supernatant fluid.....	15,360
Complete (0° control)...................	80
Without microsomes......................	20
Without Mg^{++}............................	45

(For experimental conditions see Ilan, 1968)

Other features of the transfer reaction of leucine
from transfer RNA to polypeptide are also shown. Inhibition by puromycin is almost complete and there is absolute
dependency on GTP and Mg^{++}. C^{12}-leucine has no effect on
the transfer reaction indicating unidirection of the
reaction and that there is no recharging of tRNA which
would bring about isotopic dilution and a significant decrease in incorporation. These experiments rule out the
second possibility that the transferases are limiting the
system and point to the fact that the microsomes are
saturated with transfer enzymes and are not influenced
by the addition of supernatant fluid from Tenebrio.

Table II

Requirements of aminoacyl-tRNA transfer system
on microsomes

The reaction mixture and conditions were as described
by Ilan, 1968. Each tube contained 0.35 mg of tRNA charged
with 19 ^{12}C-amino acids and ^{14}C-leucine, 1700 cpm per tube.
The concentration of protein in the supernatant fluid was
1.6 µg per ml.

Additions and omissions	Radioactivity transferred
	cpm/mg microsomal RNA
None..................................	536
With liver supernatant fluid........	526
With E. coli supernatant fluid......	232
With 2 X 10^{-4} M puromycin...........	30
With ^{12}C-leucine (4mM)..............	558
With liver supernatant fluid and ^{12}C-leucine......................	510
With E. coli supernatant fluid and ^{12}C-leucine......................	302
With insect supernatant fluid.......	558
Without microsomes..................	18
Without microsomes; with E. coli supernatant fluid.........	20
Without microsomes; with liver supernatant fluid...........	20
Without microsomes; with insect supernatant fluid.................	16
Without GTP.........................	14
Without Mg^{++}........................	12

The stimulation is due to tRNA and its activating
enzyme which are rate limiting factors in the protein
synthesizing system. The evidence is presented in
Table III.

Table III
Stimulation of ^{14}C-leucine incorporation on insect
microsomes by E. coli supernatant fluid and E. coli tRNA

Incubation was carried out for 8 min at 30°. E. coli
supernatant fluid free of tRNA was used. tRNA and E. coli
supernatant proteins were at levels of 3 mg per ml and
1.6 mg per ml, respectively, when added. (From Ilan, 1968.)

Additions	Incorporation
	cpm/mg microsomal RNA
None..	1240
With E. coli tRNA.........................	1200
With E. coli tRNA and E. coli supernatant fluid.................................	6300
With E. coli supernatant fluid...........	1230
With E. coli supernatant fluid and tRNA (less microsomes).......................	18
With E. coli supernatant fluid and tRNA (0° control).............................	45

For these studies supernatant fluid from E. coli
containing all amino acid activating enzymes for 20 amino
acids was obtained free of transfer RNA by passage through
DEAE cellulose. Neither this supernatant fluid alone nor
E. coli tRNA alone could stimulate protein synthesis on
insect microsomes above the endogenous level. However,
when both were added together five fold stimulation of
leucine incorporation into protein was observed. These
experiments indicate that the limiting factor in the
Tenebrio protein synthesizing system is transfer RNA and
its amino acid activating enzyme. Therefore, a ribosomal
cell free system from Tenebrio showing complete dependency
on transfer RNA and enzyme fraction was prepared. This
system could promote incorporation of amino acids utilizing
endogenous messenger RNA (Ilan, 1968; Ilan et al., 1970).
From the experiments with actinomycin D we deduced
that the messenger RNA for cuticular protein is stable and
exists on ribosomes at an early developmental stage and is
translated 5 to 6 days later. Moreover, microsomes iso-

48

lated from late adult development but not from early development are capable of synthesis of protein with relative high tyrosine content (Ilan and Lipmann, 1966). Since microsomes contain all the necessary factors for protein synthesis, factors associated with translational control of adult cuticular protein synthesis may be obtained from microsomes when this protein is being synthesized. It follows that the regulation of the synthesis involves a rate limiting component of the protein synthesizing machinery. We have already seen that tRNA and amino acid activating enzymes are rate limiting in the microsomal amino acid incorporation system.

Ribosomes containing the endogenous messenger RNA and capable of protein synthesis have been prepared from microsomes. These ribosomes were purified to an extent which made them completely dependent on supernatant enzymes and tRNA for incorporation activity. The supernatant enzyme was extracted from microsomes and was prepared free of tRNA. tRNA was prepared from pupae or developing adults at different time periods after the larval pupal molt.

Cuticular protein is synthesized in vivo 5 to 6 days after the larval pupal molt. As an approximation for cuticular protein synthesis in ribosomal preparations we measured ratios of tyrosine to leucine incorporation. An increase in such a ratio may indicate preferential adult cuticular protein synthesis. Experiments of this nature are summarized in Table IV.

When ribosomes from day 1 were used and the enzyme fraction and transfer RNA was from day 7 a relative high ratio of incorporation of tyrosine to leucine was observed. Both enzyme and transfer RNA must be from day 7 in order to obtain a high level of tyrosine incorporation since when a combination such as enzyme from day 7 and transfer RNA from from day 1 or enzyme from day 1 and transfer RNA from day 7 were used, a relatively low ratio of tyrosine to leucine was observed. It is important to emphasize that the low ratio is as a result of decreasing tyrosine incorporation without affecting incorporation of leucine. The incorporation of the latter is at the same level under all conditions in which the source of transfer RNA and enzyme were varied. The salient point of these experiments is that under conditions in which both enzyme and transfer RNA from day 7 are used to supplement the ribosomal protein synthesizing system a protein product is synthesized which con-

tains more tyrosine per leucine per mole product and therefore it is qualitatively different.

Table IV
Ratio of tyrosine incorporation to leucine incorporation

The reaction mixture (0.25 ml) consisted of: 0.5 mg
of ribosomal RNA of insect ribosomes; 0.5 mM GTP; 8 mM
dithiothreitol; 2 mM ATP; 8 mM phosphoenolpyruvate; 40 µg
per ml of pyruvate kinase; 40 mM KCl; 35 mM Tris-HCl, pH
7.6; 6 mM $MgCl_2$; 19 ^{12}C-amino acids, 0.06 mM each; 0.2 µCi
of ^{14}C-leucine (222 mCi per mmole) or ^{14}C-tyrosine (375 mCi
per mmole); 1 mM phenylthiourea; 2 mg per ml of enzyme
protein; 1 mg per ml of tRNA. Incubations were carried out
for 30 min at 30° (Ilan et al., 1970).

| Enzyme | | tRNA | | Tyrosine | Leucine | Tyrosine to |
day 1	day 7	day 1	day 7	cpm/mg RNA		leucine ratio
		Ribosomes from 1st day pupae				
	+		+	9,600	9,800	0.98
+		+		2,400	9,800	0.25
		+		130	150	
	+	+		2,200	10,200	0.21
+			+	2,500	9,600	0.26
	+			38	42	
+				45	51	
		Ribosomes from 7th day pupae				
	+		+	17,600	10,700	1.64
+		+		2,600	10,600	0.25
		+		120	200	
	+	+		2,000	9,900	0.23
+			+	2,400	11,600	0.21
	+			50	48	
+				46	52	

Table IV also shows the complete dependency of the ribosomal preparation on the addition of tRNA and enzyme for incorporation activity. When ribosomes from day 7 were used essentially the same results were obtained. Namely, that both tRNA and enzyme from day 7 are needed for the translation of message into protein with high tyrosine content. The higher ratio obtained on day 7 ribosomes in comparison to day 1 ribosomes is interpreted to result from a higher content of messenger for cuticular protein on day 7 ribosomes. However, both ribosomes from day 1 or day 7 translate a protein with high tyrosine content when supplemented with transfer RNA and enzyme from day 7.

If synthesis of protein with high tyrosine content represents adult cuticular protein, it implies that ribosomes from 1st day pupae contain the message for this protein. The translation of this message is controlled by tRNA and enzyme fraction. With Tenebrio it was observed that when juvenile hormone or its mimics are topically applied to 1st day pupae one can obtain a second pupal molt eight days later. When dodecyl methyl ether was applied (1 μl per pupa) on 1st day pupa (0-4 hours after emergence) a perfect second pupal molt was obtained. It was important to determine whether the newly synthesized pupal cuticular protein results from a mechanism in which juvenile hormone affects the enzyme fraction and transfer RNA.

Involvement of Juvenile Hormone in Translational Control.

Ribosomes prepared from animals seven days after the larval pupal molt were used in the experiments utilizing juvenile hormone since these ribosomes have more messenger RNA than ribosomes from first day pupae. As juvenile hormone we used dodecyl methyl ether. In one set of experiments the ribosomes were prepared from untreated animals. These ribosomes were supplemented with transfer RNA and an enzyme preparation from hormone treated animals. Extractions of enzyme and transfer RNA were made six days after treatment. The results are summarized in Table V.

Essentially the table shows that transfer RNA and enzyme from hormone treated animals separately or in combination suppress the incorporation of tyrosine without affecting the incorporation of leucine. In contrast, transfer RNA and enzyme from 7 day old untreated animals together promote a higher incorporation of tyrosine. Again

transfer RNA and enzyme from hormone treated animals supplemented to ribosomes from normal pupae shifted the
pattern of incorporation into protein which contains fewer
tyrosine units per leucine. The shift in incorporation is
determined by the transfer RNA and the enzyme fraction only,
since day 7 ribosomes from hormone treated animals behave
as normal ribosomes and can promote different patterns of
incorporation in response to varying the sources of transfer RNA and enzyme. This is illustrated in Table V.

Table V
Effect of tRNA from Hormone Treated Animals.

Ribosomes from normal or hormone treated animals were
used 7 days after the pupal molt. tRNA was prepared from
animals of the same age (normal) or from insects of the
same age which had been treated with dodecyl methyl ether
(1 µl per pupa) on their 1st day of pupal life (Ilan et al.,
1970).

Enzyme			tRNA (from day 7 pupae)			
1st day	7th day		From hormone-treated animal	From normal animals	Tyrosine	Leucine
	Normal	Hor-mone			cpm/mg	RNA
Normal ribosomes						
	+		+		2,600	11,000
	+			+	18,000	10,800
+				+	2,000	9,500
+			+		2,400	11,500
		+	+		2,100	11,100
		+		+	2,300	11,000
Ribosomes from hormone treated animals						
	+		+		2,400	11,800
	+			+	17,200	10,500
		+	+		2,200	11,200
		+		+	2,400	10,000
+				+	2,600	10,500
+			+		2,400	11,600

Characterization of the Product Containing High Tyrosine
as Adult Cuticular Protein.

Changes in the ratio of tyrosine to leucine incorporation in a cell-free preparation can serve only as an
indicator but not as proof for a shift in protein synthesis.
Therefore, a more rigorous test was conducted which involved finger printing of the proteins as follows: Adult
cuticular protein was labeled in vivo by injecting
C^{14}-leucine into animals during the late adult developmental stage. The animals were allowed to develop into adults
and the adult cuticular protein was isolated. This labeled
protein was combined with H^3-leucyl labeled protein synthesized in a cell-free preparation under conditions which
showed high tyrosine to leucine ratio of amino acid
incorporation. The combined proteins were digested with
trypsin and the tryptic digest was subjected to column
chromatography. Trypsin specifically cleaves the polypeptide chain at points where lysine occurs. Therefore,
if the protein synthesized in vitro is the same as that
synthesized in vivo the peptides resulting from the tryptic
digestion will be identical in length, in amino acid
composition and hence in charge. Cochromatography of the
tryptic digest of the in vivo and in vitro protein products
should show the same elution pattern for the C^{14}-peptides
synthesized in vivo and the H^3-peptides synthesized in
vitro.

Almost identical elution patterns were obtained when
a digest of labeled protein synthesized in a cell-free
system was cochromatographed with a digest of labeled
cuticular protein synthesized in vivo (Ilan, 1969; Ilan
et al., 1970). This is illustrated in Fig. 1a.

We have seen in Table V that addition of transfer RNA
from day 7 animals which had been treated with juvenile
hormone on day 1, is sufficient to bring about a shift in
the ratio of amino acids incorporated into protein in cell-
free preparations. A protein synthesized under such
conditions and labeled with H^3-leucine was combined with
C^{14}-leucyl labeled peptide that was synthesized with enzyme
and tRNA from day 7 animals. Both peptides were trypsin-
ized and cochromatographed on a Dowex-50-X2 column by a
gradient of pyridinium acetate as described above. Fig. 1b
shows that the profile of the H^3-leucyl labeled peptide
does not correspond in position after chromatography with

the profile of the C^{14}-leucyl-labeled peptide which represents fragments of adult cuticular protein. The only difference between the two preparations lies in the source of transfer RNA.

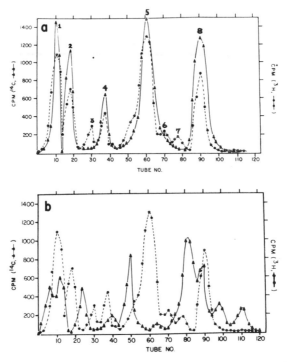

Fig. 1. Product analysis. (a) Elution profiles of tryptic digests of C^{14}-cuticular protein synthesized in vivo and digest of H^3-protein synthesized in vitro. The digests were cochromatographed. The in vitro incubation medium contained tRNA and enzyme from day 7 untreated animals. (b) Elution profiles of tryptic digests of H^3-protein synthesized in vitro as in (a) and tryptic digest of C^{14}-protein which had been synthesized with tRNA from hormone treated animals. Both digests were cochromatographed.

It appears that the tRNA from hormone treated animals can selectively translate mRNA which is not adult cuticular protein. Also it is obvious that the message for adult cuticular protein is present in the preparation.

Similar results to those obtained with tRNA from hormone treated animals were obtained with tRNA from day 1 animals.

The Role of Transfer RNA in Translational Control.

Table VI shows that addition to ribosomes of 0.5 mg of tRNA from first day pupae is saturating, since addition of 1 mg does not promote greater incorporation for leucine or tyrosine. However, when 0.5 mg of first day tRNA was added together with 1 mg of tRNA from day 7 pupae the ratio of tyrosine to leucine incorporation increased, producing an approximately six fold stimulation in tyrosine incorporation over and above the saturation level of first day tRNA.

As a control tRNA-CMP-AMP-pyrophosphorylase from rat liver was prepared. This enzyme reversibly cleaves the three terminal end nucleotides from tRNA as follows:

$$PPi + tRNA\text{-}C\text{-}C\text{-}A \rightleftharpoons tRNA + 2CTP + ATP$$

The amino acid is attached to the 3' end terminal adenylic moiety of tRNA. Therefore, if the terminal adenylic nucleotide is stripped from the tRNA the latter cannot be aminoacylated and does not function in protein synthesis. When tRNA from 7th day animals was pyrophosphorilyzed and re-isolated it lost its ability to stimulate relative tyrosine incorporation over and above the saturation point of first day tRNA. When the same tRNA preparation was reactivated by reversing the reaction and re-adding the missing CCA-end nucleotides, it regained its ability to stimulate relative tyrosine incorporation (Table VI). Therefore, it is the tRNA and not a contaminant from the tRNA fraction which is the important factor in the relative rise in tyrosine incorporation. We suggest that this is due to the degeneracy of the genetic code.

We have observed (Ilan et al., 1970; Ilan, 1969) a correlation in the timing of the appearance of new tRNA^{Leu} and its activating enzyme with the switch in protein synthesis in vivo. Fig. 2a depicts kinetics of the formation of C^{14}-leucyl-tRNA using tRNA from first day pupae and leucyl-tRNA synthetase from animals of the same age. At 45 min (arrow) more tRNA was added. This addition resulted in a second increase in leucyl-tRNA formation, indicating that at the plateau the limiting factor is the

Table VI
Effect of tRNA which had been inactivated
by pyrophosphorolysis and reactivated
on amino acid incorporation

Pyrophosphorolysis of tRNA prepared from animals 7 days after the larval pupal molt was carried out (Ilan et al., 1970). The reaction was terminated by the addition of an equal volume of freshly distilled water-saturated phenol and RNA was isolated. Reactivation was carried out in 3 ml at 37° for 60 min. The reaction mixture contained 40 mM Tris-HCl (pH 8.4), 6mM MgCl$_2$, 0.5 mM ATP, 0.5 mM CTP, 10 mM phosphoenolpyruvate, 5 μg of pyruvate kinase, 5 μg of inorganic pyrophosphorylase, 3 mg of pyrophosphorylized tRNA, and 3 mg of rat liver tRNA-CMP-AMP-pyrophosphorylase. The reaction was terminated by the addition of an equal volume of water-saturated phenol and tRNA was isolated. Experimental conditions for amino acid incorporation were as described in the legend to Table IV except that the ribosomes and enzyme used were prepared only from animals 7 days after the larval pupal molt. The total volume of the reaction mixture was reduced to 0.1 ml and tRNA was added as indicated in the table.

Addition of tRNA (mg)				Incorporation	
	From day 7				
From day 1	Un-treated	Pyrophos-phorylized	Pyrophos-phorylized and reactivated	Tyrosine	Leucine
				cpm/mg RNA	
	1.0			18,000	10,000
0.5				2,300	10,700
1.0				2,500	10,100
0.5	1.0			12,600	9,900
0.5		1.0		2,100	11,200
0.5			1.0	11,700	10,600
0.5			1.0[a]	2,200	10,400

[a]Reactivation reaction of pyrophosphorylized tRNA was carried out in the absence of CTP.

56

availability of tRNA^{Leu}. The influence of increasing amounts of leucyl-tRNA synthetase on the formation of C^{14}-leucyl-tRNA is shown in Fig. 2b, c, and d. In all cases there is a linear increase of leucine esterification and saturation is reached at about 1 mg of enzyme per ml. However, when tRNA prepared from day 7 animals was used as substrate and aminoacylated to saturation by enzyme from 1 day old pupae, addition of enzyme from day 7 after the saturation point resulted in additional charging (Fig. 2c).

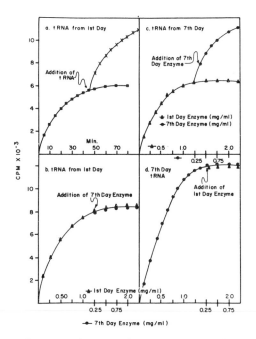

Fig. 2. Changes in leucine acceptor ability during metamorphosis. The formation of ^{14}C-leucyl-tRNA unless otherwise stated was carried out at 30° for 30 min. Microsomal wash served as enzyme. The incubation mixture (0.1 ml) contained per ml: 50 μmoles of imidazole (pH 7), 10 μmoles of $MgCl_2$, 4 μmoles of ATP, 1 μCi of ^{14}C-leucine (248 mCi per mmole), and 1 mg of tRNA from different sources as indicated above. The reaction was terminated by the addition of 5 ml of cold 5% trichloracetic acid; the precipitate was washed on a glass filter with 50 ml of cold trichloracetic acid, dried and counted (Ilan et al., 1970).

These results suggest that leucyl-tRNA synthetase prepared from 7 day old animals can recognize more or different subspecies of tRNA^{Leu}. This new leucine acceptor tRNA is not found in tRNA prepared from 1st day pupae (Fig. 2b). In contrast to the experiments shown in Fig. 2c, Fig. 2d shows experiments using tRNA from day 7 which had been aminoacylated to the point of saturation with increasing amounts of enzyme from day 7. Addition of the enzyme fraction from 1st day did not result in increased charging. This suggests that the day 7 enzyme preparation also contains the enzyme present in 1st day preparations. Alternatively, the 7th day enzyme could have all of the specificities of 1st day enzyme as well as its additional functions. tRNA and enzyme prepared from animals 7 days after the larval pupal molt behaves like enzyme and tRNA isolated from 1st day pupae, if the animals had been treated with juvenile hormone on the 1st day of pupation.

Additional evidence for the appearance of a new isoacceptor tRNA^{Leu} during development was obtained from experiments based on the following rationale. If cells from 7 day old animals contain an additional isoaccepting tRNA^{Leu} which is discriminately recognized by synthetases, this tRNA may contain a unique sequence of nucleotides. The first guanosine base in the nucleotide sequence starting from the terminal - CCA might not be in the same position in the 7th day tRNA^{Leu} as in the 1st day tRNA^{Leu}. We tested this hypothesis in the following way: First day tRNA was aminoacylated with H^3-leucine and 7th day tRNA with C^{14}-leucine. The mixture was digested to completion with T1 ribonuclease. Some aminoacyl oligonucleotides from the 7th day tRNA differed in length from the aminoacyl oligonucleotides produced from identically treated 1st day tRNA. T1 ribonuclease hydrolyzes at the guanosine-phosphate bond exclusively. Oligonucleotides were fractionated according to their length on a column of DEAE cellulose. The position of the oligonucleotide in the elution gradient at pH 5.5 is largely a function of the number of phosphorous atoms in the fragment. Under these conditions the ester bond is stable and the terminal oligonucleotide fragment possesses the radioactive amino acid and was thus identified.

It is seen from Fig. 3 that tRNA from 1st day animals contains 5 different oligonucleotides which represent the 3' end with the H^3-leucine still attached. 7th day tRNA^{Leu}

when charged with C^{14}-leucine using enzymes from day 7, contained all 5 fragments observed for day 1 $tRNA^{Leu}$ as well as a pronounced new terminal fragment of C^{14}-leucyl-oligonucleotide (Fig. 3 arrow). This additional fragment resulted from $tRNA^{Leu}$ which is genetically different from that obtained from 1st day $tRNA^{Leu}$. The distance between the leucine and the first guanosine residue is not the same as that observed for 1st day $tRNA^{Leu}$.

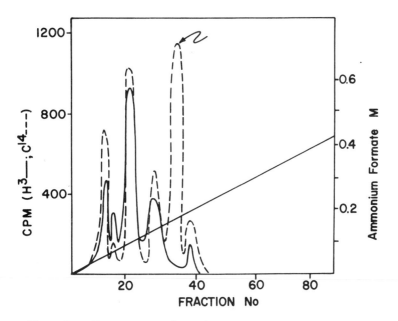

Fig. 3. Chromatography of T1 RNase digestion products of leucyl-tRNA. tRNA preparations from day 7 were charged with C^{14}-leucine and tRNA from day 1 with H^3-leucine as described in Fig. 2. The isolated aminoacyl tRNAs were deproteinized and then mixed and 500 μg of the mixture digested with 500 units of T1 RNase at 37° for 45 min in 2 mM EDTA in sodium acetate buffer pH 5.5. The digest was applied to a 1 cm x 5 cm column of DEAE cellulose and eluted at 4° using a linear gradient of ammonium formate at pH 5.5 in the presence of 7M urea.

The genetic code specifies six codons for leucine. This implies six tRNA^{Leu} which differ at least in the anticodon sequence of nucleotides. It remains to be shown that the new tRNA^{Leu} from the 7th day which differs at the 3' end from that of 1st day tRNA^{Leu} varies also in the anticodon sequence.

Gene Activity and Rates of mRNA Translation.

Most examples brought to show differences in gene activity imply that genes are "turned on" or "turned off". In liver cells the gene for albumin is "turned on" as though genes existed in only two alternative states, active and inactive. However, there is evidence that the same gene can be active to varying degrees. Isozymes are an example. In case of lactic dehydrogenase there are five isozymes and any cell that has one usually has all. But the cells of different tissues or organs, or the same tissue or organ at different stages of development, have different proportions of the five isozymes. The difference is in the relative activity of the two genes. Another example is tyrosine transaminase in mammalian liver, a basal level of which is always present. The level of the enzyme can be elevated (induced) by treatment with hydrocortisone. This phenomenon has been interpreted to result from different rates of gene transcription at various times. Alternatively, this may be due to differences in rates of translation of mRNA at different stages. For instance, the basic level of tyrosine transaminase in liver is quite high and cannot be suppressed by Actinomycin D. After a short period of induction by hydrocortisone, addition of the antibiotic overstimulates enzyme induction (Garren et al., 1964). This may suggest translational control.
It is attractive to suggest, that since the rate of translation of specific natural mRNA can be differentially slowed or stimulated in vitro by simple deletion or addition of a tRNA fraction, a similar control mechanism might occur in the cell in vivo, by the reduction or elevation in the concentration of a specific tRNA species.
We carried out in vitro experiments in which ribosomes from animals 7 days after the larval-pupal molt were incubated with limiting amounts of enzyme isolated from animals of the same age. A constant amount of tRNA from

day 7 animals, and varying amounts of tRNA extracted from animals of the same age which had been treated with juvenile hormone were added. Reverse experiments in which a constant amount of tRNA from hormone treated animals and varying amounts of tRNA from normal 7th day animals, were carried out. These experiments are summarized in Table VII.

Table VII

Effect of combining different concentrations of tRNA
from normal and hormone treated animals
on amino acid incorporation

Addition of tRNA isolated from 7th day pupae		Incorporation	
Hormone treated animal	Normal	Tyrosine	Leucine
mg		cpm/mg RNA	
1.0		2,300	10,500
0.5		2,600	11,800
0.5	0.5	5,400	10,600
0.5	1.0	12,600	9,500
	1.0	18,400	11,400
	0.5	18,300	10,600
0.5	0.5	5,900	11,400
1.0	0.5	2,800	10,100
0.5	1.0[a]	2,300	10,800
1.0[a]	0.5	18,000	11,400

[a]Treated with rat liver tRNA-CMP-AMP-pyrophosphorylase.

It is clear that the ratio of incorporation of tyrosine to leucine is proportional to the amount of tRNA added above the amount present from each source. The ratio may, therefore, express rates of translation controlled by rare tRNA.

Similar observations on a rate limiting tRNA species which regulates the rate of translation of bacterial or mammalian mRNA were reported recently. Anderson (1969) has

studied the effect of different tRNA species on the rate of
translation of artificial mRNA templates in vitro in an
E. coli system. He suggested that AGA and AGG might be
regulatory codons in E. coli. Both are code words for
arginine. The rate of polypeptide synthesis was stimulated
in direct proportion to the amount of arginine tRNA
corresponding to AGA and AGG, when poly AG was used as a
message. These findings indicate that E. coli extract
contained only a rate limiting amount of the above species
of arginine tRNA. Therefore, it would follow that any
change in the abundance of the individual tRNA species
would be potentially capable of changing the rate of
translation of mRNA. There are indications that such
regulation is also present in mammalian and insect systems.
It was shown by Weisblum et al., (1965) that tRNA^{Leu} can be
separated into two fractions. These two fractions insert .
leucine into different positions in the hemoglobin chain.
This work has been extended to show that a similar phenomenon exists for tRNA carrying serine, arginine or glutamic
acid. Since different species of tRNA can be responsible
for inserting the same amino acid into a hemoglobin chain,
the presence of limiting amounts of one species might
produce a reduced rate of mRNA translation at a given
point. Recently, Anderson and Gilbert (1969) presented
evidence that unequal chain synthesis of chains of hemoglobin in vitro, could be mediated by tRNA. They concluded
that even though the alpha and beta chain both contain all
twenty amino acids, the alpha chain must contain at least
one codon which is used either less often, or not at all
in beta chain synthesis. If such control also operates
in developing systems it may partially explain the rise in
amount of enzyme and structural protein.

Evidence that the Translational Control of Protein
Synthesis is at the Chain Elongation Level.

We have shown that tRNA is involved in translational
control of protein synthesis. Juvenile hormone promotes
changes in tRNA thereby discriminating which mRNA is to be
translated. tRNA is involved in the translational
machinery in at least three points: at peptide chain
initiation, at peptide chain elongation and at the termination of the polypeptide chain. Regulation may occur at
each of these levels. Therefore it was important to

determine the point of regulation. First we examined the
capacity of the system to initiate polypeptide chain
synthesis. Table VIII shows that when microsomal preparations are incubated with C^{14}-algal hydrolysate and the
incorporation of C^{14}-amino acids into NH_2-terminal position
is measured, 5 to 10% of the labeled amino acids are in the
NH_2-terminal position. Conversely, on purified ribosomes
no incorporation into NH_2-position was observed.

Table VIII

Chain initiation in cell-free system

Incubation conditions as described in Table IV, except
that ^{14}C-algal hydrolysate was used and in some experiments
microsomes were used. The hot trichloracetic acid precipitate was washed with ether. The protein (3 mg per sample)
was suspended in 3 ml of H_2O in excess of fluorodinitrobenzene for 80 min at pH 9 and 40°. The pH was maintained
by addition of 2 N NaOH. Excess of fluorodinitrobenzene
was extracted with ether and the solution was acidified to
6 N HCl and hydrolyzed for 16 hours at 100°. The precip-
itated 2,4-dinitrophenyl derivatives were separated by
centrifugation, resuspended in ether, and aliquots were
counted. Portions from the supernatant fluid of the 2,4-
dinitrophenyl derivatives served for measurement of internal peptide labeling. The recovery of radioactivity was
close to 70%.

Experiment	Conditions	Incorporation	
		NH_2-terminal	Internal
		cpm/mg protein	
1	Microsomes	516	5974
2	Microsomes	354	5863
3	Ribosomes	0	7956
4	Ribosomes	0	8211

It is possible that the lack of NH_2-terminal labeling
on purified ribosomes might be a result of a blocked amino
group at the NH_2-terminal position of the polypeptide

chain. However, it seems more likely that the purified
ribosomes have lost chain initiation factors, since the
purification involves three washings in 0.5 M KCl (Ilan,
1968). Such a procedure is known to remove initiation
factors from bacterial ribosomes. Moreover, reticulocyte
ribosomes purified in the same manner lost their ability
to incorporate C^{14}-valine into the NH_2-terminal position
of hemoglobin (Bishop, et al., 1960).

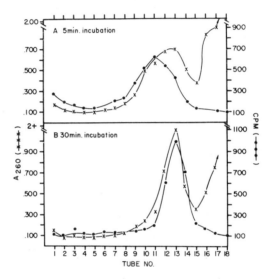

Fig. 4. Localization of newly synthesized polypeptide
during incubation of purified ribosomes. Incubations were
carried out as described in the legend to Table IV except
for the time as indicated above. After incubation the
tubes were placed in ice and their contents were layered
on a 10 to 40% sucrose gradient (4.5 ml). After centrifugation for 90 min at 39,000 rpm. drops were collected
from the bottom (2 drops per sample), diluted to 1 ml for
optical density determination, after which 5 ml of 5%
trichloracetic acid were added and the samples were heated
for 20 min at 90°. The protein was collected and washed
on Millipore filters and counted (From Ilan et al., 1970).

Next we looked for chain termination on purified
ribosomes. We had previously observed that a crude microsomal system is capable of releasing about 30% of the

labeled protein (Ilan et al., 1970). However, chain termination does not occur in the purified ribosomal system. This is evident from the following experiment: when a complete reaction mixture was cooled after 5 minutes of incubation and analyzed by sucrose gradient sedimentation most of the protein that was synthesized in the cell-free system is in the polysome region.

The same analysis was applied to a sample after 30 minutes of incubation. From previous kinetic studies it was known that the reaction is over after 30 minutes (Ilan, 1968). The polysomes had broken down to monosomes. However, the newly synthesized protein was not released from the monosomes (Fig. 4). Therefore, the involvement of tRNA in regulation of mRNA translation is not at the chain termination level. The only remaining possibility for involvement of tRNA in mRNA translation is in regulation at the chain elongation level.

Summary and Conclusions

Many processes of growth and development in higher plants and animals are controlled by hormones. The emphasis in hormone research has been on the transcription of DNA. Much of the current thinking and experimental design in the field of growth and differentiation is based on the model for gene expression suggested by Jacob and Monod (1961). Although this model was proven to be essentially correct for some bacterial systems, it has not been adequately tested for multicellular organisms.

Many variations and modifications of this model have been suggested for higher organisms. For insects it was first proposed by Karlson (1963) that ecdysone acts directly on the gene to produce mRNA for a specific protein enzyme, dopa decarboxylase. An inhibition of the hormonal effect by actinomycin D was interpreted as a proof for direct hormonal involvement in the transcription of DNA into messenger RNA. The experiments with ecdysone were performed on the blowfly Calliphora during puparium formation. The ligated larvae were treated with ecdysone and the induced enzyme appeared in the epidermal cells twenty hours later. Since ecdysone is known to stimulate cell division in the epidermis the daugher cells are the ones likely to contain the induced enzyme. Therefore, the cells treated with ecdysone are probably not those which contain high dopa decarboxylase.

A prerequisite for regulation of gene expression as put forth by Jacob and Monod is that the mRNA must be a short-lived intermediate. Thus the synthesis of the final gene product, the protein, could be "turned on" or "turned off" by turning on or off the synthesis of mRNA. It is well established in many developing systems as well as in insect development that many mRNA's are stable. Moreover, there is usually a lag period between the synthesis of mRNA and its translation. Therefore in cells containing stable mRNA some of which is not immediately translated, other mechanisms must be responsible for gene expression. These mechanisms must be at the translational or post transcriptional level.

Here we have presented evidence for the regulation of the synthesis of one protein, adult cuticular protein during Tenebrio adult development. Our experiments show that the control of gene expression mediated by juvenile hormone is at the translational level and involves the appearance of new tRNA and its activating enzyme. The mRNA for cuticular protein is formed well in advance but is not immediately translated. tRNA and enzyme from the differentiated stage can direct the reading of this specific mRNA. Moreover, tRNA from hormone treated animals added to normal ribosomes, which contain mRNA for adult cuticular protein cannot permit the synthesis of this protein.

The identification of the protein product of the cell-free system was achieved by cochromatography of the tryptic digest together with digest of cuticular protein synthesized in vivo. We have also shown that it is the tRNA fraction and not a contaminant in the tRNA preparation which is important. This was achieved by inactivation and reactivation of tRNA with tRNA-CMP-AMP-pyrophosphorylase. The fact that the enzyme fraction is also needed is interesting, because such a requirement could provide a double filter mechanism. We have never observed more than one peak of activity of leucyl-tRNA synthetase from a chromatographic profile. Therefore, the additional functions of this enzyme at day 7 of development might result from an alteration at the macromolecular level.

We have also shown that on purified ribosomes neither chain initiation nor chain termination of polypeptide take place. Therefore, the translational effect is at the level of chain elongation and involves a rate limiting species of tRNA. We have shown the appearance of new isoacceptor tRNA^{Leu} which is genetically different from the five iso-acceptor tRNA^{Leu} present during early development. There is no direct evidence of involvement of this subspecies of tRNA with the switch in protein synthesis but there is indirect evidence. The timing of the appearance of new leucyl-acceptor-tRNA is correlated to the shift in protein synthesis. Also, the fact that enzyme and tRNA are required from a late developmental stage for the switch in protein synthesis may suggest the existence of a link between the acceptor activity and the switch in protein synthesis. We would like to stress that the appearance of new leucyl specific tRNA during development is not unique for insects and has been reported for many developing systems (Lee and Ingram, 1967). Leucyl-tRNA is in a suitable position to regulate protein synthesis. There are six code words for leucine, UUA, UUG, CUU, CUC, CUA, CUG. Each one of them inserts leucine into polypeptide chain and requires tRNAs which are different from each other at least in the anticodon sequence.

We imagine that in some developmental systems the mRNAs are stable and programmed in advance. In others, some of the mRNA is stable while in some is turned over. However, a group of mRNAs share a common code for a rare tRNA. The appearance of a rare tRNA either as a result of direct effect of the hormone on DNA, or by activation of pre-existing tRNA, will trigger the translation of these mRNAs. Since the code is degenerate, other messages, which do not share this particular code word, are independent of the hormone and can be translated. It is known that tRNA can exist in two stages, native and denatured (Lindahl, et al., 1967). Moreover, certain drugs will mediate the conversion of tryptophan tRNA from an inactive to an active state (Muench, et al., 1966).

References

W.F. Anderson, **Proc**. Nat. Acad. Sci. U.S., 62, 566 (1969)

W.F. Anderson and J.M. Gilbert, Cold Spring Harbor Symposia on Quantitative Biology, 34, 585 (1969)

J.O. Bishop, J. Leahy and R.S. Schweet, Proc. Nat. Acad. Sci. U.S., 46, 1030 (1960)

L.D. Garren, R.R. Howell, G.M. Tomkins and R.M. Crocco, Proc. Nat. Acad. Sci. U.S., 52, 1121 (1964)

P.R. Gross and G.H. Cousineau, Biochem. Biophys. Res. Commun., 10, 321 (1963)

J. Ilan, J. Ilan and J.H. Quastel, Biochem. Journ., 100, 441 (1966)

J. Ilan and F. Lipmann, Acta Biochem. Polon., 13, 353 (1966)

J. Ilan and J.H. Quastel, Biochem. J., 100, 448 (1966)

J. Ilan, J. Biol. Chem., 243, 5859 (1968)

J. Ilan, Cold Spring Harbor Symposia on Quantitative Biology, 34, 787 (1969)

J. Ilan, J. Ilan and N. Patel, J. Biol. Chem., 245, 1275 (1970)

F. Jacob and J. Monod, J. Mol. Biol., 3, 318 (1961)

F.C. Kafatos and J. Reich, Proc. Nat. Acad. Sci. U.S., 60, 58 (1968)

P. Karlson, Perspectives Biol. Med., 6, 203 (1963)

J.C. Lee and V.M. Ingram, Science, 158, 1330 (1967)

T. Lindahl, A. Adams, M. Geroch and J.R. Fresco, Proc. Nat. Acad. Sci. U.S., 57, 178 (1967)

P.A. Marks, E.R. Burka and D. Schlessinger, Proc. Nat. Acad. Sci. U.S., 48, 2163 (1962)

A.A. Moscona, M.H. Moscona and N. Saenz, Proc. Nat. Acad. Sci. U.S., 61, 160 (1968)

K.H. Muench, Cold Spring Harbor Symposia on Quantitative Biology, 31, 539 (1966)

D. Nathans and F. Lipmann, Biochim. Biophys. Acta, 43, 126 (1960)

H.A. Schneiderman and L.I. Gilbert, Science, 143, 325 (1964)

R.W. Seed and H.I. Goldberg, Proc. Nat. Acad. Sci. U.S., 50, 275 (1963)

R.W. Seed and H.I. Goldberg, J. Biol. Chem., 240, 764 (1965)

M. Sussman, Proc. Nat. Acad. Sci. U.S., 55, 813 (1966)

B. Weisblum, F. Gonano, G. von Ehrenstein and S. Benzer, Proc. Nat. Acad. Sci. U.S., 53, 328 (1965)

BIOLOGICAL ACTIVITY AND BIO ASSAY OF

JUVENILE HORMONE ANALOGS

Gerardus B. Staal
Zoëcon Corporation, Research Laboratory
Palo Alto, California 94304

Abstract

Of the known insect hormones only juvenile hormone analogs (JHA) are at present considered to have immediate promise for insect pest control. Biological impact of these compounds (including natural juvenile hormones) and their bio-assay technology are discussed in the light of possible applications.

Introduction

Recent papers (1,2,3,4,5,6,7,8,9,10,11,12,13, 14,15,16,57) give accounts of some of the present knowledge of structure activity relationships of representatives of certain structural groups of JHA. Although the diversification and the number of structures is impressive, absolute specificity for species does not exist, family specificity is rare and some relative order specificity is the rule. Little evidence is reported for other than quantitative differences in biological activity between compounds. Qualitatively different effects are often obtained when JHA are applied at different moments in the life cycle, but our experience has shown that a correlation between activities measured in bio assays on different stages of the life cycle in the same insect holds good for nearly all compounds. A qualitatively different factor of utmost importance for practical applications must be the rate of degradation in different environmental situations and perhaps also in the target organism. In laboratory screening this degradation period should be as short as possible in order to minimize this factor. Special degradation studies must be very carefully planned in order to yield useful results.

Sensitive periods for JHA action are always limited, but the effects are often delayed (sometimes up to several months), and knockdown effects do not occur. Evaluative scoring may be complicated since death of the insect is not usually a direct effect of these compounds and more complicated phenomena have to be considered.

Standardization of assay animals and assay conditions is perhaps not fully possible but standardization of evaluation techniques and statistical expression is certainly desirable. In this way figures may be compared between laboratories.

Since JH is a major regulator of the insect's development, not only of metamorphosis and oogenesis, but also of a variety of other processes, exposure to exogenous JHA at a moment of low endogenous titer is very disruptive. What makes the impact of exogenous JHA so dramatic at the moment that induction of metamorphosis requires a low JH titer, is the irreversibility of the effect due to the fixation of morphological characters in the exoskeleton during the molt and subsequent ecdysis, abnormal behavior patterns, etc. During metamorphosis a temporary low JH titer is required for the degeneration of the prothoracic gland so that the adults will not molt (46). Partially inhibited intermediates but sometimes also adults that have been exposed to low exogenous JH levels as larvae will therefore often initiate a molting that is doomed to fail because adult cuticle lacks the proper ecdysis mechanism. The mentioned effects, readily produced by exogenous JHA, have been known for many years as a result of corpora allata implantations, parabioses, and other surgical techniques. The fact that all of

these earlier obtained results could be duplicated
by exogenous application of JHA came as a very
pleasant surprise when practical applicability was
considered, because there is no obvious advantage
to an insect to have a cuticle that can be pene-
trated by a juvenile hormone mimicking compound,
or even its own hormone.

Much less predictable was the finding that
JHA can disrupt embryonic development in the early
egg stages or even through application to the
female prior to oviposition.

Sensitive Stages in the Insect Development

Larval Development. There is no evidence for
any direct effect of excess juvenile hormone on
larval development prior to metamorphosis in most
non social insects. When active corpora allata
are implanted in young larval instars as a rule
nothing happens before the usual time of metamorphosis. Since metamorphosis takes place when the
corpora allata are shut off and a low titer of
juvenile hormone results, any excess juvenile
hormone, through topical applications, injections,
or through the implantation of excess corpora
allata is disruptive. The remanence of exogenous
JHA applied in earlier larval instars seems to be
largely a function of the chemical compound in
question and of the insect taxon, but generally
this remanence is very low. The Endopterygota in
particular have efficient mechanisms to metabolize
JH at the onset of metamorphosis, probably through
a stepping up of an always present JH breakdown
mechanism (17) and also through a varying ability
to postpone the pupal molt induction until the
titer of JH is sufficiently low. However, when
such a delay is abnormally long, normal pupation
and further development rarely occurs.

Exopterygota cannot escape through postpon-
ing the metamorphic molt. If this is inhibited
usually an accelerated larval molt ensues. Most
likely because of this reason the remanence of
JHA in this group is usually higher when applied
to earlier instars. The application of JHA to

first instar aphid nymphs has produced increased
mortality in the next larval molt (18). This
effect has been confirmed in our laboratories
while using highly purified JHA (19). The mechanism involved has not been studied in detail.

The morph determination in aphids is most
likely not directly mediated by JH. In the castes
in bees, termites and other social insects, JH
probably plays an important role, but the complexity of this phenomenon necessitates further investigation (20,21). The influence of high JH titers
in the nymphs of grasshoppers and locusts is well
defined. They respond by forming green pigment in
the blood and the integument under the simultaneous disappearance of dark pigments in the exocut-
icle (22,23,24,8). This effect signals a special
function of extra high titers that have otherwise
little morphogenetic effect in the nymphs. This
"phase" phenomenon plays a role in the ecological
adaptation of the population (24). Further analysis shows that the induction periods for pigmentation and for morphogenetic inhibition are different in the last larval instar so that green
adults can form. The exact consequences of an
artifically induced solitary pigmentation in the
field are not known but are probably not very
impressive since this phenomenon is reversible
before lethal effects on metamorphosis are
induced.

Very high JHA pulse doses may indirectly
stimulate the prothoracic gland to secrete a critical dose of molting hormone somewhat prematur-
ely, which can lead to an effect on the development program resulting in more larval instars(81).
The spectacular morphological differentiation from
larval instar to larval instar in certain insects
like the Cecropia silkworm ("heteromorphosis")
cannot be influenced directly by manipulations
with JHA (25).

Metamorphosis. In Exopterygota the sensitive
period is restricted to the last larval instar,
in Endopterygota with a two stage metamorphosis
the pupal stage is again sensitive. However, the
changes in the exoskeleton are actually only part

of the overall effect. Metamorphosis of internal organs like the nervous system and associated behavioral changes and metabolic changes are not as thoroughly studied but may be of tremendous impact on the ultimate survival of the individual. It has been demonstrated in Galleria that the induction periods for the metamorphosis of the different organs and structures are generally not coinciding (26,27,28,29,79). Application of JHA at different moments therefore can lead to the inhibition of a different complex of responding organs or tissues. The maximum result in the form of extra larval instars can only be obtained by application of JH early in the last larval instar or by continuous exposure. Extra larval instars may consume more food and molt again to larval instars, but do not produce normal adults under most experimental conditions. In most Lepidoptera the prepupa cannot transform into a full extra larva any more but most of the exoskeleton can still be inhibited. Application at this stage leads to unviable intermediates that often have great difficulties in ecdysis. Even in species that lead a hidden life during most of their larval development, often the mature larva leaves the foodplant in search of a pupation site and just happens to be very sensitive at this stage. This can give some hope for control purposes.

We have observed that Plodia interpunctella can respond to exogenous JHA by almost unlimited postponement of the pupal molt until death ensues months later. Larvae of Hyalophora cecropia do not readily respond to any type of exogenous application. The response therefore can be very different even within orders of insects. Lepidoptera usually can make intermediates between larvae and pupae of either a homogenous type or a mosaic type, depending on the method and timing of the application. Coleoptera and Diptera are much more resistant in these respects. However, intermediates in these orders are more difficult to recognize because of the rather undefined character of the transparent pupal cuticle. In beetles like Diabrotica retention of an unpigmented pupal patch in the compound eyes is the most conspicuous scoring character, whereas pupal cuticle on the abdomen and pupal genitalia and urogomphi only occur under the influence of higher doses.

Mosquito and fly larvae always develop into pupae, and there are no well documented cases of extra larval instars or intermediates as a result of exposure to JHA prior to pupation. The effects are only observed later in the development of the adults.

Beetle larvae generally can respond by long delays in pupation. The delay is somehow related to a failure in the molting hormone secretion. Application of combinations of molting hormone and juvenile hormone, appropriately timed, may lead to all possible intermediates.

Most Endopterygota species are usually very sensitive during the first hours or days of pupal life. Diapausing pupae only become sensitive at the resumption of development although earlier applications can show remanency. In pupae complete exoskeletal inhibition is easily achieved. When treated pupae are left undisturbed, a repeated ecdysis to new extra pupal instars may be observed, indicating either cyclic sensitivity to a pool of remanent molting hormone, or repeated secretion of molting hormone. In no case will the extra pupae be able to extricate themselves from the earlier pupal skins.

Some toxic compounds are known to produce pseudo juvenilizing effects (30). We have observed for instance that pupae of Tenebrio may show a JH response to Fenthion. Certain inhibitors of mitosis are known to block differentiation resulting in pseudo-juvenilizing effects.

Embryonic Development. The sensitivity of early embryonic stages of exogenous JH was first described by Slama and Williams in 1966 (74). It has since been found to be a general phenomenon in all insects for which sufficiently active JHA are known (31,32,33,34,35,36). The nature of the disruption of embryonic development is described as either a differentiation failure or a toxic effect (35) but the mechanism is still obscure.

The observed responses are the failure to close the dorsal suture connecting the embryo with the yolk sack, muscle atrophy in the appendages, etc., all leading to failure in hatching (31,35,36,73). Full grown embryos may fail not only in the embryonic molt but also later, in the first larval instar, after having hatched normally, indicating internal abnormalities. An isolated observation on eggs of Dermestes vulpinus in our laboratory is that sublethal doses of JHA supplied to young eggs may result in viable larvae with very reduced setae. These larvae later molt into normal second instar larvae. This is strongly suggestive of a molting hormone action since reduced setae have been readily produced by the author in Actias selene (Lepidoptera) larvae by injection of mas-sive doses of molting hormones. In this case, the effect was correlated with a shortening of the intermolt period. Here, also the condition was often non lethal and was repaired in the next molt. (Setae are formed anew in every instar).

The effects on eggs seem useful for practical application, but are somewhat restricted because of the limited sensitivity window (Fig. 1).

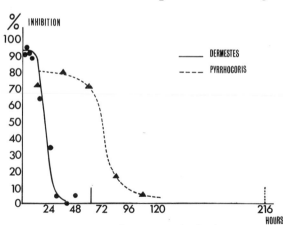

Fig. 1 The decrease in sensitivity to JHA in eggs of 2 insect species as a function of time. Eggs of Dermestes vulpinus and Pyrrhocoris apterus treated with a high dose of JHA.

The effect on embryonic development may be ampli-
fied by application to females prior to oviposition (33,38), but it remains largely theory because
except Pyrrhocoris and Dysdercus few insects are
sensitive enough to yield female sterilization by
topical application of JHA in reasonable doses.
With more potent JHA, however, the effects may
well be obtained. The sensitivity of females of
Pyrrhocoris is so exceptionally high that sterility may also be obtained even through contact with
contaminated males (37).

Oogenesis and Adult Diapause

Juvenile hormone is an indispensable factor
in the egg formation in many groups of insects
(22,39,40,41). Particularly those that have not
matured all their eggs at the moment of adult
ecdysis usually show only restricted egg ripening
when the corpora allata are taken out. Several
nocturnal Lepidoptera emerge with fully developed
eggs and in this case JH withdrawal through allatectomy has little effect. The effects of massive
overdoses of JHA on oogenesis have been insuffic-
iently studied, they tend to be obscured by more
spectacular effects on embryogenesis. Masner
(42), however, already pointed out that the differentiation of follicular epithelium requires a
period of absence of juvenile hormone. Studies
in our laboratories indicate that doses higher
than those necessary for effects on embryogenesis
often reduce fecundity. This will have to be
studied by detailed dissection and histology in
order to find the causal relationships.
Several insect species undergo an adult diapause preceeding reproduction. In the females at
least, diapause termination and oogenesis are both
dependent on JH. Exogenous JH can break diapause
and induce egg ripening simultaneously (43).
There are observations indicating that the length
of diapause interruption and the number of eggs
produced are proportional to the amount of JH
administered (80). After having responded to a
small dose of JH by breaking diapause females may

76

later return to the diapause condition, or die pre-
maturely for unknown reasons. Complete breaking
of diapause probably requires more than only a JH
stimulus, and the latter alone may therefore induce
an abnormal and morbid condition. Nevertheless,
diapause disruption with JHA has found a use in
insect breeding (43).

Other types of diapause in Saturnidae can be
broken with large doses of JH, but there is good
evidence that this is an indirect JH influence
affecting molting hormone secretion (45). Depending on the mode of administration, this so-called
prothoracotropic effect may or may not be accompan-
ied by juvenilization at the same time since the
induction periods do not seem to coincide (44).
The role of hormones in larval diapause prior to
pupation is not well understood. However, it must
be ultimately linked to a molting hormone deficiency. This condition may be also associated with a
high JH titer and there is indeed no evidence that
exogenous JHA can break it. The molt delaying
influence of JHA in many Endopterygota suggests
that it is a similar phenomenon induced artifically.

Direct male sterilization has not been reported for JHA, but through the failure of normal
genital rotation as a marginal JHA effect in Diptera, functional mechanical sterility has been
achieved (47).

Female accessory glands can be dependent on
JH for their synthesis of the normal secretion
products. This has been utilized for a JH bioassay
on ligated adult cockroaches, in which the secretion products after JHA administration can be chemically evaluated (48).

Programming of Development. No good explanation for the mechanism of regulating larval development has been presented. Many insects go
through a fixed number of instars after which the
JH secretion stops and metamorphosis follows. In
other insects, the number of instars is less fixed
and dependent on environmental and genetical factors. In both cases, the premature onset of metamorphosis would be detrimental. What exactly shuts

off the JH secretion in the corpora allata at the precise and critical moment is not known. Humoral control, as well as nervous induction from a central organ, has been considered. Effects on programming, or deferred effects, as distinguished from direct effects have been obtained by JHA applications (34,36,49). The effect may become apparent only when the exogenous induction has long worn off and JHA is no longer detectable (50). Whatever the mechanism is, if these effects can be shown to occur in other insects too, it would be of great practical consequence.

Effects on Behavior. Many aspects of behavior are only related to stages in the metamorphosis and diapause and do not have to be discussed here. Direct and short term effects of JH on behavior have not been reported so far. JHA may affect the secretion of sex pheromones and thus influence male behavior indirectly (39) but the possible control aspects of this have not been studied.

BIOASSAY OBJECTIVES AND CHOICE OF BIOASSAY

Since all the effects that are known from endogenous JH may theoretically be used for bioassays, the possibilities are manifold. Good consideration should therefore be given to the objectives. Five types of assays may be distinguished.
1. Titer determinations in different physiological stages in insects.
2. Evaluation of purification and isolation of endogenous JH for the purpose of identification of new JH structures from extracts.
3. Determination of structure activity relationships for different compounds and insects.
4. Studies on specificity and activity.
5. Evaluation for the possibility of practical application, ranging from laboratory to field assays.
The requirements for these five categories are very different. Titer determinations and JH

isolation procedures require extremely sensitive
assays with adequate reproducibility and good
quantitation. Only one assay, the pupal wax test
on certain species of Lepidoptera, has been ful-
filling these requirements so far. Its use may
be limited to insect hormones with a specificity
similar to that of Cecropia JH. The isolation of
new JH of different insects certainly needs
exploration and comparison with more species
specific assays. Successful purification of
Cecropia JH has been completed through use of an
assay technique on Tenebrio pupae (51). Although
the identified materials are not the most potent
JHA existing for beetles, they come close to that
on Lepidoptera. The possibility that a different
beetle JH exists cannot be excluded as yet.

Structure activity correlations for JHA are
the most common objective and since usually
greater amounts of synthetic compounds are available, these tests do not have to be so extremely
sensitive. It nevertheless pays off to select the
most sensitive stage of the prospective test
insect for the test because it allows for greater
reproducibility. Accurate synchronization of the
animals in days and sometimes even hours after an
easily observed process like for instance a behavior change, ecdysis, spinning, apolysis, oviposition etc. is always a basic requirement.

Since most evaluations are directly or indirectly aiming at ultimate application purposes,
topical tests should be preferred. The inherent
variance in all JH tests can usually be decreased
by taking larger numbers of test animals when
compound availability is no limiting factor.

Evaluation for practical purposes suggests
the use of asynchronous colonies under conditions
that approach those of the field situations. The
use of plants, animals or stored commodities as
the insect's substrate, may require an entirely
different application approach. For stored food
pests, the short cut of overlapping of objectives
3 to 5 exists. Actual bioassays for both can be
done by mixing the compound into the commodity
and infesting it with the insect - be it as a
synchronous, or, as an asynchronous population.

Results from work on asynchronous populations are very difficult to evaluate and to interpret and may require repeated observations after the actual treatment. We do see it as the ideal situation when this work can be backed up by a complete profile of activities on any given moment in the development cycle of the insect compiled from assays on synchronous batches.

BIOASSAY TECHNOLOGY

There are many ways of administering JHA for evaluation purposes and only the most important ones can be mentioned. Gilbert and Schneiderman published a comprehensive paper on the subject (52), but many other papers mention specially adapted techniques.

No clear picture has evolved explaining why certain JHA have a higher activity than others. With our present knowledge we have to admit that we do not know whether a JHA is more active because it penetrates more rapidly or more slowly through the cuticle, binds easier or less easy to a carrier in the bloodstream, breaks down more or less rapidly when exposed to the insect's metabolism, etc. The different possible types of tests on one single insect species may differ tremendously in their sensitivity, depending probably on factors related to penetration, critical sensitivity periods, speed of breakdown at all levels, etc.

Pupal Wax Test. This highly sensitive test (in our laboratories, the Galleria unit corresponds to 5×10^{-6} micrograms of Cecropia JH) is laborious, but the only one sensitive enough for the #1 objectives (53,54,75). In young Galleria pupae, a small section of epidermis plus cuticle is removed and the wound is sealed with a molten mixture of solid paraffin wax and a dilution in mineral oil of the compound or extract to assay. The regenerating epidermis proves to be highly sensitive to exogenous JH and will secrete a local patch of pupal cuticle once again when JH is present. This pupal cuticle is conspicuously different from adult cuticle. The explanation of

the high sensitivity may be in the sealing
mixture that hardens to a paraffin skeleton in
which the oil circulates continuously and contact
with the regenerating integument is maximized.
Serial logarithmic dilutions with a factor of 10
usually yield a distinct curve (even from as
little as 5 to 10 animals per concentration) of
which the intersection with the 50% response line
indicates the active concentration or inhibition
dose (ID 50). In our test procedure, only positive and negative responses are distinguished. No
synthetic material equals the Cecropia JH activity
in this test. The wax test values obtained with
other JHA are not well correlated with values
obtained by topical application on intact animals,
and are therefore no reliable indicators for
practical evaluation.

Injection Tests. Pupal injection tests do
not have the high sensitivity of the wax test.
The variation used by Röller et al. (51) is in
reality a hybrid test. A quantity of material is
deposited by injection locally under the abdominal
cuticle. The test produces a local cuticle effect
which explains the higher sensitivity compared
with injections in the haemocoele, which produce
general effects. Yet this test is approximately
40 times less sensitive than the Galleria waxtest.
Injection in a test needs oil as a carrier. The
use of any water soluble carrier like propylene
glycol and of emulsified preparations is futile
since they do not afford any protection to the
compound against rapid metabolic breakdown in the
insect. Injection of pure materials is equally
useless and is technically difficult for microgram
quantities.

Topical Application. This is by far the most
practical and reproducible method when solvent
dilutions are used. Most insects take 1 microliter of acetone or any other volatile solvent
without difficulty, but others may show adverse
effects (55). Different solvents often consequently yield different quantitative results. When
Cecropia JH is evaluated in the Galleria pupal
wax test concurrently with the topical test on
intact pupae, the latter shows a sensitivity

10,000 x lower. Yet this latter test can record ID 50 values in the range between 0.005 and 100 micrograms and the sensitivity is therefore sufficient for JHA evaluation. The ultimate effect of topical application can probably be compared with that of oil injection. The lipophilic cuticle may act as a sink as well as a slow release mechanism at the same time. Abrasion prior to topical application was used in the very early days as a potentiating factor (56), but newer and more active JHA do not require such preparations. Quite recently synergistic effects were described for certain fatty materials. (5).

Application with an oil carrier will, in general affect the pattern of response, and it may be nearly impossible to make exact comparisons between results with and without oil admixture. With 1 microliter of acetone on a medium sized insect, as a rule, the whole insect will show a general response. The solvent will usually run through all the intersegmental membranes, but even when the application is made more locally under the wing pads for instance, general affects are common. We have observed in Pyrrhocoris, however, that certain compounds with very low activity may occasionally show local effects only. Topically applied compounds will not only affect the exoskeleton, but also act internally, as can be demonstrated by the delay of the metamorphic molt and the female "sterilization," particularly when fecundity is involved. Topical application can be used on all insect stages, including eggs. Sticking the eggs to tape, prior to application, can be a great help. Surface tensions in the solvent may create great practical difficulties with very small insect larvae, for which special techniques have to be worked out.

Substrate Treatment. Small insects can often be conveniently treated by allowing them to contact a surface treated with the compound. A treated plant surface is of course an almost natural situation. Very effective also is the prolonged contact with treated filter paper. The explanation of this may be sought in a slow

release administration that in itself, is potentiating, and also in the deduction that cellulose
is an excellent protective absorbent as was observed in the work on the "paper factor" (76,77).

In aquatic larvae, water treatment expressed
as parts per million is customary. Introduction
in acetone solution even when larvae are present,
is acceptable provided that the ultimate acetone
concentration does not exceed 1%. Many JHA are
not soluble at high doses and may exert their
effect on the surface layer, which will be fre-
quented by many aquatic larvae and pupae for
respiration. This may obscure the dose response
curve for JHA with low activity.

Food Treatment. In no feeding experiment
done so far, certainty exists as to the exact
route of entry of the compound (it may enter
through the alimentary canal, the cuticle, or
through the trachea in vapor form). Food treatment has shown very good and reproducible effects
on chewing insects when fed on bulk treated food
materials (artificial media, grains, and other
particulate foods, etc.). Continuous exposure may
be the explanation of the excellent effects at
doses sometimes lower than 1 part per million in
situations that approximate natural conditions.
When following a whole generation cycle in a
closed system exposed to a critical dose of JHA,
it becomes obvious that metamorphosis is indeed
the most sensitive life stage and that particularly long delayed metamorphic molts are a common
result.

Systemic Application. Certain compounds have
been shown to have systemic activity when painted
on stems and leaves of plants (58). Very careful
elimination of contaminating factors (more specifically vapors) is an absolute requirement for this
type of work.

Assay of Vapor Effects. Experiments set up
to demonstrate vapor activity, have often been
successful. Particularly in cases of very short
sensitive periods, good evidence for a true vapor
effect was obtained (36). Effects after expos-
ures of longer duration, however, turned out to

be ambiguous. We have experienced that JHA vapors
will condense on any cage surface, on paper, and
even on the cuticle of the assay animals. Untreated animals can readily pick it up by contact
from any of these surfaces, including the insects.
This type of experiment, therefore, cannot lead
to the conclusion that the action was through the
respiratory system exclusively (80).

Large scale JH experiments require special
facilities like non return air conditioning to
avoid all possible vapor effects. The use of
incubators must be strongly discouraged, it is
usually a waste of time and material when JHA are
involved.

Spray Applications. The spraying of food
plants with or without insects usually requires a
water formulation in order to achieve a reproducible "run off" dose, to avoid phytotoxicity and
adverse effects on the insects. Different compounds may require different formulations for
optimal results but for reasons of comparison,
standardization of the formulation is desirable.
We found .1% of Tween 20 and 1% acetone   a
practical formulation for most JHA.

SCORING AND EVALUATION

Every insect species and every stage will
require a special scoring system unlike the
evaluation of insecticides. Fortunately, often a
test can be devised that uses a simple positive
or negative score, for instance, where non-
emergence is a possible result.

Two types of scoring can generally be distinguished:

A. Graded Scoring - When different steps
of intermediates can be recognized. Some of
these scoring methods are published, new ones are
devised frequently and they usually reflect the
personal bias of the investigator. Rarely is
such a scoring system immediately final after its
inception. After more experience, modifications
may be necessary. An unaffected animal should
receive a zero score; a maximum observed response

and not the maximum <u>theoretical</u> response should
set the highest number, with the intermediates
arbitrarily fixed in between. The total score
can then be calculated as a percentage of the
observed maximum and plotted on semi-logarithmic
paper as a log dose response curve. The intersection of this curve with the 50% response line,
yields the ID 50 response figure. One should
realize that probit conversion of this type of
curve is not likely to result in a straight line,
because of the fact that the grading system is
arbitrary. If controls are positive (up to 20%),
correction of all the values with Abbott's formula is desirable. With more than 20% positive
response in the control, revising the assay will
be necessary.

B. <u>Quantal Scoring</u> - If the results can be
evaluated as clear cut positive or negative, the
response percentage can be easily calculated and
plotted. As attractive as this may seem, it has
some inherent disadvantages compared with graded
scoring. Graded scoring reveals more information
and therefore requires fewer animals for the same
variance in the end result. Unfortunately also,

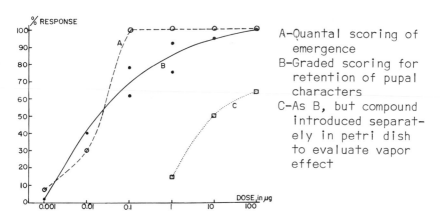

A-Quantal scoring of
   emergence
B-Graded scoring for
   retention of pupal
   characters
C-As B, but compound
   introduced separat-
   ely in petri dish
   to evaluate vapor
   effect

Fig. 2 Cocoons of Potato tubermoth (Phtorimoea
operculella) treated with different doses of
Cecropia JH. Each dot represents 15 animals.

the more clear cut the result is, the less specific it usually is for JH action. (e.g. the housefly pupal assay). Certain assays like the topical pupal assay in Galleria allow for both scoring systems simultaneously and experience teaches that they are usually reasonably well correlated (Fig. 2). Yet we have to attach more significance to the graded score for an equal number of animals. Quantal scoring results lend themselves very well to probit conversion.

Egg assays can usually be scored in both ways too, especially for those eggs in which the chorion can be cleared in Clorox to allow for internal inspection. Half developed embryos may then be detected and unfertile eggs can be discounted.

A bioassay scoring system should be restricted to one subsequent instar if possible. For instance, when treated larvae only partly develop into pupae, the assay should be scored on the pupae, however attractive it may be to wait until the present pupae have developed into adults. The effect on the adult stage should be the subject of a new and specially designed assay.

The results are best expressed as the ID-50, IC-50, IC-95, etc., when applied to direct morphogenetic effects. For an evaluation of reproductive potential a comparison with a control group of animals will yield a percentage reduction in reproductive potential.

SPECIFIC TARGET ORGANISMS AND REPORTED EFFECTS OF JHA

Lepidoptera - Much work has been done in this group on all the sensitive stages: eggs, larvae, pupae, (topical application to cocoons also yields good results) and adults. Since the remanence is very low, timing or contact with a residual deposit should be optimal to obtain useful results. Treatment against stored food moths can be very effective, and illustrates what is theoretically achievable for pests under more difficult field situations through the use of ideal formulations.

Coleoptera will respond in the same life stages as Lepidoptera, with some exceptions. In many beetles the adults over-winter in a diapause condition, offering an additional target stage. Beetle as well as moth larvae may go into extended diapause when exposed to JHA as mature larvae.

While most moths will readily respond to larval treatments with a spectrum of intermediates between larvae and pupae, this is not so common in beetles. The response usually only surfaces in the adults, but is often not clear cut. Diabrotica larvae treated with massive doses of JHA show no direct response except for mortality and delay of pupation, but adults later show dose related symptoms. Unpigmented eye segments and some retention of urogomphi and unpigmented abdominal cuticle are most prominent. Wings will not expand but look otherwise normal and so does the rest of the body, including head and legs. Leptinotarsa responds similarly, the clear black abdominal spots of the adults lose their distinction and merge, terminal abdominal segments retain pupal shape and wings are abortive. Head and legs, however, are very insensitive. Other beetles species, like Tribolium, Dermestes and Tenebrio may show a full range of intermediates involving additional structures. The Tenebrio pupae test is established as a standard JHA test in many laboratories and makes comparison of data possible(60).

Hymenoptera - Very little information is available (59). Social insects are likely to be affected when active materials are introduced in the colonies for instance by foraging workers. This group counts more beneficial parasites than actual pests, and honeybees are indispensable for many fruit and seed producing crops. More information is therefore needed.

Diptera - Good larvacidal JHA compounds are available for mosquitos and flies (61,62,63,64,65, 47,66). No extra larval instars and no lengthy delays of puparium formation are reported. However, morphogenetic effects are usually as insignificant as in certain beetle species. Quantal

scoring of adult emergence is therefore the most
practical technique. Sensitivity occurs in the
latter half of the last larval instar, the pupa is
entirely insensitive. However, the puparium stage
of houseflies is sensitive until tanning proceeds.
The effects on adult flies (non emergence, some
repression of adult structures on the abdomen and
occasionally only non rotation of the male genitalia) are not very characteristic for hormones.
The delayed character of the response and the
correlation in activities of JHA with those on
other insects, points to a juvenilizing response.
Toxic materials would always produce more immediate responses. The accelerated receptivity of
female mosquito adults when exposed to JHA immediately after emergence may qualify as the fastest
bioassay for JHA, but has not been used for comparative studies (71).

Homoptera - Aphids in particular seem to be
more sensitive to substrate treatment rather than
to direct topical application, in contrast to the
response to insecticides (19). Effects on morphogenesis are observed in alatae as well in apterae
but are more conspicuous in the former. Reproduction is not impaired by alary inhibition, but by
stimultaneous inhibition in the formation of the
adult genital plate and cauda (19), which prevents the disposition of fully formed embryos.
Spontaneous alary intermediates, as often seen in
the pea aphid (Macrosiphum pisi), do have adult
genitalia and reproduce normally. The onset of
embryogenesis in early larval instars of partheno-
genetic forms make aphids a prime target for JH
effects, since early treatments effectively block
this process, even when the remanence is not
enough to produce morphogenetic intermediates
later. Thus, non reproductive adults result. The
reported first instar mortality needs further investigation (18). The alatae/apterae dimorphism
may be directly influenced by JHA, depending
on the species and the critical induction
periods (18,19,72,78).

Scale insects have shown to be most sensitive in the crawler stage, responding with either

inhibition of further development or with
inhibition of the final metamorphic molt. The
early sensitivity may indicate a different development pattern in this specialized group of
insects (19).

Leafhoppers do respond especially well to
plant surface treatments with the partial inhibition of metamorphosis. A peculiar cuticular
melanosis has resulted from the treatment with JHA
in any larval instar in the normally cream colored
corn leafhopper (Dalbulus maidis) (67). This
effect was reversible and non lethal, and showed
an induction period different from that for morphogenetic effects, comparable to the green pigment induction in Acrididae.

Hemiptera - Only the Pyrrhocoridae and
Lygaeidae have shown excellent responses to some
compounds, that are almost inactive on other
insects. Other families, particularly the more
economically important Miridae and Pentatomidae
are more refractory. JHA activities on these
groups at present may not be sufficient for
control purposes.

Orthoptera - Good effects on morphogenesis
have been obtained in Acrididae like Locusta and
Schistocerca, but the effective doses for larval
application seem too high for practical consideration (10 - 100 micrograms/animal) (8). Identification of the natural JH might lead to a breakthrough. In cockroaches morphogenetic effects are
reported, but the practicality for control purposes is low because of the long development
periods for these insects. There are no data for
remanence, but because of the long development
time, the expectations should be low. Recently
significant effects on reproduction in Periplaneta
were obtained with some JHA (5).

Acarina - Spider mites and ticks are not
known to use a JH in their development. Consequently, no significant progress has been made
in the study of developmental inhibitions since
the JHA active on other insect groups do not seem
to have significant effects on nymphs or eggs in
this group.

Isoptera - Termite nymphs are known to respond to JHA with polymorphic changes in caste development (20,21). Introduction of JHA in a colony may therefore disrupt the social organization and lead to its destruction. Effects on reproduction, embryogenesis and metamorphosis proper are not reported so far, but could add to the total impact.

Anoplura - Impressive effects were obtained by Vinson and Williams (68). The gigantic extra larval instars obtained do not point to direct applicability, but less of an overdose may produce greater mortality and better control.

Mallophaga - Good activities are reported by Hopkins, Chamberlain and Wright (69).

Other Orders - Although several other orders present important economic and health aspects, little work with JH has been reported for these and no predictions can be made.

CONCLUSION

Although an impressive amount of work has been done in basic endocrinology and applications of JHA, only the surface has been scratched. Full evaluation of the potentials for control will require extensive studies on many delayed and deferred effects and their impact on survival of the population. These studies and also a more comprehensive integration of isolated phenomena observed throughout the life cycle into the evaluation may improve the outlook for JHA type compounds considerably beyond the present slightly short sighted comparison with direct kill insecticides. Peculiarities in the action of JHA make the development of special formulations with slow release characteristics very desirable (70).

REFERENCES

1. Schneiderman, H.A., A. Krishnakumara, V.G. Kulkarni and L. Friedman, J. Insect Physiol. 11, 1641-1649.
2. Bowers, W.S., Mitt. Schweiz. Entomol. Ges. 44 (1971) 115-130.
3. Bowers, W.S. in Naturally Occurring Insecticides, edts. M. Jacobson and D.G. Crosby, New York (1971) 307-332.
4. Cruickshank, P.A., Mitt. Schweiz. Entomol. Ges. 44 (1971) 97-113.
5. Cruickshank, P.A. and R.M. Palmere, Nature 233 (1971) 488-489.
6. Jarolim, V., K. Hejno, F. Sehnal and F. Sorm, Life Sciences 8 (1969) 831-841.
7. Mori, K., Mitt. Schweiz. Entomol. Ges. 44 (1971) 17-35.
8. Nemec, V., Life Sciences 9 (1970) 821-831.
9. Pallos, F.M., J.J. Menn, P.E. Letchworth and J.B. Miaullis, Nature 232 (1971) 486-487.
10. Poduska, K., F. Sorm and K. Slama, Z. Naturforsch B. 26B (1971) 719-722.
11. Redfern, R.E., T.P. McGovern, R. Sarmiento and M. Beroza, J. Econ. Entomol. 64 (1971) 374-376.
12. Slama, K., Ann. Rev. Biochem. 40 (1971) 1079-1102.
13. Slama, K., K. Hejno, V. Jarolim and F. Sorm, Biol. Bull. 139 (1970) 222-228.
14. Sorm, F., Mitt. Schweiz. Entomol. Ges. 44 (1971) 7-16.
15. Wigglesworth, V.B., J. Insect Physiol. 15 (1969) 73-94.
16. Zaoral, M. and K. Slama, Science 170 92-93.
17. Slade, M. and C.Zibbitt, Proc. 2nd I.U.P.A.C. Int. Congress Pesticide Chemistry: Israel 1971 Pub. Gordon & Breach London (in press).
18. White, D.F., J. Insect Physiol. 14 (1968) 901-912.
19. Nassar, S. and G.B. Staal, (in preparation).
20. Lüscher, M. and Springhetti, J. Insect Physiol. 5 (1960) 190-212.

21. Lüscher, M., Proc. 16th Int. Congress Zool. Wash. D.C. 1963, 4 (1965) 244-250.
22. Joly, L. Functions des corpora allata chez Locusta migratoria L. These, Strasbourg (1960) 1-93.
23. Joly, P., C.R. Acad. Sc. Paris. 268 (1969) 1634-1635.
24. Staal, G.B., Publ. Fonds. Landb. Export Bur. 40 (1961) 1-125.
25. Staal, G.B., XIII Int. Congr. Ent. Moscow (1968) 442.
26. Schwartz, J.L., Gen. Comp. Endocrinol. 17 (1971) 293-399.
27. Sehnal, F., J. Insect Physiol. 14 (1968) 73-85.
28. Sehnal, F. and A.S. Meyer, Science 159 (1968) 981-983.
29. Piepho, H., Arch. Entw. Mech. Org. 141 (1942) 500-583.
30. Smith, R.F., J. Invert. Path. 17 (1971) 132-133.
31. Novak, V.J.A., J. Embryol. Exp. Morph. 21 (1969) 1-21.
32. Retnakaran, A., Can. Entomologist 102 (1970) 1592-1596.
33. Riddiford, L.M. and C.M. Williams, Proc. Nat. Acad. Sci. U.S 47 (1967) 595-601.
34. Riddiford, L.M., Science 167 (1969) 287-288.
35. Matolin, S., Acta Entomol. Bohemoslov. 67 (1970) 9-12.
36. Walker, W.F. and W.S. Bowers, J. Econ. Entomol. 63 (1970) 1231-1233.
37. Masner, P., K. Slama, J. Zdarek and V. Landa J. Econ. Entomol. 63 (1969) 706-710.
38. Patterson, J.W., Nature New Biology 233 (1971) 176-177.
39. Bell, W.J. and R.H. Barth, Jr., J. Insect Physiol. 16 (1970) 2203-2313.
40. Cassier, P., Ann. Biol. 5 (1967) 596-670.
41. Pan, M.L. and C.R. Wyatt, Science 174 (1971) 503-505.
42. Masner, P., Acta Entomol. Bohemoslov. 66 (1969) 81-86.

43. Bowers, W.S. and C.C. Blickenstaff, Science 154 (1966) 1673-1674.
44. Krishnakumaran, A. and H.A. Schneiderman, J. Insect Physiol. 11 (1965) 1517-1532.
45. Gilbert, L.I. and H.A. Schneiderman, Nature 184 (1959) 171-173.
46. Gilbert, L.I., Nature, Lond. 193 (1962) 1205-1207.
47. Spielman, A. and C.M. Williams, Science 154 (1966) 1043-1044.
48. Bodenstein, D. and E. Shaaya, Proc. Nat. Acad. Sci. U.S. 59 (1968) 1223-1230.
49. Riddiford, L.M., Develop. Biol. 22 (1970) 249-263.
50. Willis, J.H., J. Embryol. Exp. Morphol. 22 (1969) 27-44.
51. Röller, H., J.S. Bjerke and W.H. McShan, J. Insect Physiol. 11 (1965) 1184-1197.
52. Gilbert, L.I. and H.A Schneiderman, Trans. Am. Micros. Soc. 79 (1966) 38-67.
53. Wilde, J. de, G.B. Staal, C.A.D. deKort, A. deLoof and G. Baard, Proc. Koninkl. Ned. Akad. Wetenschap. c71 (1968) 321-326.
54. Wilde, J. de, C.A.D. deKort and A. deLoof, Mitt. Schweiz. Entomol. Ges. 44 (1971) 79-86.
55. Hintze-Podufal, C., Experientia 9 (1971) 476-477.
56. Wigglesworth, V.B., J. Insect Physiol. 2 (1958) 74-84.
57. Wakabayashi, N., M. Schwarz, P.E. Sonnet, R.M. Waters, R.E. Redfern and M. Jacobson, Mitt. Schweiz. Entomol. Ges. 44 (1971) 131-140.
58. Babu, T.H. and K. Slama (in press).
59. Hsiao, C. and T.H. Hsiao, Life Sciences 8 (1969) 767-774.
60. Rose, J., J. Westermann, H. Trautmann, P. Schmialek and J. Klauske, Z. Naturforsch. 23B (1968) 1245-1248.
61. Ashburner, M., Nature 227 (1970) 187-189.
62. Srivastava, U.S. and L.I. Gilbert, J. Insect Physiol. 15 (1969) 177-189.
63. Srivastava, U.S. and L.I. Gilbert, Science 161 (1968) 61-62.

64. Wright, J.E., J. Econ. Entomol. 63 (1970) 878-883.
65. Wright, J.E. and G.E. Spates, J. Agr. Food Chem. 19 (1971) 289-290.
66. Spielman, A. and V. Skaff, J. Insect Physiol. 13 (1967) 1087-1095.
67. Staal, C.B. and D. Cerf, (in preparation).
68. Vinson, J.W. and C.M. Williams, Proc. Nat. Acad. Sci. U.S. 58 (1967) 294-297.
69. Hopkins, D.E., W.F. Chamberlain and J.E. Wright, Ann. Entomol. Soc. Amer. 63 (1970) 1361-1363.
70. Staal. G.B., Bull. World Health Organ. 44 (1971) 391-394.
71. Gwadz, R.W., L.P. Lounibos and G.B. Craig, Jr., Gen. Comp. Endocrinol. 16 (1971) 47-51.
72. Lees, A.D., Adv. Ins. Phys. 3 (1966) 207-277.
73. Riddiford, L.M., Mitt. Schweiz. Entomol. Ges. 44 (1971) 177-186.
74. Slama, K. and C.M. Williams, Nature 210 (1966) 329.
75. Meyer, A.S., Mitt. Schweiz. Entomol. Ges. 44 (1971) 37-63.
76. Slama, K. and C.M. Williams, Proc. Nat. Acad. Sci. U.S. 54 (1965) 411-414.
77. Williams, C.M. and K. Slama, Biol. Bull. 130 (1966) 247-253.
78. White, D.F. and K.P. Lamb. J. Insect Physiol. 14 (1968) 395-402.
79. Hintze-Podufal, C., Z. Naturforsch. 26 (1971) 154-157.
80. Masner, P. and G.B. Staal, (unpublished).
81. Staal, G.B., J. Endocrinol. 37 (1967) XIII-XIV.

JUVENILE HORMONE AND INSECT EMBRYONIC DEVELOPMENT: ITS POTENTIAL ROLE AS AN OVICIDE

Lynn M. Riddiford

The Biological Laboratories
Harvard University
Cambridge, Massachusetts 02138

Abstract

Juvenile hormone (JH) blocks embryonic development when applied either to the female insect or to the freshly laid egg. High doses given to the female during the terminal phases of oogenesis prevent germ band formation. Lower doses to the female or application to the egg interfere with blastokinesis. This difference in the stage blocked was shown to be due to the developmental stage of the egg rather than to a differential rate of metabolism of JH by the female. JH applied to the egg after germ band formation did not prevent hatching. But it had delayed effects in postembryonic life, thus preventing the formation of reproducing adults. These delayed effects were shown to be due to an effect of the applied JH on the development of the corpus allatum. The use of JH as an ovicide is discussed, particularly with respect to the effectiveness of a single application to the female and the relative effectiveness of JH and its analogs on metamorphosis and on embryonic development.

Introduction

Sláma and Williams (1) first showed that juvenile hormone disrupted insect embryogenesis. Application of the juvenile hormone analog juvabione either to the female bug <u>Pyrrhocoris</u> <u>apterus</u> or to the freshly laid eggs prevented hatching. The same effect has also been found after application of juvenile hormone (JH) and its analogs to the females or eggs of the wild American silkmoth <u>Hyalophora</u>

cecropia and the Chinese oak silkmoth, Antheraea pernyi (2)
and subsequently in numerous other species (3) including
Oncopeltus fasciatus, Lygaeus kalmii, Tenebrio molitor,
Manduca sexta, and Samia cynthia in this laboratory (Riddiford, unpublished). This ovicidal action appears to be one
of the most promising means of insect control by JH.

The purpose of this paper is to explore the mode of
action of JH on insect embryonic development. The insect
egg is fertilized at oviposition and cleavage begins immediately. Due to the large amount of yolk, no cells are
formed but rather just nuclei with surrounding cytoplasmic
islands. After a set number of divisions, the cleavage
nuclei migrate to the cortical cytoplasm around the peri-
phery and form a single layer of cells called the blastoderm. Depending upon where the nuclei fall, some will
form the germ band, while others form the extra-embryonic
membranes. The germ band then forms, elongates, segments,
and finally develops appendages. Next closure of the embryo along the dorsal midline begins followed closely by
a series of morphogenetic movements known as blastokinesis
which culminate in a revolution of the embryo in the egg
so that the now closed dorsum is toward the chorion.
Blastokinesis occurs about midway through embryonic development and signals the beginning of the differentiation of
the first instar larva. In many insects, a molt with the
formation of the first instar larval cuticle occurs shortly
after blastokinesis (4). According to the dosage and time
of application of JH, embryonic development is blocked
either at blastoderm stage or at blastokinesis, or delayed
effects are seen in postembryonic life.

Each of these three effects will be explored in detail below. Most of the studies utilized a mixture of synthetic JH analogs (JH-A) (5), but a synthetic preparation
of dl-C18 Cecropia JH (JH-C) (6) yielded identical results.

JH Application to the Female

When JH or its analogs was applied to either Cecropia
or Pyrrhocoris females, it became apparent that the effectiveness of a given dose of a specific compound was dependent upon the time of application, relative to the time of
oviposition (2,7,8). The effectiveness of a compound
could be judged, firstly by its prevention of hatching and
secondly, by the stage of embryogenesis which was blocked.

The more effective compounds at critical times prevented hatching by stopping embryonic development in the blasto-derm stage. Lower doses or high doses applied at other times blocked development later at blastokinesis.

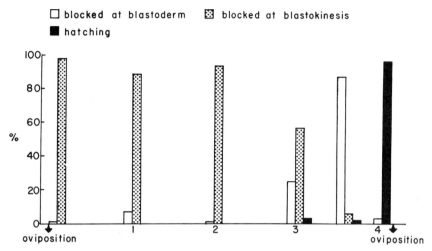

TIME OF APPLICATION (DAYS AFTER LAST OVIPOSITION)

Fig. 1. The effects of application of 10µg dl–C18 Cecropia juvenile hormone to Pyrrhocoris apterus females at various times during the oogenesis cycle. Day 0 refers to appli-cation to female shortly after a batch of eggs was laid; day 4 application was about 4 hours prior to oviposition.

This phenomenon can best be illustrated by Fig. 1 in which 10 µg JH–C was applied to female Pyrrhocoris at various times during the oviposition cycle. When it was applied less than 4 hours before oviposition, hatching of the eggs was not prevented, but the subsequent batch, 4 days later, was blocked at blastokinesis. When applied during the first three days of the 4-day oviposition cycle, JH blocked hatching, again primarily at blastokinesis. But application 12-14 hours before oviposition blocked de-velopment earlier at the beginning of germ band formation. Even 0.1 µg JH–C applied 12 hours before oviposition blocked 83% of the eggs at the blastoderm stage.

Since the corpora allata of Pyrrhocoris females nor-mally secrete JH at the outset of the oviposition cycle to

promote vitellogenesis and yolk deposition (9), it seemed
possible that the apparent difference in effectiveness
might merely be due to a higher rate of metabolism of JH
during the first days of the cycle than in the last day.
Therefore, female <u>Pyrrhocoris</u> were treated with 1 μg tritiated JH-C (specific activity 5x10^5 dpm/μg) (New England
Nuclear Corporation) at various times during the oviposition cycle (Ajami and Riddiford, unpublished). As seen in
Fig. 2, the amount of JH-C remaining in the blood was not

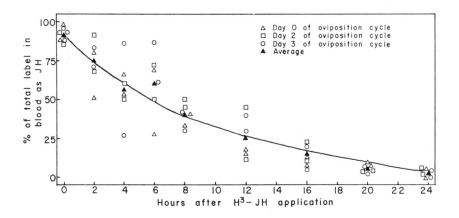

Fig. 2. The amount of juvenile hormone remaining in the
blood of <u>Pyrrhocoris</u> <u>apterus</u> females at various times
after application of 1μg H^3<u>dl</u>-C18 Cecropia juvenile hormone (specific activity 5x10^{5}dpm/μg). One μl blood samples were taken from the tip of the leg or antennae,
extracted with 10 μl 2:1 ether-ethanol, and chromatographed
on silica gel sheets (Eastman Chromagram 6061) with 1:3
ethyl acetate:hexane. After two elutions the zone which
co-chromatographed with unlabeled C18 Cecropia juvenile
hormone was removed and counted in Aquasol. Tritium counts
were assumed to represent unmetabolized juvenile hormone.
Each point represents the average of determinations done
on 3 different females; the different symbols indicate the
day of the oviposition cycle when the JH was applied. The
curve is drawn through the average of all determinations
made at a certain time after application. Thus, the half-
life is found to be about 6 hours.

dependent upon the stage of the oviposition cycle. The large scatter reflects considerable individual variation, most likely due to the fact that in these preliminary experiments no correction was made for blood volume and body weight. The average half-life for JH in the blood was found to be about 6 hours, about twice the time necessary for equilibration in the blood after topical application.

Thus, the extreme sensitivity to JH 12 hours before oviposition must be correlated with the events in oogenesis occurring at that time. Using Trypan blue as an indicator of pinocytotic uptake of protein into the oocyte (10), we have shown that yolk deposition occurs during the first three days of the oviposition cycle (11). During the final 24 hours the egg is hydrated, the cortical cytoplasm is laid down, and the chorion is formed. A similar short period of high sensitivity of the eggs to JH was also found in Cecropia females (8). Fig. 3 shows the effective-

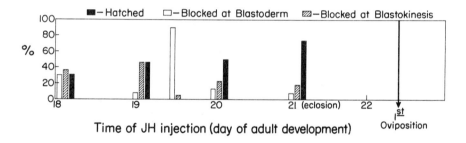

Time of JH injection (day of adult development)

Fig. 3. The effects of a single injection of 5 mg of the Williams-Law mixture of juvenile hormone analogs (50 µg of this preparation in the Polyphemus pupal assay (12) produced a 3+ pupal-adult intermediate) into developing Hyalophora cecropia females before and just after eclosion. These females routinely mated the first night after eclosion and began laying eggs the second night. The percentages are based on the total number of eggs laid over 4 to 5 nights, although usually 30-50% were laid the first night. Each histogram set represents an average of two females treated at that time.

99

ness of a JH-A preparation when injected into Cecropia females at various times prior to mating and oviposition.
Clearly, the eggs were most sensitive at day 19-1/2 of
adult development, about 1-1/2 to 2 days before emergence
and 3 days before the first oviposition. At this time
vitellogenesis is completed in the majority of follicles
and the ovaries have entered the terminal phases of oogenesis (10). During the next 2 to 3 days protein-containing
refractile bodies are deposited in the cortex of the egg,
the egg is hydrated, and the chorion is formed.

Thus, it appears that to block germ band formation,
JH must be present at the time that the cortical cytoplasm
is being laid down. Since the cortical cytoplasm determines the fate of the nuclei which migrate into it, possibly JH interferes with either the deposition or utilization of this determinative information. Germ band formation can also be blocked by actinomycin D (13) which suggests that the messenger RNA provided by the maternal
genome during oogenesis is sufficient for development up
to the blastoderm, but no further. Support for this view
is also afforded by the formation of the blastoderm but
never of an organized germ band in Cecropia eggs subjected
to artificial parthenogenesis (7). Therefore, the transition from blastoderm to germ band signals the switchover
of the use of information from the maternal genome to that
of the zygotic genome. It is this transition that can be
blocked by JH application to the female during the terminal
phases of oogenesis.

JH Application to the Egg:
Effects on Embryonic Development

Once the egg is fertilized and oviposited, JH no longer blocks development at the blastoderm stage, but only
later at blastokinesis. When Cecropia eggs were treated
with either JH-A or JH-C immediately after oviposition,
hatching was blocked (2,7). The unhatched embryos routinely had not completed blastokinesis. Some had not differentiated beyond this stage, but most showed varying degrees
of larval differentiation, at least externally.

After application of JH to early Pyrrhocoris embryos,
development is blocked in blastokinesis (11,14,15). A careful examination of the internal morphology of these
blocked embryos showed one very striking internal anomaly

in the development of the nervous system. Normally, between 24 and 30 hours after blastokinesis, the abdominal
ganglia consolidate and fuse with the thoracic ganglia to
form one large ganglionic mass (16). But, as seen in Fig.
4, in the JH-treated embryos this consolidation had not

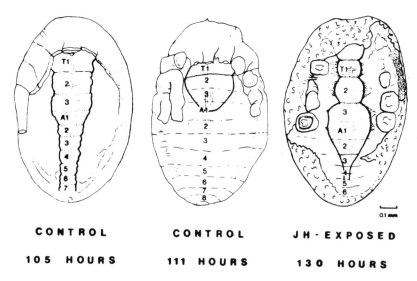

CONTROL

105 HOURS

CONTROL

111 HOURS

JH-EXPOSED

130 HOURS

Fig. 4. Diagram showing the effects of the application of
the Williams-Law mixture of juvenile hormone analogs to
the freshly oviposited egg on the development of the nervous system of the Pyrrhocoris apterus embryo. The normal
control embryo at 105 hours of development (left) has a
segmentally arranged system which then rapidly fuses into
a ganglionic mass containing the thoracic ganglia and first
abdominal ganglion at 111 hours (center). By contrast,
after treatment with juvenile hormone little or no ganglionic fusion is seen (right).

occurred by the normal hatching time, although the embryos
had subsequently pigmented and shown other signs of external larval differentiation (11,15).

Thus, JH applied to the early embryo or to the female
in low doses blocks embryonic development at the embryonic-
larval transition. In this respect its action resembles
its status quo effect on metamorphosis.

101

JH Application to the Egg:
Delayed Effects on Postembryonic Life

As the germ band forms, the eggs become progressively
less sensitive to JH (1,2). Those individuals which
hatched after JH treatment appeared as perfectly normal
first instar larvae, but later in postembryonic life development was often blocked (7,17). The Cecropia silkworm
proved to be an ideal insect for investigating these delayed effects because each larval instar has its own
characteristic coloration and tubercle morphology. This
so-called larval heteromorphosis has been attributed to a
declining titer of JH (12).

When JH was applied to Cecropia eggs before blastokinesis (7), the animals which hatched often showed delayed effects during larval life (Fig. 5). These effects
were usually manifest as the reformation of certain external characteristics of the preceding instar. Such inter-
mediate-type larvae often molted to another intermediate
but never completed metamorphosis. Many larvae died during the molt or immediately thereafter.

When JH was applied after blastokinesis (7), i.e., during the larval differentiation phase of embryonic development, most individuals hatched. Larval life proceeded
normally, but metamorphosis was prevented (Fig. 5). In
treated Cecropia the larval-pupal transformation was most
often affected. In many individuals development stopped
at the time of gut evacuation, during spinning, or at the
beginning of pupal development. Others formed pupae which
retained external larval characters such as the dorsal tubercles; many of these did not survive the pupal ecdysis.
Occasionally an individual from a treated egg formed a normal pupa, but then did not complete adult development.

All these delayed effects can also be obtained by the
contemporaneous application of juvenile hormone (7,18).
But the doses required were at least tenfold higher than
that applied to the embryo to obtain the same effect. For
instance, daily application of 5 μg JH-A throughout larval
life was necessary to produce larval intermediates whereas 0.16 μg JH-A applied to germ band embryos was sufficient
(7). Also, to obtain pupae with reformed larval tubercles,
60 μg JH-A must be applied 2 to 3 days before gut evacuation (18). Similar animals were obtained after only 1.6
μg JH-A was applied to the late egg (7).

DELAYED EFFECTS OF TREATMENT OF CECROPIA EMBRYOS WITH A JUVENILE HORMONE ANALOGUE

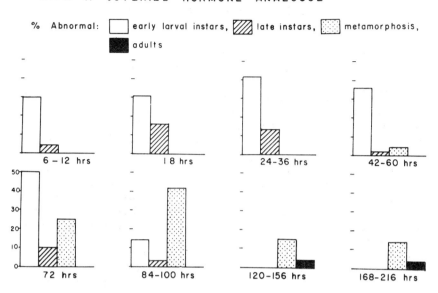

Fig. 5. Effects of application of the Williams–Law mixture of juvenile hormone analogs at various times during embryonic development of <u>Hyalophora</u> <u>cecropia</u> (25 µg of this preparation in the Polyphemus pupal assay (12) produced a 3+ pupal-adult intermediate). The treatment produced abnormalities which were manifest during postembryonic life. "Early larval instars" are the first to third stages; "late larval instars" are the fourth and fifth stages; "metamorphosis" refers to the larval-pupal transformation; and "adults" include individuals which either did not initiate or complete adult development or were sterile adults. The timing of the stages of embryonic development are as follows: blastoderm formation at 18 hours, beginning of dorsal closure at 72 hours, and blastokinesis from 96 to 108 hours. The data are taken from Riddiford (7,8).

The disparity of the respective doses clearly shows that the delayed effects cannot be due to the persistence of applied hormone in the insect throughout larval life. Rather, the applied JH must have a direct effect on the embryos, either on the programming of the cells <u>per</u> <u>se</u> or on the programming of the corpora allata as first suggested by Willis (19).

JH Application to Late Embryos:
Action on the Corpus Allatum

The delayed action of juvenile hormone on metamorphosis after application to the late embryo was also seen in Pyrrhocoris (17). Normally during the molt to the fifth instar the corpus allatum stops secreting JH, and the larva molts to an adult 7 days later. If, however, active corpora allata are implanted or JH is applied at the outset of the fifth instar, then the individual molts after 5 days to a supernumerary sixth instar larva (20). A supernumerary seventh instar larva may also be produced by similar treatment of the sixth instar larva. Application of JH-A to the Pyrrhocoris embryo after blastokinesis also produced sixth instar larvae (17). Some of these giant larvae molted again to seventh instar larvae, but they never metamorphosed.

To test the hypothesis that the JH application somehow affected the development of the corpus allatum, so that it did not shut off normally, the following experiments were performed (21). Fertile Pyrrhocoris eggs 24 to 36 hours before hatching were treated with JH-A. Then 24 hours after the molt of the resulting larvae to the fifth instar, the corpus allatum was removed and implanted into a normal host of the same age. As seen in Table 1, the allatectomized treated bugs molted to normal adults. By contrast, many of the normal hosts which had received the corpus allatum implants showed marked JH effects. Table 1 also shows that such effects were not seen when the corpus allatum from untreated fifth instar larvae was implanted into a normal host. Adultoids produced by implantation of corpora allata from treated individuals did not show as pronounced effects as seen in intact treated adultoids, apparently because of a variability in the functioning of the implanted allata. To test this hypothesis, normally functional corpora allata from a series of freshly molted fourth instar larvae were implanted into freshly molted fifth instar larvae. Upon the next molt, the hosts showed effects ranging from supernumerary sixth instar larvae to normal adults.

From these data, it is clear that juvenile hormone applied to the late embryo somehow affects the corpus allatum so that it does not shut off normally at the beginning of the fifth instar. Also, since the allatecto-

TABLE 1

Application of Juvenile Hormone Analogs to Late
Pyrrhocoris Embryos: Effects on the Corpus Allatum

	Number	% Normal Adults	% Adultoids				
			+1	+2	+3	+4	+5
Treated	36	14	8	16	19	33	6
Treated allatectomized..........	23	87	13	0	0	0	0
Treated allatum implanted into normal host........	40	47	31	22	0	0	0
Treated allatum removed and reimplanted.........	5	40	20	20	20	0	0
Normal allatum implanted into normal host...................	42	100	0	0	0	0	0

mized treated bug formed a perfectly normal adult, the
applied JH was not still present in the bug at the outset
of the fifth instar as suggested by Willis and Lawrence
(22).

Mode of JH Action on Embryonic Development

Fig. 6 summarizes the effects of JH application to the
egg on the insect's life history.
Embryonic development can be thought of as a progres-
sive utilization of genetic information.   In the insect
embryo the two major critical steps are the switching-on
of the zygotic genome at blastoderm formation, then of the
larval genome at blastokinesis.   Just as in postembryonic
development where JH is thought to prevent the derepres-

sion of new information (23), so it seems that it has a
similar action in embryonic development. Application of
JH to the female during the terminal   phases of oogenesis

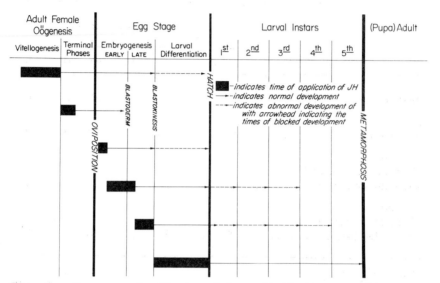

Juvenile Hormone Application to the Insect Egg:
Effects on Embryonic and Postembryonic Development

Fig. 6. Summary of effects of juvenile hormone application to the egg on embryonic and postembryonic development
of insects.

blocks her eggs at the first step--the activation of the
zygotic genome. Once the egg is fertilized and laid, JH
can no longer block the formation of the germ band, but
only later at the embryonic-larval transition.

When JH is applied after germ band formation (i.e.,
after the turning-on of the embryonic genome), it has progressively less effect on embryonic development and more
effect in postembryonic life. This delayed action appears
to be due to its action on the developing corpus allatum,
such that its secretions do not ebb and flow in the normal
manner.

It is interesting to note that JH can exert these
effects on embryonic development, although it normally
plays no role in these events. Also, it acts in the absence of ecdysone, unlike its action in postembryonic life.

Potential Applications of Embryonic Action
of JH for Insect Control

Juvenile hormone can thus act as an ovicide if given
to the adult female or to her freshly laid eggs. This
action of JH would seem to be the most practical means of
using JH for insect control. One then can eliminate the
potentially harmful larval stages as well as the next generation. And even if the application is not early enough
to prevent hatching, the delayed effects will prevent metamorphosis into a normal reproductive adult.

But, as has been shown in this paper, to utilize the
JH most effectively, one must have sufficient knowledge
about the life history of the pest insects under field conditions. For instance, as seen above, the half-life for
JH-C in the Pyrrhocoris female is only 6 hours and the
most sensitive stage of oogenesis to JH application is 12-
14 hours before oviposition. Therefore, to be able to
utilize the smallest effective dose of this JH, the timing
of the application must be quite precise. Yet Fig. 7 shows
that, in spite of the short half-life, the ovicidal effectiveness of a single application may last through several
egg batches and sometimes throughout the lifetime of the
female as was the case in 20% of the females given 10 μg
JH-C. When 10 μg JH-C is given daily for 5 days beginning
the day after adult ecdysis and ending at the time of the
first egg batch, the eggs are all blocked at the blastoderm stage. But, more importantly, the successive egg
batches throughout the female's lifetime (about 30-40 days)
also do not hatch (Riddiford, unpublished). Yet the oviposition cycle, mating behavior, and viability of the
treated female is apparently unimpaired. Similar lifetime
sterilization effects of methyldichlorofarnesoate in
Pyrrhocoris (24) and of various JH analogs in this laboratory (Riddiford, unpublished) have also been seen in
O. fasciatus, L. kalmii, and H. cecropia.

Therefore, JH analogs can be found which have a long-
lasting ovicidal action. But one must be careful about
basing relative ovicidal effectiveness of JH analogs on its
morphogenetic effects at metamorphosis. Table 2 shows for
Pyrrhocoris the relative effectiveness of several analogs
at different stages in its life history. Each compound
shows a somewhat different relationship between the dose
necessary to produce a larval-adult intermediate, that

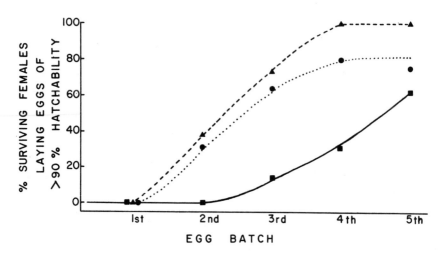

Fig. 7. The long-term effectiveness of a single dose of
dl-C18 Cecropia juvenile hormone on Pyrrhocoris apterus
females as indicated by the hatchability of successive
batches of eggs. Each dose was applied to 15 females after
deposition of one egg batch. The cumulative percentage of
females laying normal eggs (> 90% hatchability) is plotted
for each successive batch after application. Often the
batch preceding the normal one showed intermediate hatchability (25-75%). The doses used are indicated as follows:
▲ – 0.1 µg, ● – 1.0 µg and ■ – 10 µg.

required to sterilize 90% of the females, that required
to prevent hatching of 90% of the treated eggs, and that
required to prevent 90% of the treated late embryos from
attaining adulthood. Even among the three different preparations of JH-A, striking variations are found. For
instance, although JH-A-1 was only about half as effective
at metamorphosis as the other two preparations, it was
2 to 16 times as effective in producing delayed effects.
Despite certain anomalies, the following two generalizations
can be made from this table:

    1) The SD_{90} for the female and the LD_{90} for the egg
is of the same order of magnitude.

    2) The amount necessary to cause delayed effects is
about 3 to 10 times the amount necessary to prevent hatch-

ing except for methyl dichlorofarnesoate.

Once more compounds are systematically assayed on different insects in such a way, we will be able to see whether these and additional generalizations can be made.

TABLE 2

Relative Effectiveness of Juvenile Hormone and Its Analogs
on Different Stages of Life Cycle of
Pyrrhocoris apterus

Compound	MD_{50}[*] 5th	SD_{90}[*] Female	LD_{90}[*] Early Eggs	MD_{90}[*] Late Embryos
C18 Cecropia JH	0.35µg	5.2µg	2 µg	10µg
JH-A-1[**]	0.01µg	≤1 µg	0.16µg	0.54µg
JH-A-2[**]	0.004µg	–	0.55µg	8.3µg
JH-A-3[**]	0.004µg	<0.5µg	0.4µg	1.1µg
ethyl dichloro-farnesoate [†]	0.005µg	<2.5µg	0.6µg	1.5µg
methyl dichloro-farnesoate (25)	0.01µg	<10 µg	0.4µg	27µg

[*]MD_{50} 5th is the amount necessary to produce a larval-adult intermediate (III) when applied to the freshly molted fifth instar (20). SD_{90} female is the amount necessary to give to a female to prevent hatching of 90% of the subsequent two egg batches. LD_{90} early eggs is the amount necessary to apply to eggs within 4 hours of oviposition to prevent 90% from hatching. MD_{90} late embryos is the amount necessary to apply to eggs after blastokinesis to prevent normal metamorphosis of 90% of the treated individuals.

[**] Three different preparations of the Williams-Law mixture of juvenile hormone analogs (5).

[†] Prepared by addition of hydrogen chloride to farnesenic acid ethyl ester. Products used without further purification.

If such generalizations are valid, then they would serve as a guideline for the testing of new compounds as potential ovicides.

Acknowledgments

Supported by NSF and Rockefeller Foundation. I wish to thank Professor Carroll M. Williams for providing the various preparations of the mixture of juvenile hormone analogs (JH-A) and the ethyl dichlorofarnesoate, Professor E. J. Corey for providing the C18-Cecropia juvenile hormone, Dr. Karel Sláma for providing the methyl dichlorofarnesoate, Miss Saundra Tróisi for technical assistance, and Dr. James Truman for a critical reading of the manuscript.

References

1. Sláma, K. and C. M. Williams, Nature 210, 329 (1966).
2. Riddiford, L. M. and C. M. Williams, Proc. Natl. Acad. Sci. U.S. 57, 595 (1967).
3. Novák, V. J. A., J. Emb. and Exp. Morph. 21, 1 (1969); Retnakaran,A.,Can. Entomol. 102, 1592 (1970); Retnakaran, A. and D. Grisdale, Ann. Ent Soc.Am.63, 907 (1970); Spielman, A. and C. M. Williams, Science 154, 1043 (1966); Vinson,J. W. and C. M. Williams, Proc. Natl. Acad. Sci. U.S. 58, 294 (1967); Walker, W. F. and W. S. Bowers, J. Econ. Ent. 63, 1231 (1970).
4. Mueller, N. A. S., Ph.D. Thesis, Univ. of Wisconsin (1962); Cobban, R. H., Evolutionary Trends in Heteroptera. Part I. Eggs, architecture of the shell, gross embryology, and eclosion. Center for Agriculture Publishing and Documentation, Waegeninen (1968).
5. Law, J. H., C. Yuan, and C. M. Williams, Proc. Natl. Acad. Sci. U.S. 55, 576 (1966).
6. Corey, E. J., J. A. Katzenellenbogen, N. W. Gilman, S. A. Roman, and B. W. Erickson, J. Amer. Chem. Soc. 90, 5618 (1968).
7. Riddiford, L. M., Develop. Biol. 22, 249 (1970).
8. Riddiford, L. M., Mitt. Schweiz. Ent. Ges. 44,177(1971).
9. Sláma, K., J. Insect Physiol. 10, 283 (1964).
10. Telfer, W. H. and L. M. Anderson, Develop. Biol. 17, 512 (1968).
11. Enslee, E., Ph.D. Thesis, Harvard University, in

preparation.
12. Williams, C. M., Biol. Bull. 121, 572 (1961).
13. Lockshin, R. A., Science 154, 775 (1966).
14. Matolin, S., Acta ent. bohemoslav. 67, 9 (1970).
15. Enslee, E. and L. M. Riddiford, Amer. Zool. 10, 527 (1970).
16. Seidel, F., Z. Morph. Ökol. Tiere 1, 429 (1924).
17. Riddiford, L. M., Science 167, 287 (1970).
18. Riddiford, L. M., Biol. Bull., in press.
19. Willis, J. H., J. Embryol. exp. Morph. 22, 27 (1969).
20. Sláma, K., Zool. Jb. Physiol. 70, 427 (1964); Williams, C. M. and K. Sláma, Biol. Bull. 130, 235 (1966).
21. Riddiford, L. M. and J. W. Truman, Manuscript in preparation.
22. Willis, J. H. and P. A. Lawrence, Nature 225, 81 (1970).
23. Williams, C. M., The Nature of Biological Diversity, ed. J. M. Allen. McGraw-Hill Book Co., p. 243 (1963); Williams, C. M. and F. C. Kafatos, Mitt. Schweiz Ent. Ges. 44, 151 (1971); ibid, this volume.
24. Masner, P., Sláma, K. and Landa, V., J. Emb. exp. Morph. 20, 25 (1968).
25. Sláma, K., M. Romanuk, and F. Sôrm, Biol. Bull. 136, 91 (1969).

FIELD EXPERIENCES
WITH JUVENILE HORMONE MIMICS

R. W. Bagley and J. C. Bauernfeind

Hoffmann-La Roche Inc.
Chemical Research Department
Nutley, New Jersey 07110

Abstract

Three compounds, namely, synthetic Roeller compound, methyl 10, 11-epoxy-7-ethyl-3, 11-dimethyltridecadienoate (mixture of 8 isomers); Romanuk compound, ethyl trans-7, 11-dichloro-3, 7-11-trimethyl-2-dodecenoate (the trans isomer) and Bowers compound, 6, 7-epoxy-3, 7-dimethyl-1-[3, 4-(methylenedioxy)-phenoxy]-2-nonene (mixture of 4 isomers) were synthesized by Hoffmann-La Roche and made available for laboratory, greenhouse and field studies at a relatively high state of purity in 3 to 10 kilogram lots. Exploratory trials were undertaken on insects and related pests attacking fruit, cotton, tobacco, grain, forage crops and stored crops as well as mosquitoes and other pests of man and animals. Synthetic juvenile hormone compounds offer a certain potential for use as a sole or integrated control agent for insects. Effective compounds have high biological activity, narrow or intermediate specificity, apparent low mammalian toxicity and short environmental persistence. Limitations are in the efficacy pattern of the insect's life cycle and their lack of persistence in the field. More stable compounds, improved formulations and better methods of application are needed.

Introduction

Synthetic chemicals which act as insect growth regulators so modify the growth, metamorphosis, sexual maturation or reproductive cycle of an insect that they bring about its eventual inability to be harmful or annoying to man, animals or crops. Juvenile hormone mimics are members of this class. In recent years, attempts have been made to apply such compounds in the field to disrupt naturally occurring insect populations.

Over 35 years ago the distinguished insect physiologist, V. B. Wigglesworth, described the juvenile hormone as inhibiting or preventing metamorphosis at critical periods in the insect life cycle. In a series of classical experiments using decapitated bugs, parabiosis and transplanted organs, Wigglesworth (68) demonstrated that the juvenile hormone was secreted by the corpora allata and that the hormone from one insect species would also affect other species. Introduced into a nymph of a hemimetabolic species like Rhodnius prolixus, for example, at the time when this bug would normally transform into the adult stage, the active substance caused a molt into another immature nymphal stage. The presence of juvenile hormones at this critical time interferes with normal metamorphosis. The juvenile hormone must likewise be absent during the pupal-adult transformation of holometabolic insects such as the cecropia silk moth. Treatment of a pupa with juvenile hormones results in an abnormal molt to a pupal-adult intermediate or the pupa may simply molt to a second pupa.

In 1956, Williams (70) extracted crude juvenile hormone from the abdominal lipids of the male cecropia moth, Hyalophora cecropia. This ether extract proved to be active not only in other lepidoptera like the cabbageworm, Pieris brassicae, but also in the yellow mealworm, Tenebrio molitor; the roach, Periplaneta americana; and a bug, Rhodnius prolixus. In 1965, Roeller et al. (44,46) reported an isolation of the hormone and Williams and Law (72) isolated a highly active fraction from "cecropia oil". After a decade of work, Meyer, Schneiderman and Gilbert (33, 34) also isolated the juvenile hormone from the cecropia moth. Two years later it was identified by Roeller, Dahm, Sweely and Trost (47) as methyl trans, trans, cis-10, 11-epoxy-7-ethyl-3, 11-dimethyl-2, 6-tri-decadienoate with a molecular weight of 294 and the empirical formula, $C_{18}H_{30}O_3$. A number of syntheses (11, 16, 22, 28, 36, 41, 52), some stereo-selective (1, 15, 17, 19, 29, 31, 45, 53, 64, 78) have been achieved. A lower homologue of the above compound (7-methyl) was identified in the cecropia moth by Meyer et al. (34) in 1968. Other similar or related juvenile hormone structures are believed to exist and with the passage of time, more will probably be identified (8, 61).

These hormones appear to be quite active when applied at critical stages of the life cycle for various orders of insects such as the Lepidoptera, Hemiptera, Coleoptera, Orthoptera, etc. When supplementary juvenile hormones are externally or internally applied to the insect (18, 33, 51), the normal physiological process may be interrupted and one or more of the following phenomena may occur:

1. An action on epidermal cells and an influence on the kind of cuticle secreted at the molt.
2. An effect on internal organs such as brain, gonads and mid-gut and an influence on their metamorphosis.
3. An effect on embryonic development (when juvenile hormone is applied to adult females or laid eggs) which leads either to a block of embryonic development or a later block in post-embryonic development (a potential chemosterilant role) (42, 75).

Juvenile hormone appears to affect cells which are synthesizing DNA and may be involved in the control of genetic information, needed for new cell syntheses. A particularly serious deficiency in our knowledge of the insect juvenile hormones is the lack of basic information (6) on juvenile hormone biosynthesis and metabolism in insects, although some concepts have been discussed (3, 33, 45, 50, 55, 69, 71).

Some juvenile hormone structures are almost species-specific in their activity, for example, juvabione from the balsam fir, the so-called "paper factor" (58) which is extremely potent for pyrrhocorid bugs. This material was identified by Bowers, et al. (10) and synthesized by several groups (2, 4, 5, 37, 39). The identification of the juvenile hormones and the presence of juvenile hormone active structures in a variety of natural sources (20, 25, 49, 73) has prompted chemists to synthesize thousands of related molecules (55) in an attempt to find compounds which might have future utility in insect control. Discussions of the chemical structural requirements for juvenile hormone activity have been published (27, 55, 69).

Present-day criticism by society is that currently used insecticides are (a) too toxic to man, or (b) are unusually persistent in the ecosystem, or (c) not effective against newly evolved insect strains possessing a high resistance or tolerance to the pesticide. However, insects must be controlled if man is to produce the food he needs and maintain high standards of health for the future. In addition to man's food, insects destroy forage, pasture and grain needed to produce livestock. Insects may also carry and transmit many diseases to plants and animals which further limit the food supply. It becomes obvious and has been previously stated (6, 38, 43, 51, 57, 62, 66, 67, 70, 71, 74) that if synthetic insect growth regulators of the juvenile hormone-type could be produced economically in volume, and were found to possess the desirable lethal or debilitating characteristics for insects without development of resistance, yet be relatively harmless to mammalian species and be biodegradable in the environment, that a new mode of insect control may be possible, either practiced alone or in an integrated control concept.

To test the concept that insect juvenile hormone active structures would have some future potential in insect control, a number were prepared in kilogram quantities so that trials could be conducted outside the laboratory, such as greenhouse tests, micro-plot evaluations, and small-scale field studies.

Compounds

Three compounds (Table 1) namely, the Roeller compound or synthetic juvenile hormone (16), a Romanuk compound or DDFAE (32, 48), and a Bowers compound (7) or the methylenedioxyphenoxy terpenoid ether mimic, were synthesized in 3 to 10 kilogram lots at a relatively high state of purity. The synthetic juvenile hormone (mixed isomers), herein designated as the Roeller compound, is most similar to the single naturally occurring trans, trans, cis isomer. The Romanuk compound is interesting for its demonstrated activity and high selectivity for certain insects (32, 56, 69). The Bowers compound, also a synthetic mixed isomer preparation, is one of the more active juvenile hormone mimics having a fairly wide spectrum of activity (7, 8). This "hybrid" molecule combines the cyclic portion of an insecticide synergist with the branched chain of the juvenile hormone. The biological activities of the individual isomers of the synthetic juvenile hormone mixture (17, 41, 45, 69) and the Bowers compound (40) have been reported.

Some chemical characteristics (Table 2) of the three preparations were determined. They were in the range of 90% to 95% pure compounds. Characteristically, these synthetic compounds are colorless or pale yellow clear oils of low viscosity, decidedly lipophilic, and very sparingly soluble in water. Juvenile hormone mimics are soluble in acetone, ether, methylene chloride, alcohols, vegetable and petroleum oils.

The three compounds were subjected to oral, intraperitoneal, and subcutaneous administration in acute toxicological trials with various animal species. Acute dermal and eye irritation tests were included. Included in the toxicology program were the mouse uterus tests in which uterus and thymus weights were taken, and rat male organ tests where testes, thymus and related organs were observed. None of these tests (Table 3) indicated any degree of significant acute toxicity or sensitivity and hence, based on these short term observations, the compounds are regarded as relatively safe. Lack of high toxicity to mammals has recently been reported for one of the juvenile hormone analogs by Siddall and Slade (54) with the observation that the LD$_{50}$ for mice by the oral route was greater than 5,000 mg/kg.

Laboratory Studies

Before undertaking larger scale trials, laboratory data were collected on the three compounds. Since juvenile hormone activity is commonly judged by the highly sensitive yellow mealworm, Tenebrio molitor, assays were conducted at 5 different laboratories. While some differences can be noted (Table 4), depending on the age of the pupae and the method of evaluation employed, all agree that the Bowers compound is the most active, the Romanuk compound, the least active and the Roeller compound, intermediate. On the other hand, the response of the milkweed bug, Oncopeltus fasciatus, to the three compounds (Table 5), shows the Romanuk compound to be the most active. The biological profile of the three compounds on a variety of insects (Tables 6-8) confirms the general understanding that activity depends on (a) the particular species of insect, (b) its critical phase of the life cycle, (c) the mode of administration, as well as (d) the concentration of the active substance. Certain specificity is clearly indicated.

Preliminary testing in the laboratory was usually done by topical application to last instar nymphs (or larvae) or just before or after the pupal molt at levels varying from 100μg to 0.001μg of synthetic compound/insect applied in 1 μl acetone. Eggs, particularly early in embryonic development, may also be very sensitive to such juvenile hormone treatments. Normal fecundity and egg viability may be affected by exposing adult females to synthetic juvenile hormone mimics. Modified topical applications can be made with larger volumes of acetone/water solutions of test compound. Test organisms can be dipped or sprayed with solutions containing a little surfactant to aid uniform wetting and penetration. Either acetone or alcohol can be used to disperse candidate sub-

stances in water for assay on mosquito larvae which are
often sensitive to concentrations well below 1 ppm. Another technique is to expose test insects to filter paper,
cloth pads or leaves treated with the candidate compound
at the rate of 0. 01 - 10 μg/cm². Many synthetic juvenile
hormone mimics are highly active as vapors even when
insects are prevented from contacting the residue. Either
superficially applying the compound or mixing it with the
artificial laboratory diet subjects the feeding insects to
both contact and ingestion.

The laboratory studies served to point out the phases
of the insect life cycle sensitive to the hormone-like substances and established criteria for evaluating the possible
effects on field populations.

Micro-Plot and Field Trials

Contrary to the presently used quick killing insecticides, it must be recognized that the juvenile hormone
action is considerably slower and may involve effects on
the F_1 or F_2 generation of the treated insect population.
Field tests, therefore, may be conducted in a screened-in
facility with a captive insect population for the growing
season (and perhaps even to be carried over to the next
season). This may be necessary to keep out of the test
area flying and crawling insects that have not been exposed
to the experimental compound. Secondly, new criteria for
judging compound efficacy may need to be developed in
order not to overlook residual or long-term effects. Even
where field cages are used, it may be highly desirable to
bring samples of the treated insect population into the laboratory for closer study and correlation with field observations.

Advanced greenhouse investigations and preliminary
field work were carried out in cooperation with the branch
stations of the USDA-ARS, Entomology Research Division,
university experiment stations or by contract testing
agencies. Most of the field trials were conducted with an
emulsifiable concentrate formulation, diluted with water,
and sprayed like a conventional insecticide. Special tests

119

required oil solutions, dust formulations or a granular form.

Both the pure compounds and formulated material in closed containers can be stored for many months in the refrigerator. Even at room temperature, storage stability is satisfactory, but excessive heat and particularly sunlight must be avoided. Spray preparations diluted to field use levels were not carried over in these trials from one day to the next. The suspected instability of the juvenile hormone mimics prompted the recommendation in the microplot and field trial work to use reasonably high concentrations and to apply treatments frequently to assure the exposure of the pest population to the compound.

The objective of these microplot and small-scale field studies was to ascertain whether synthetic compounds with juvenile hormone activity would be a practical approach to insect control. Exploratory trials were undertaken on insects and related pests attacking fruit, cotton, tobacco, grain and forage crops, as well as mosquitoes and other pests of man and animals.

Fruit Crops

The scale insect pests of citrus are tiny insects that build up to large numbers over a period of many months before they are considered an economic problem. One or two full-coverage sprays a year are usually applied to suppress populations in commercial groves. Petroleum spray oils are often mixed with scale control materials to enhance their effectiveness. These factors make the diaspine scales ideal targets for population control by means of a slow-acting hormonal agent.

Both the Roeller and the Romanuk compounds were tested on the citrus snow scale, Unaspis citri, under field conditions. Five sprays were applied to mature trees at 10-day intervals using 1 lb. active ingredient in 700 gallons of water per acre. Neither the total population nor individuals examined under a microscope showed abnormalities from treatment with these juvenile hormone-type compounds. Although the 1 lb. per acre rate might be

considered low, treatments were applied much more frequently than necessary with conventional insecticides, yet,
no adverse effects on development and sexual maturity of
these citrus snow scales were observed.

In the laboratory, more promising results were obtained with two compounds on another species of diaspine scale,
Aonidiella aurantii, or red scale in California. However,
a very high concentration of synthetic juvenile hormone
mimic appears to be required for complete population suppression of the California red scale on dipped fruit. The
effectiveness of the Roeller compound falls off rapidly at
concentrations under 1%. Somewhat more promising is the
Bowers compound which begins to "break" at 0.2% under
the same conditions. Field trials are underway to further
explore the prospects of hormonal control of this pest of
world-wide importance (35).

The brown soft scale, Coccus hesperidum, is not one
of the armored or diaspine scales, but belongs to a distinct
group of lesser economic importance. It is still somewhat
unexpected, however, to find that this coccid insect appears
to be highly susceptible to concentrations as low as 100
ppm of the Romanuk compound. This material had no
effect at primary screening rates on the diaspine scales
again showing the specificity often encountered in the activity of synthetic juvenile hormone mimics. Most of the
soft scales remain small and die without reproducing.
Others appear normal. Since scale development is not
uniform, it is possible that survivors were not in a susceptible stage at the time of treatment. Scales proved
most susceptible to juvenile hormone mimics just prior to
molting. This interesting activity has not yet been verified
under field conditions in Texas.

Completely negative results were obtained on the citrus red mite, Panonychus citri, eggs, immature forms
and adults reared on fruit dipped in 1,000 ppm solutions of
these hormonal agents. This lack of activity is consistent
with the fact that, to date, juvenile hormone mimics have
not shown juvenilizing action on mites, ticks, spiders or
other similar organisms outside of the insects.

Prospects for the practical application of insect population regulants of the juvenile hormone type to control fruit insects appear very limited based on the results of initial investigations. Following some positive indications from work in Switzerland, however, exploratory studies have been initiated on codling moth, Carpocapsa pomonella, the major insect pest of apples and pears.

Cotton and Tobacco

The two major problems on cotton in the United States are the boll weevil, Anthonomus grandis, and the bollworm complex. The most difficult to control of the "bollworms" is the tobacco budworm, Heliothis virescens. This noctuid is highly resistant to conventional organic insecticides.

Field-cage trials with insect growth regulator compounds were conducted during the summer of 1970 on cotton artificially infested by periodic release of Heliothis virescens moths. Materials were applied in an emulsifiable spray formulation at the rate of one pound of active ingredient per acre for a total of 10 applications at weekly intervals. Observations were made in the field cages on the abundance of eggs and larvae. Samples were brought into the laboratory for hatching, pupation and to investigate possible hormonal effects on reproduction (21). The trial could hardly be considered a successful one, particularly from the point of view of protecting the crop. Although up to 60% decrease in egg viability and possibly 25% failure to pupate were indicated in certain treatments, the bollworm populations were uncontrolled.

No significant data on boll weevil were obtained in the same field-cage trial in Texas. Laboratory investigations have since shown that the species is not very susceptible to synthetic juvenile hormone mimics. The Bowers compound is decidedly more active than the Roeller compound or the Romanuk compound on boll weevil pupae but this sensitive stage is not exposed in the field.

Of other cotton insects, the tarnished plant bug, Lygus lineolaris, appears to be quite susceptible as does the cotton aphid, Aphis gossypii. In small-scale application studies of spray formulations against tarnished plant bug,

122

nymphs and established colonies of cotton aphids, morphogenetic abnormalities and death during molting stage were
observed. More extended studies on a larger scale would
be necessary to appraise the practical significance of insect growth regulators as a mode of insect control for
these insects.

Spray trials on field grown tobacco in South Carolina
showed no visible effects on larvae of Heliothis virescens
with any of the three compounds applied at one pound or two
pounds of active ingredient per acre. On the other hand,
some striking results were seen on tobacco hornworm,
Manduca sexta, larvae invading these same plots. As a
result of treatment with the Bowers compound, tobacco
hornworm larvae completely lacked melanization and these
whitish larvae eventually attained a size considerably larger
than normal hornworms. Attempts were made to rear a
few of these visibly affected tobacco hornworms. They all
failed to pupate.

In trials at another location, observations were made
on larvae and eggs of Manduca sexta treated with juvenile
hormone mimics. The larval stage was lengthened with
the feeding of the Bowers compound, the most active compound, with supernumerary molts to the 6th and 7th instar.
Survival was reduced with all three compounds, death often
preceeded by an attempt to molt; in most instances, pupae
were badly deformed and did not survive to adult form to
reproduce. Egg treatment with juvenile hormone mimics
did not significantly reduce the percent hatch.

The juvenilizing effects detected in some of the lepidopterous larvae in these field plots did not deter injury to
the valuable crop. Immediate prospects for practical
applications of juvenile hormone-type materials in cotton
and tobacco do not appear favorable.

Grain and Forage Crops

Field corn, wheat, oats, soybeans and alfalfa are cultivated over large acreages and can tolerate a certain amount
of insect damage. These crops lend themselves well to the
concept of pest management which may provide opportunit-

ies for a physiological approach to insect control. On the other hand, the value of these grain and forage crops is relatively low, hence if synthetic juvenile hormone mimics find applications on such crops, their use will have to be tailored to a very low cost per acre.

Several important lepidopterous larvae have been shown to be susceptible to juvenile hormone mimics, the European corn borer, Ostrinia nubilalis; the fall army-worm, Spodoptera frugiperda; and the army cutworm, Chorizagrotis auxiliaris. The Bowers compound was consistently the most active. The Roeller compound showed moderate activity on lepidoptera while the Romanuk compound showed little activity. Classical symptoms are:

1. A supernumerary molt or prolonged last larval instar.
2. Failure to pupate.
3. Failure to emerge from the pupal stage.
4. Emergence as imperfect adults with pupal appendages or defective wings, generally short-lived and incapable of reproduction or survival.

The method used to evaluate synthetic juvenile hormone mimics on the European corn borer, Ostrinia nubilalis, involves the treating of the larval diet in individual containers with several concentrations of candidate compounds applied in acetone solution and rearing the insects through to normal pupation. A clear juvenile hormone response is seen in this species which will remain for extended periods in the larval stage and often undergo supernumerary molts. All three compounds are being investigated in field-cage studies.

The larvae of the army cutworm, Chorizagrotis auxiliaris, is susceptible to juvenile hormone mimics in a series of tests in which varying degrees of response were recorded on mortality, intermediate forms and deformed, wingless adults. Juvenilization was strongly noted with the Roeller compound, while the Romanuk compound was less effective at 25 ppm in the larval diet. In a single test, topical application of the Bowers compound was superior to the Roeller compound on large, 6th instar larvae.

The most dramatic response was that individuals

escaping larval mortality, lack of pupation, and pupal-adult intermediate deformation, generally survived as wing-less adults. This phenomenon noted at low dosages even on large larvae might be used in the field to prevent the May migration of adults from crop fields to the mountain wilderness. Mortality during this critical period could re-duce the population that returns to the cultivated areas in the fall to oviposit.

Soil insects, particularly the economically important corn rootworm complex, provide a potential target for synthetic juvenile hormone mimics in grain and forage crops. Synchronization of the insect life cycle with the planting operations and other cropping practices is critical. False chemical messengers might disrupt normal insect development and offer a tool to control soil insect popu-lations on an area-wide basis.

The southern corn rootworm, Diabrotica undecimpunct-ata howardi, showed morphogenetic effects in screening tests. Soil in pots treated with Romanuk and Bowers com-pounds showed marked inhibition of adult emergence. The Roeller compound was less effective. Preliminary work with the Bowers compound on the eggs of the western corn rootworm, Diabrotica virgifera, indicates that this syn-thetic juvenile hormone mimic is ovicidal.

In the southeast, all three synthetic juvenile hormone mimics were screened in soil at a rate of three pounds per acre with negative results on the larvae of southern potato wireworm, Conoderus falli. Mortality in any treatment did not exceed the check, pupation was not inhibited and all emerged adults appeared normal.

All juvenile hormone compounds gave negative results on the Japanese beetle, Popillia japonica, in field trials. Larvae in the soil under turf were drenched at a rate of ten pounds of active ingredient per acre. Adults emerging from the 1/100th acre plots were trapped in conical wire cages covering five square feet each. Neither morpho-genetic abnormalities nor effects on reproduction were noted in the beetles collected from any of the field plots.

Subsequent laboratory findings revealed that the larvae

are virtually immune but the early pupal stage is susceptible to synthetic mimics. The timing of the summer treatments was evidently inappropriate for contacting the pupae
during the sensitive period.

Preliminary work with Graphognathus peregrimus, the
white-fringed beetle, in Mississippi, in soil in large pots
with screened cages placed out-of-doors indicates that this
flightless curculionid is susceptible to the juvenile hormone
action of certain synthetic mimics. White-fringed beetles
in the last instar and pre-pupal stage were collected in the
field and placed in a standard greenhouse soil mixture. The
soil had been previously blended with a dust containing one
percent active ingredient at the rate of five pounds active
ingredient per acre. The caged pots were infested with
insects and planted to peanuts to provide the larvae with food
and observed for emerging adults.

Results with the Romanuk compound were quite encouraging. In all evaluations, feeder larvae were more
susceptible than prepupae to hormone mimics. A few
feeder stage larvae introduced into soil containing the
Romanuk compound emerged as adults. No significant
differences were noted in the number of eggs deposited or
in the percent hatch among adults which emerged from the
treatments evaluated. Emerging adults in all treatments
appeared phenotypically normal. Trials with the Roeller
and Bowers compounds are also in progress. It remains
to be seen whether this initial promise can be developed
into a practical control. Researchers are pursuing the
idea with considerable interest since the only reliable
method of control known is with DDT.

A more sophisticated approach may be taken with the
cereal leaf beetle and the alfalfa weevil. Synthetic population regulants of the juvenile hormone type have been
shown to break adult diapause in the laboratory. This
response, possible morphogenetic effects, and prolonged
exposure to hymenopterous parasites might be used to disrupt field populations.

Bowers and Blickenstaff (9) showed that adult diapause
could be broken in the alfalfa weevil, Hypera postica, by

126

topical applications of 10, 11-epoxy farnesenic acid methyl ester. Although the amount required was quite high (50 to 100 μg per weevil), this standard compound had an advantage as a laboratory rearing aid because it does not affect egg viability. Further studies have shown that the Romanuk, Roeller and Bowers compounds screened on diapausing adult alfalfa weevils cause some interruption of diapause. The Romanuk compound was as effective as the standard in terminating adult diapause. The Bowers compound was indicated to be even more active but also quite toxic at 100 μg per weevil. The Roeller compound was considerably more active than the chemically related standard material 10, 11-epoxy farnesenic acid methyl ester. Even the lowest rate tested, 1 μg per weevil, broke reproductive diapause and initiated egg laying within ten to twenty days after topical treatment.

Theoretically, a break in reproductive diapause at an unfavorable time of year would cause heavy mortality of the immature stages and reduce the population potential for the following season. One difficulty with the alfalfa weevil, however, is that tests to date have shown this action occurs only on adults already in diapause, individuals which in nature are found only in protected niches and not readily accessible to chemical treatments.

The breaking of adult diapause in the chrysomelid beetle Oulema melanopus, cereal leaf beetle, with hormone-like chemicals has been recorded in the literature by Connin, et al. (14). However, the methyl ester of 10, 11-epoxyfarnesenic acid is only active in breaking diapause and the rate required is rather high. Since, as already mentioned, it is not practical to reach the diapausing field population, a hormonal agent is needed that would prevent beetles from going into diapause.

Initial studies show that juvenile hormone mimics are capable of preventing, as well as breaking, adult diapause. Sprays of the Roeller compound and the Bowers compound to plants under greenhouse conditions, as well as topical treatments appeared to successfully interrupt diapause and initiate oviposition. Since there were some eggs produced

127

in the untreated checks, however, these more advanced
studies were repeated. In a subsequent study in caged pots
of barley, the Bowers compound applied at a rate of two
pounds per acre gave evidence of egg production, greater
feeding and adult activity in units infested with pre-dia-
pause adult cereal leaf beetles. Although the number of
eggs produced was small, the results provide a potential
in preventing adult diapause. Field work is being considered. The pre-diapausing stage of this insect is not only exposed and feeding on its host plants, but populations are
concentrated on late grain fields during the month of July.

An entirely unrelated species, a leafhopper, Draecul-
acephala crassicornis, also responds to the synthetic
Roeller compound when in reproductive diapause. Kamm
and Swenson (30) have reported that females exposed to
topical applications or vapors completed ovarian development and commenced oviposition in greenhouse tests.
Attempts to duplicate this response in field-cages this year
however, were unsuccessful.

Under laboratory conditions, a number of synthetic
juvenile hormone mimics have been demonstrated to be
active on diapausing pupae of the lepidoptera such as the
cecropia moth. Bowers (8) recently reported similar
effects on tobacco hornworm pupae, Manduca sexta, as well
as adult bugs, e.g. the linden bug, Pyrrhocoris apterus,
and boxelder bug, Leptocoris trivittatus.

To summarize the prospects of using synthetic juvenile
hormone mimics for controlling insect pests of grain and
forage crops, a number of lepidoptera and coleoptera have
shown morphogenetic responses. Reproductive diapause
has been interrupted by topical treatments to many unrelated species. A rather atypical soil insect, the white-fringed beetle, has been demonstrated susceptible to one of the
compounds. Responses have been obtained in corn pests.
Even if these promising leads are reconfirmed under
more extensive field conditions, however, practical applications may well involve population control concepts that
are not in general commercial use today.

Field Tests on the Alfalfa Weevil

The alfalfa weevil is an important agricultural pest in many areas of the United States. This weevil was select- ed as a target for field control studies because of its sus- ceptibility to synthetic juvenile hormone mimics in the laboratory. Both morphogenetic effects in the immature stages and interruption of adult diapause have been demon- strated. Exploratory field trials were conducted at four locations during the 1971 season to determine what effects might be induced in natural populations of the alfalfa weevil, Hypera postica, in the East, and the Egyptian alfalfa weevil, Hypera brunneipennis, in the West.

The field test on irrigated alfalfa in Arizona this spring serves to illustrate the experimental procedure used to evaluate these juvenile hormone-type materials. There were eight treatments: the Roeller compound at 0.25 lbs., 1.0 lbs., and 4.0 lbs. active ingredient per acre; the Bowers compound at 0.25 lbs., 1.0 lbs. and 4.0 lbs. per acre; diazinon insecticide at 0.5 lbs. per acre and an un- treated check. Individual plots were 30 feet wide by 72.6 feet long or 1/20th of an acre. Each treatment was repli- cated three times in a randomized block design.

All chemicals were applied as emulsifiable concentrate formulations diluted with water. Applications were made with a tractor-mounted flat boom sprayer equipped with Teejet 80015 nozzles spaced 20 inches apart. The spray system was under constant pressure of 40 psi from a nitrogen tank and calibrated to deliver 15 gallons per acre at a speed of 3 mph. Measurement of the spray solution remaining in the small containers after each treatment indicated that actual delivery was 5 percent to 7 percent below the desired rates of treatment.

Multiple applications were made with the synthetic juve- nile hormone mimics while the conventional insecticide was applied only once as normally done in commercial practice. All applications were made between 4:30 and 7:30 PM MST to avoid intense sunlight during the 12-hour period immediately after spraying. Each of the hormone mimic plots was treated three times, April 1st, 18th and

27th. On April 1st, weevil larvae in all instars, but primarily in the third and fourth instars, were actively feeding on terminal growth of the alfalfa which was 12-14 inches tall. On April 18th, the larvae, primarily fourth instar, were on the ground as a result of the recent mowing, raking and baling. A few pupae were present in all plots. Only alfalfa stubble without new growth was present on this date. On April 27th, the weevils were primarily in the adult stage. The alfalfa on that date had about two inches of new growth. The standard treatment of diazinon insecticide was made once on March 24th. At that time, most of the larvae were in the second and third instars and were actively feeding on the terminal growth of alfalfa 8-10 inches tall.

Two methods of sampling, sweep net and time-search of ground trash, were used with the method dependent on the location of the various stages of the weevil population. Fourth instar larvae obtained during samplings after the first and second applications were held with alfalfa in petri dishes for observation. Unsexed adult weevils collected following the second and third application were caged over alfalfa to observe oviposition response.

The diazinon treatment was applied earlier than the experimental materials to follow the commercial practice of controlling the peak population of small larvae before extensive feeding injury occurs. Diazinon gave good control during the week after treatment, however, the April 6th and 9th readings show higher populations than are normally considered desirable.

It is evident that the larval populations increased between the time the juvenile hormone-type sprays were applied on April 1st and the April 6th reading. The only reduction of larvae occurred in the plots treated with the Roeller compound at 4 pounds per acre. This observation was also supported by the April 9th readings. Thereafter, however, subsequent sprays of the hormonal materials did not appear to affect the insect population level. Counts were similar to those obtained in the untreated check.

The rearing of last instar larvae to the adult stage was

fairly successful. Of prime interest among the rearing
results was the frequency of deformed pupae and to a lesser extent, deformed adults resulting from treatment with
the Bowers compound at 4 pounds per acre. The deformit-
ies noted were primarily in the wing pads of the pupae and
the elytra of the adults. Most deformed pupae eventually
died. The few deformed adults were able to walk, but were
definitely flightless. On the other hand, from approximately 300 unsexed adults brought into the laboratory, only one
egg mass was obtained. Apparently none of the spray treatments stimulated oviposition and all adults, including the
untreated weevils, entered the normal summer diapause.

Similar mild morphogenetic effects were seen in small
plot tests conducted in Maryland and Pennsylvania, particularly with the 4 pound rate of the Bowers compound.
The most common symptom was prolongation of the last
larval instar which remained feeding longer than insects in
the untreated checks. Adults from all treatments appeared
normal and there were no discernible effects on their diapause condition.

Under the conditions of the Arizona test, phytotoxicity
was noted with both the Roeller and Bowers compounds at
the 4 pound rate and took the form of tan necrotic spotting
of the foliage. Significant injury was not recorded at two
locations in the East nor observed in any of the 4 tests at
the 1 pound rate. No other adverse side effects were
detected.

These test results on the alfalfa weevil can be considered typical of the attempts to date to evaluate spray treatments of synthetic juvenile hormone compounds on agro-
nomic crops. Minor morphogenetic effects can be seen
generally in a small percent of the treated insect populations following multiple applications of rather high rates of
chemical. Instability of the compounds (40) in the environment is suspected to be a major factor.

Beneficial Insects

Only preliminary laboratory studies have been undertaken with insect parasites and predators. Sensitivity

varies greatly with the compound; the species involved and the life stage treated. Hymenopterous parasites are not particularly susceptible to juvenile hormone-type materials, but Apanteles and Trichogramma wasps can apparently be affected by the Bowers compound. Chrysopa lacewings, hemipterous predators and coccinellid lady beetles show morphogenetic responses to the Roeller compound, and the Bowers compound. What this may imply under field conditions remains to be determined.

Hsiao and Hsiao (24) have shown a juvenilizing response with topical applications of the Roeller compound on the alkali bee, Nomia melanderi.

Stored Products

Synthetic juvenile hormone type compounds would appear to have many advantages as control agents for stored product insects and reasonable residual action could be expected in enclosed storage facilities. Thomas and Bhatnagar-Thomas (63) used the methyl ester of the Romanuk compound to demonstrate the inhibition of development in stored food of the red flour beetle, Tribolium castaneum, and two other pests, Stegobium paniceum and Bruchus chinensis. In the test with Tribolium, wheat flour was thoroughly treated with 100 ppm to 1,000 ppm of the compound dissolved in ether.

More recent laboratory tests in Florida have shown that the Bowers compound is particularly effective against both the Indian-meal moth, Plodia interpunctella, and the red flour beetle (1 ppm to 25 ppm). The Roeller compound was somewhat less effective in preventing the pupation of emergence of these same species (10 ppm to 250 ppm).

Studies using the Indian-meal moth indicated high dosages of the Roeller compound greatly stimulated feeding. (However, dosage levels can be selected that do not greatly enhance feeding but do greatly delay pupation). At slightly lower dosages, the larval-pupal molts resulted in the production of non-viable intermediate forms. Although some lower levels did not affect pupation, they did prevent eclosion. Therefore, careful selection of dosage and uni-

132

form distribution on the commodity will have to be critical-
ly considered in developing a possible method of insect
control.

Tests in progress indicate that the juvenilizing agents
are fairly stable on the commodity and do not lose appreciable activity over a period of several months.

Pests Affecting Man and Animals

A field test with synthetic juvenile hormones demonstrating the control of biting lice (Mallophaga) on Angora
goats was reported by Chamberlain and Hopkins (13) at
Kerrville, Texas.

Multiple treatments at 14-day intervals were employed
using the Roeller compound as a 0.1% spray. No immediate effect on the population of the Angora goat-biting louse,
Bovicola limbata, was recorded, but the infestation dropped off sharply between the 4th and 6th week of the test,
and was essentially eliminated about 3 weeks after the third
spray. Larger scale tests using a power sprayer on about
20 goats showed that two well-timed spray treatments could
clean up infestations of biting lice. Single treatments of
0.25% concentration, however, were inadequate. Symptoms,
such as lack of normal melanization in the nymphs, supernumerary nymphal molts, and failure to complete development have been described by Hopkins, et al. (23) and
Chamberlain and Hopkins (12).

Preliminary laboratory work on a related species,
Bovicola bovis, that attacks cattle has shown that both the
eggs and immature stages are affected by the Roeller compound through topical application, ingestion with the laboratory diet and exposure to vapors. Romanuk compound
was ineffective and the Bowers compound was only slightly
active in these studies.

Sucking lice (Anoplura) are more widespread as livestock pests than the biting lice (Mallophaga). The species
attacking man has been reported to be susceptible to juvenile hormone compounds by Vinson and Williams (65).
Recent tests on Pediculus humanus humanus tend to confirm this earlier study although the slow action of juvenile

133

hormone makes it undesirable for public health use. The
three juvenile hormone mimics were tested against Pediculus humanus humanus by spraying cloth patches with a 1%
solution and exposing adult colonies to the treated patches
for 24 hours. The Bowers compound caused an immediate
total ovicidal effect on eggs laid by exposed adults. The
Roeller and Romanuk compounds were less effective when
tested in this manner.

The Bowers compound is among the most active juvenile
hormone mimics tested to date on the immature stages of
the stable fly, Stomoxys calcitrans, and the horn fly,
Haematobia irritans. Eggs and adults appear to be unaffected although partial sterility was reported in the house fly,
Musca domestica, by one worker.

Wright and Spates (76, 77) have developed an assay to
select candidate compounds with juvenile hormone activity
in the stable fly. The Bowers compound was the only one
of the three materials to warrant advanced testing. In recent field-cage studies, the Bowers compound applied as a
spray to fly rearing media sharply reduced or completely
prevented adult emergence. Although relatively high rates
of 1 gram to 5 grams per square foot were used in these
initial trials, the results obtained by Wright are quite encouraging.

The practice of larviciding is widely used in mosquito
control programs in the United States. Since late instar
larvae are highly susceptible to the action of synthetic
juvenile hormone mimics, these new chemicals have been
tested in a manner similar to insecticides. Many compounds have been demonstrated effective in the laboratory
(26, 59, 60) on mosquito larvae of the genera Aedes,
Anopheles and Culex. Less specificity is noted with mosquitoes than with flies. Larvae exposed to juvenile hormone mimics either fail to pupate or do not emerge as
adults, hence providing control equivalent to toxicants.
The concentration of hormonal agent required to achieve
such control in the laboratory, on the other hand, is
extremely high compared to active insecticides. The physiological approach to control of mosquito larvae, however,

appears to hold a great deal of promise. The methylene-dioxy phenoxy compound of Bowers has consistently been the most active on mosquitoes and control of a field population was recently demonstrated in a small scale trial in California.

When considering the potential of synthetic juvenile hormone mimics as chemical control agents for pests of man and animals, it must be remembered that the leads from the field to date indicate fairly specific uses. Although restricted in the number of susceptible species and slow acting, this physiological approach has the advantage of safety and effectiveness against insects resistant to conventional insecticides. Louse control on cattle, goats and possibly sheep and hogs looks promising. Fly control in manure and other breeding media offers a potential if effectiveness can be demonstrated and appropriate methods of application developed. Mosquito abatement through treatment of waters where larvae are developing is being explored at a number of laboratories across the United States.

Discussion

Synthetic juvenile hormone compounds offer a certain potential for use as control agents for insects. Some juvenile hormone-type compounds are highly active and under controlled conditions, they disrupt metamorphosis, reproduction or cause death when applied topically to the insect at dosage levels in the nanogram range or when ingested at concentrations of less than I ppm. They penetrate the egg chorion or insect cuticle and hence, are active by contact. Some are sufficiently volatile to act like fumigants. The juvenile hormone compounds affect developmental stages including eggs, fullgrown larvae or nymphs, prepupae, pupae and female adults.

It must be considered that the use of juvenile hormone mimics may be useful as part of an integrated control program and not necessarily as a sole treatment. Trends favor the future acceptance of synthetic hormone mimics to selectively regulate insect pest populations if they are truly effective under field conditions. A considerable effort will be needed to reduce theoretical advances to actual practice during the next decade.

On the favorable side, it may be said that the better juvenile hormone compounds developed have, (a) high biological activity even against insecticide resistant strains (b) narrow or intermediate specificity, (c) low vertebrate or mammalian toxicity and (d) short persistence in the environment. Another potential advantage that has been declared for juvenile hormone compounds is that insects will not readily become resistant to hormonal chemicals; however, there is no assurance that resistance would not eventually develop.

Field experiences during the past two years serve to underscore the negative aspects of insect control with hormonal agents. The juvenile hormone compounds do not inactivate or kill the growing larvae or nymphs which are the most destructive stages of plant feeders. Also, for effective control, the juvenile hormone compound must be applied in the insect's environment at a sensitive stage of the insect cycle and for a sufficient period of time to insure that large numbers of the insect population are exposed and will be subject to their lethal or debilitating action.

There is also the subject of persistence of juvenile hormone-type compounds in the field and the question of whether it will be necessary to use repeated applications which of course will adversely influence economics. More stable compounds, improved formulations and better methods of application are clearly needed.

The relative activity of the three synthetic juvenile hormone mimics field tested shows a considerable amount of selectivity that is difficult to classify along broad phylogenetic lines.

Although only intermediate in activity level, the Roeller compound has shown a fairly wide spectrum. In laboratory screening it demonstrated moderate activity on lepidopterous larvae like the fall armyworm, Spodoptera frugiperda; the European corn borer, Ostrinia nubilalis; and the army cutworm, Chorizagrotis auxiliaris. At relatively high treatment levels, the Roeller compound gives a juvenile hormone response in coleoptera like the yellow mealworm, Tenebrio molitor, and the boll weevil, Anthonomus grandis. Preliminary results in potted soil on southern corn rootworm, Diabrotica undecimpunctata howardi, appear negative. It is quite active in breaking adult diapause in the alfalfa weevil, Hypera postica. A low order of activity has also been recorded on dipterous stable flies, Stomoxys calcitrans, and mosquito larvae, Culex pipiens quinquefasciatus and Anopheles quandrimaculatus. Slight activity was seen with certain hemiptera, tarnished plant bug, Lygus lineolaris; milkweed bug, Oncopeltus fasciatus; cotton aphid, Aphis gossypii, and California red scale, Aonidiella aurantii, but not on other species like the brown soft scale, Coccus hesperidum. The Roeller compound gave good residual control of Angora-goat biting lice, Bovicola limbata, on animals in field trials. In the laboratory, the Roeller compound is the standard hormonal agent for cattle lice, Bovicola bovis, being superior to Bowers compound for this insect. Field work on cattle lice and further evaluation for the control of livestock ectoparasites are planned or in progress. Field sprays of the Roeller compound at 1 pound to 4 pounds per acre on cotton, alfalfa, tobacco and citrus were ineffective against tobacco hornworm, Manduca sexta; tobacco budworm, Heliothis virescens; alfalfa weevils, Hypera spp. and citrus snow scale, Unaspis citri. Trials on soil insects in the field, e.g. Japanese beetle, Popillia japonica and the southern potato wireworm, Conoderus falli, gave negative results.

The Romanuk compound was highly active on only two species of hemiptera, the milkweed bug, Oncopeltus fasciatus, and the brown soft scale, Coccus hesperidum. It failed on the tarnished plant bug, Lygus lineolaris, and the armored scales, Aonidiella aurantii and Unaspis citri. In the laboratory trials, high rates of the Romanuk compound showed a mild to good response in certain lepidoptera and coleoptera. In the field, however, negative results were obtained in the 4 trials in which it was included.

The Bowers compound was the most active of the mater-

ials in this three-compound study. Comparative tests showed its superiority on coleoptera like the yellow mealworm,
Tenebrio molitor; the alfalfa weevil, Hypera postica; the
boll weevil, Anthonomus grandis, several lepidopterous
larvae like the army cutworm, Chorizagrotis auxiliaris;
the European corn borer, Ostrinia nubilalis, and the
tobacco budworm, Heliothis virescens, dipterous pests
such as the stable fly, Stomoxys calcitrans, and mosquito
larvae, Culex and Anopheles spp. and certain hemiptera
like the tarnished plant bug, Lygus lineolaris. Preliminary results were also promising in potted soil against the
southern corn rootworm, Diabrotica undecimpunctata
howardi. The Bowers compound was included in the tobacco field test and the cotton field trial. Positive responses were seen on lepidopterous larvae under the same conditions where no effects were noted with the Roeller compound and the Romanuk compound. With the tobacco hornworm, Manduca sexta, larvae/treated plots lacked melanization, had an extended larval period and apparently produced supernumerary instar larvae which failed to pupate.
On cotton, Heliothis virescens, tobacco budworm larvae
had a prolonged larval period possibly with supernumerary
instars and lack of pupation was also observed.

The Roeller compound showed a fairly broad spectrum
and interesting activity. Potential prospects for livestock
insect control has been demonstrated. The Romanuk compound was highly active in a few instances but had the nar-
rowest spectrum of activity. Of the three compounds
investigated, the Bowers compound showed the most activity and the broadest spectrum. An observation
most apparent is that each juvenile hormone compound
will have its own characteristic profile of activity and no
single one will meet all insect control requirements.

Some of the results with juvenile hormone-active
synthetics in small-scale field trials and cage tests indicate
promise for control or were of scientific interest because
a juvenile hormone response was obtained. How do we
translate the disruptive effects of the insect hormonal chemicals observed under laboratory conditions into practical

terms for future insect control? Field tests such as the
type discussed in this paper can provide us with some of
the needed answers.

Summary

Small scale field trials were conducted with three
synthetic juvenile hormone mimics: the Roeller compound,
methyl 10, 11-epoxy-7-ethyl-3, 11-dimethyltridecadienoate,
(mixture of 8 isomers), Romanuk compound, ethyl trans-
7, 11-dichloro-3, 7-11-trimethyl-2-dodecenoate (the trans
isomer), and Bowers compound, 6, 7-epoxy-3, 7-dimethyl-
1- [3, 4-(methylenedioxy)-phenoxy] -2-nonene (mixture of
4 isomers). Distinct spectra of activity were apparent,
for example, the Roeller compound was the only one effective on Angora goat biting lice, Bovicola limbata, and the
Romanuk compound was fairly specific for the brown soft
scale, Coccus hesperidum. The Bowers compound was
the most active and showed positive responses on the
tobacco hornworm, Manduca sexta, and the Egyptian alfalfa
weevil, Hypera brunneipennis, under the same conditions
where little or no effects were noted with the other compounds. Mosquito control by treating late instar larvae in
water was also demonstrated. In most cases, relatively
high rates were required to produce mild juvenilizing
activity in insects probably due to lack of stability of these
compounds in the environment. The responses recorded
were not always useful in protecting the crop from insect
damage.

It is apparent that each juvenile hormone compound will
have its own characteristic profile of activity and no single
one will have utility in over-all insect control. While the
juvenile hormone approach possesses some merit as a
means of insect control, there are still many scientific
and practical aspects requiring further study and resolution.

Acknowledgement

We wish to acknowledge the cooperation of the Branch
Stations of the USDA, ARS, Entomology Research Division,

the USDA-ARS, Market Quality Research Division, and University Agricultural Experiment Stations in conducting studies on these juvenile hormone mimics. We also acknowledge efforts of the Roche Chemical, Toxicological, and Biological Laboratories in Basle and Nutley in providing data cited in these studies.

References

1. R. J. Anderson, C. A. Henrick and J. B. Siddall, J. Amer. Chem. Soc. 92, 735 (1970).
2. K. S. Ayyar and G. S. K. Rao, Canad. J. Chem. 46, 1467 (1968).
3. G. Baumann, J. Insect Physiol. 14,1459 (1968); Nature 223, 316 (1969).
4. A. J. Birch, P. L. MacDonald and V. H. Powell, Tetrahedron Lett. 351 (1969).
5. J. F. Blount, B. A. Pawson and G. Saucy, Chem. Commun. , London 715 (1969).
6. W. S. Bowers, Science 161, 895 (1968).
7. W. S. Bowers, Science 164, 325 (1969).
8. W. S. Bowers, Juvenile Hormones-Naturally Occurring Insecticides (edited by Jacobson and Crosby) Marcel Dekker Inc. , 307 (1971).
9. W. S. Bowers and C. C. Blickenstaff, Science 154, 1673 (1966).
10. W. S. Bowers, H. M. Fales, M. J. Thompson and E. C. Uebel, Science 154, 1020 (1966).
11. B. H. Braun, M. Jacobson, M. Schwarz, P. E. Sonnet, N. Wakabayashi, and R. M. Waters, J. Econ. Ent. 61, 866 (1968).
12. W. F. Chamberlain and D. E. Hopkins, Ann. Ent. Soc. 63, 1363 (1970).
13. W. F. Chamberlain and D. E. Hopkins, J. Econ. Ent. 64, 1198 (1971).
14. R. V. Connin, O. K. Jantz and W. S. Bowers, J. Econ. Ent. 60, 1752 (1967).
15. E. J. Corey, J. A. Katzenellenbogen, N. W. Gilman, S. A. Roman, and B. W. Erickson, J. Amer. Chem. Soc. 90, 5618 (1968); Tetrahedron Lett. , 1821 (1971).

16. K. H. Dahm, B. M. Trost and H. Roeller, J. Amer. Chem. Soc. 89, 5292 (1967).
17. K. H. Dahm, H. Roeller and B. M. Trost, Life Sci. 7, (Pt. 2) 129 (1968).
18. F. Engelmann, Ann. Rev. Entom. 13, 1 (1968).
19. D. J. Faulkner and M. R. Peterson, J. Amer. Chem. Soc. 93, 3766 (1971).
20. L. I. Gilbert and H. A. Schneiderman, Trans. Amer. Micr. Soc. 79, 38 (1960).
21. A. A. Guerra, D. A. Wolfenbarger and M. J. Lukefahr, Presentation at National Meeting Ent. Soc. Amer. , Miami Beach, Fla. Nov. 30-Dec. 3 (1970).
22. W. Hoffmann, H. Pasedach and H. Possimer, Liebigs Ann. Chem. 729, 52 (1969).
23. D. E. Hopkins, W. F. Chamberlain and J. E. Wright, Ann. Ent. Soc. 63, 1360 (1970).
24. C. Hsiao and T. H. Hsiao, Life Sci. 8, (Pt. 2) 767 (1969).
25. M. Jacobson and R. E. Redfern, J. Amer. Oil Chem. Soc. 48, 93A (1971).
26. W. L. Jakob, Presentation at 27th Annual Meeting Amer. Mosquito Control Assoc. , Denver, Colorado, March 21-24 (1971).
27. V. Jarolim, K. Hejno, F. Sehnal and F. Sorm, Life Sci. 8, (Pt. 2) 831 (1969).
28. W. S. Johnson, T. Li, D. J. Faulkner and S. F. Campbell, J. Amer. Chem. Soc. 90, 6225 (1968).
29. W. S. Johnson, T. J. Brocksom, P. Loew, D. H. Rich, L. Werthemann, R. A. Arnold, T. Li and D. J. Faulkner, J. Amer. Chem. Soc. 92, 4463 (1970).
30. J. A. Kamm and K. G. Swenson, J. Econ. Ent. in press (1971).
31. P. Loew and W. S. Johnson, J. Amer. Chem. Soc. 93, 3765 (1971).
32. P. Masner, K. Slama and V. Landa, J. Embryol. Exptl. Morphol. 20, 25 (1968); Nature 219, 395 (1968).
33. A. S. Meyer, E. Hanzmann, H. A. Schneiderman, L. I. Gilbert and M. Boyette, Arch. Biochem. Biophys. 137, 190 (1970).

34. A. S. Meyer, H. A. Schneiderman and L. I. Gilbert, Nature 26, 272 (1965).
35. D. S. Moreno, J. Fargerlund and J. G. Shaw, Presentation at Pacific Branch Meeting, Ent. Soc. Amer., Sacramento, Calif., June 22-24 (1971).
36. K. Mori, B. Stalla-Bourdillon, M. Ohki, M. Matsui and W. S. Bowers, Tetrahedron 25, 1667 (1969).
37. K. Mori and M. Matsui, Tetrahedron 24, 3127 (1968).
38. K. K. Nair, Naturwissenschaften 54, 494 (1967).
39. B. A. Pawson, H. C. Chueng, S. Gurbaxani and G. Saucy, Chem. Comm. 1057 (1968); J. Amer. Chem. Soc. 92, 336 (1970).
40. B. A. Pawson, F. Scheidl and F. Vane, in press this volume (1972).
41. A. Pfiffner, Terpenoids in Plants (Edited by Goodwin) Academic Press, 95-133 (1971).
42. L. M. Riddiford, Science 167, 287 (1970).
43. W. E. Robbins, Presentation at the Nat. Acad. Sci. Symp. on Pest Control Strategies for the Future, Wash. D. C., April 14-16 (1971).
44. H. Roeller, J. Bjerke and W. H. McShan, J. Insect. Physiol. 11, 1185 (1965).
45. H. Roeller and K. H. Dahm, Recent Programs in Hormone Research, Academic Press 24, 615 (1968).
46. H. Roeller and K. H. Dahm, Naturwissenschaften 57, 454 (1970).
47. H. Roeller, K. H. Dahm, C. C. Sweely and B. M. Trost, Angew. Chemie Intern. Ed. 6, 179 (1967); Chem Eng. News 45, 48 (1967).
48. M. Romanuk, K. Slama and F. Sorm, Proc. Nat. Acad. Sci. USA 57, 349 (1967).
49. H. A. Schneiderman and L. I. Gilbert, Biol. Bull. 115, 530 (1958).
50. H. A. Schneiderman and L. I. Gilbert, Science 143, 325 (1964).
51. H. A. Schneiderman, A. Krishnakumaran, P. J. Bryant, and F. Sehnal, Agr. Sci. Rev. 8, 13 (1970); Presentation at the Symposium on Potentials in Crop Protection, N. Y. S. Agr. Exp. Sta., May 20 (1969).

52. U. Schwieter and A. Pfiffner, Presentation at the 148th Meeting, Schweizerische Naturforschende Gesellschaft Einsiedeln, Switzerland, Sept. 27-29 (1968).

53. H. Schulz, H. and I. Sprung, Angew. Chem. Intern. Edit. 8, 271 (1969).

54. J. B. Siddall and M. Slade, Nature, New Biol. 229, 158 (1971).

55. K. Slama, Ann. Rev. Biochem. 40, 1079-1102 (1971).

56. K. Slama, M. Romanuk and F. Sorm, Biol. Bull. 136, 91 (1969).

57. K. Slama, M. Suchy and F. Sorm, Biol. Bull. 134, 154 (1968).

58. K. Slama and C. M. Williams, Proc. Nat. Acad. Sci. USA 54, 411 (1965); Nature 210, 329 (1966); Biol. Bull. 130, 235 and 247 (1966).

59. A. Spielman and C. M. Williams, Science 154, 1043 (1966).

60. A. Spielman and V. Skaff, J. Insect Physiol. 13, 1087 (1967).

61. V. S. Srivastava and L. I. Gilbert, Science 161, 61 (1968).

62. M. Suchy, K. Slama and F. Sorm, Science 162, 582 (1968).

63. T. P. Thomas, P. L. Bhatnagar-Thomas, Nature 219, 949 (1968).

64. E. E. van Tamelen, P. McCurry and U. Huber, Proc. Natl. Acad. Sci. USA 68, 1294 (1971).

65. J. W. Vinson and C. M. Williams, Proc. Nat. Acad. Sci. USA 58, 294 (1967).

66. W. Vogel, Presentation at the International Pesticide Congress, Tel Aviv, February 21-28 (1971).

67. P. D. Walton, Intern. Pest Control 10, 13 (1968).

68. V. B. Wigglesworth, Quart. J. Microscop. Sci. 77, 191 (1934); ibid 79, 91 (1936); J. Exptl. Biol. 17, 201 (1940).

69. V. B. Wigglesworth, Nature 221, 190 (1969); J. Insect. Physiol. 15, 73 (1969).

70. C. M. Williams, Nature 178, 212 (1956).

71. C. M. Williams, Sci. Amer. 217, 13 (1967).

72. C. M. Williams and J. H. Law, J. Insect Physiol. 11, 569 (1965).
73. C. M. Williams, L. V. Moorhead and J. F. Pubis, Nature 183, 405 (1959).
74. C. M. Williams and W. E. Robbins, Bioscience 18, 79 (1968).
75. J. H. Willis and P. A. Lawrence, Nature 225, 81 (1970).
76. J. E. Wright, J. Econ. Ent. 63, 878 (1970).
77. J. E. Wright and G. E. Spates, J. Agr. Food Chem. 19, 289 (1971).
78. R. Zurflüh, E. N. Wall, J. B. Siddall and J. A. Edwards, J. Amer. Chem. Soc. 90, 6224 (1968).

Table 1

Structure and Chemical Name of the Juvenile Hormone Compounds

Roeller
Compound

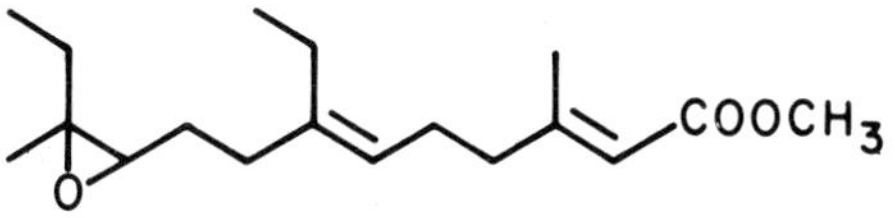

Methyl 10, 11-epoxy-7-ethyl-3, 11-dimethyltridecadienoate (mixture of 8 isomers)

Romanuk
Compound

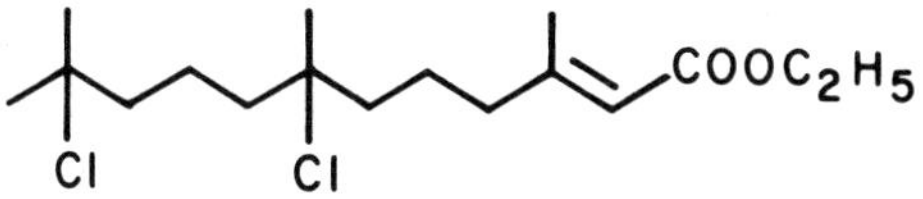

Ethyl trans-7, 11-dichloro-3, 7-11-trimethyl-2-dodecenoate (the trans isomer)

Bowers
Compound

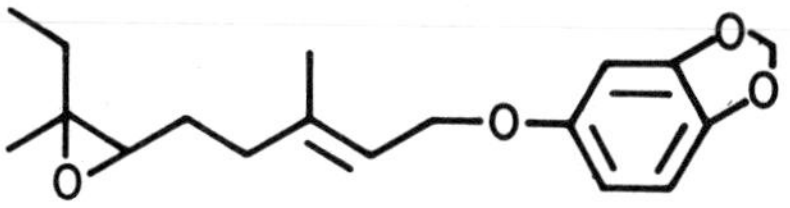

6, 7-Epoxy-3, 7-dimethyl-1- [3, 4-(methylenedioxy)-phenoxy]-2-nonene (mixture of 4 isomers)

145

Table 2

Physical Properties of the Juvenile Hormone Compounds

Compound	Molecular Weight	Color	Isomers	Refractive Index	Boiling Point (C)	Purity	Solubility
Roeller $C_{18}H_{30}O_3$	294.42	colorless liquid or pale yellow	cis, trans mixture, 8 isomers	$n_D^{25°}$ 1.4784	106°/0.001 mm Hg	90+	ins. water; v. s. organic solvents
Romanuk $C_{17}H_{30}O_2Cl_2$	337.34	colorless liquid or pale yellow	essentially all-trans, 90%	$n_D^{20°}$ 1.4841	decomposes upon distillation	95%	ins. water; v. s. organic solvents
Bowers $C_{18}H_{24}O_4$	304.4	colorless liquid or pale yellow	cis, trans mixture, 4 isomers	$n_D^{23°}$ 1.5240	150°/0.005 mm Hg	95%+	ins. water; v. s. organic solvents

Table 3

Toxicological Data on the Juvenile Hormone Compounds

Roeller Compound

Acute toxicity $LD_{50}.>$ 4,000 mg/kg p. o. (mice)
                    LD_{50} > 2,000 mg/kg i. p. (mice)
                    LD_{50} > 2,000 mg/kg s. c. (mice)
                    LD_{50} > 4,000 mg/kg p. o. (rats)
                    LD_{50} > 2,000 mg/kg i. p. (rats)
                    LD_{50} > 2,000 mg/kg p. o. (rabbits)
                    LD_{50} > 320 mg/kg p. o. (dogs)
                    LD_{50} 800 ± 65 mg/kg p. o. (neonatal rats)

Skin absorption test >   4,000 mg/kg (mice)
Uterus test - negative, 1 mg/0. 1ml/d 3x (mice)
Male test - negative, 2 mg/0. 2 ml s. c. 2x (rats)
Eye irritation test - slight conjunctival redness, 0. 1 ml (rabbits)
Abraded skin test - non-irritating, 0. 1 ml (rabbits)

Romanuk Compound ·

Acute toxicity LD_{50} > 5,000 mg/kg p. o. (mice)

Uterus test - negative, 1 mg/0. 1ml/d 3x (mice)
Male test - negative, 2 mg/0. 2 ml s. c. 3x (rats)
Eye irritation test - non-irritating, 0. 1 ml (rabbits)
Abraded skin test - non-irritating, 0. 1 ml (rabbits)

Bowers Compound

Acute toxicity LD_{50} 3,900 ± 240 mg/kg p. o. (mice)   ·
                    LD_{50} > 2,000 mg/kg i. p. (mice)
                    LD_{50} > 2,000 mg/kg s. c. (mice)
                    LD_{50} > 4,000 mg/kg .p. o. (rats)
                    LD_{50} 3,250 ± 115 mg/kg i. p. (rats)
                    LD_{50} > 2,000 mg/kg p. o. (rabbits)
                    LD_{50} 530 ± 33 mg/kg p. o. (neonatal rats)

Skin absorption test >   4,000 mg/kg (mice)
Eye irritation test - slight conjunctival redness, 0. 1 ml (rabbits)
Abraded skin test - non-irritating, 0. 1 ml (rabbits)

Table 4

Comparative Results of Topical Assays of the Juvenile Hormone Compounds on the
Yellow Mealworm, Tenebrio molitor,
Conducted by Five Different Laboratories

Compound	Rate[1] μg/Pupa	Juvenile Hormone Activity: Score 0 - 100				
		A	B	C	D	E
Roeller	10	93	100	76	84	64
	1	64	58	0	31	18
Romanuk	10	0	25	16	12	8
Bowers	10	100	100	96	100	86
	1	100	100	90	100	86
	0.1	97	80	1	90	88
	0.01	73	10	1	-	30

[1] All applied in 1 μl acetone to ventral abdominal segments of pupae less than
8 hours old (B & D) or less than 16 hours old (A & C), or less than 24 hours
old (E).

Table 5

Juvenile Hormone Topical Bioassay on the Large Milkweed Bug,
Oncopeltus fasciatus

Compound	Dosage[a] μg/bug	Average Score 0 to 3 Juvenile Hormone Activity
Roeller	10	3.0
	1	0.2
Romanuk	10	3.0
	1	3.0
	0.1	3.0
	0.01	3.0
	0.001	1.0
Bowers	10	3.0
	1	0.4
Sesamex	10	2.9
Acetone Check		0.0

148

Table 6

Activity of the Roeller Compound in Laboratory Tests

Order and Species	Life Stage	Method of Application	Effective Concentration	Observed Activity
Orthoptera Blattella germanica	Nymphs	Filter Paper	10^{-3} g/cm^2	70% deformed insects
Hemiptera Dysdercus cingulatus	Adult	Filter Paper	10^{-6} g/cm^2	68% sterility
Homoptera Aphis fabae	Adult	Seedling	10^{-4} g/plant	99% less reproduction
Coleoptera Sitophilus granaria	Adult	On Grain	10^{-4} g/g grain	92% ovicidal
Leptinotarsa decemlineata	Larvae	Topical	10^{-5} g/animal	80% less emergence
Lepidoptera Carpocapsa pomonella	Larvae	Contact	10^{-5} g/cm^2	100% less emergence
Ephestia kuhniella	Larvae	On Flour	10^{-4} g/g flour	100% less reproduction
Prodenia litura	Larvae	Spray	10^{-3} g/ml	82% less emergence
Tineola biselliella	Adult	Cloth Discs	10^{-4} g/cm^2	100% ovicidal 55% sterility
Diptera Musca domestica	Larvae	Topical	10^{-5} g/larva	100% less emergence

Table 7

Activity of the Romanuk Compound in Laboratory Tests

Order and Species	Life Stage	Method of Application	Effective Concentration	Observed Activity
Orthoptera				
Blatella germanica	Nymph	Filter Paper	10^{-5} g/cm^2	90% less adults
Hemiptera				
Dysdercus cingulatus	Nymph	Topical	10^{-7} g/animal	100% disturbed metamorphosis
Homoptera				
Aphis fabae	Adult	Seedling	10^{-5} g/plant	93% less reproduction
Coleoptera				
Anthrenus vorax	Adult	Contact	10^{-4} g/cm^2	71% sterility
Sitophilus granaria	Adult	On Grain	10^{-3} g/g grain	97% ovicidal
Leptinotarsa decemlineata	Pupae	Topical	10^{-4} g/animal	60% less emergence
Lepidoptera				
Vanessa io	Larvae	Topical	10^{-6} g/animal	10% less emergence
Carpocapsa pomonella	Larvae	Contact	10^{-5} g/cm^2	80% less emergence
Ephestia kühniella	Eggs	Filter Paper	10^{-5} g/cm^2	84% ovicidal
Prodenia litura	Eggs	Contact	10^{-8} g/egg	8% ovicidal

Table 8

Activity of the Bowers Compound in Laboratory Tests

Order and Species	Life Stage	Method of Application	Effective Concentration	Observed Activity
Orthoptera				
Blatella germanica	Nymphs	Filter Paper	$10^{-4} g/cm^2$	100% deformed insects
Homoptera				
Aphis fabae	Adult	Seedling	$10^{-4} g/plant$	45% mortality 80% less reproduction
Coleoptera				
Tribolium casteneum	Adult	on Flour	$10^{-4} g/g$ flour	100% less reproduction
Sitophilus granaria	Adult	On Grain	$10^{-5} g/g$ grain	79% less reproduction
Epilachna varivestis	Larvae	Topical	$10^{-5} g/larva$	91% disturbed metamorphosis
Lepidoptera				
Tineola biselliella	Adult Eggs	Cloth Disc	$10^{-3} g/cm^2$	100% ovicidal 51% induced sterility
Ephestia kühniella	Eggs	Filter Paper	$10^{-4} g/cm^2$	100% ovicidal
Pieris brassicae	Larvae	Topical	$10^{-5} g/larva$	100% less emergence
Diptera				
Aedes aegyptii	Larvae	to Water	$10^{-7} g/ml$	100% less emergence
Musca domestica	Eggs	Contact	$10^{-4} g/ml$	7% ovicidal

151

PART II

BIOCHEMICAL ASPECTS

METABOLISM OF CECROPIA JUVENILE HORMONE IN INSECTS AND IN MAMMALS

Michael Slade* and Charles H. Zibitt

Zoëcon Corporation Research Laboratories
Palo Alto, California 94304

Abstract

In vivo metabolism of the juvenile hormone of the silk moth *Hyalophora cecropia* modifies the observable activity of the hormone (methyl *trans, trans, cis*-10,11-epoxy-7-ethyl-3,11-dimethyltrideca-2,6-dienoate) in inhibiting metamorphosis in many orders of insects. Using 2-^{14}C-labelled hormone, studies *in vivo* and *in vitro* have shown that with *Manduca sexta* (tobacco hornworm) the mechanism of inactivation involves hydrolysis of the ester group followed by hydration of the epoxide. Qualitative differences have been shown to occur with *Hyalophora cecropia* (robin moth), *Schistocerca vaga* (vagrant grasshopper), and *Sarcophaga bullata* (flesh-fly). All of the metabolic pathways investigated and their possible relationships to the feed-back mechanisms which control development of insects have been considered.

The metabolism of Cecropia juvenile hormone by mice *in vivo* has also been studied and compared with that which occurs in insects.

Introduction

Even though the natural occurence of an insect juvenile hormone and of a C-17 homolog (compounds I and II respectively in figure I) has been elucidated in only two

---

*Senior Scientist to whom correspondence should be addressed.
Present address: 127-20th Ave., San Francisco, Calif. 94121

species of insects, both belonging to the lepidopteran genus *Hyalophora* (1-3), the activity of these compounds in inhibiting metamorphosis appears to be order-nonspecific (4). Because of this, it has been proposed (5) that insect hormones and related compounds can be effective pest control agents. Their overall effectiveness as pest control agents, however, would be dependent upon a number of things controlling their activity; and of prime importance in this regard is their *in vivo* deactivation, or metabolism.

The metabolism of the moulting hormone, ecdysone, has been studied quite extensively (6). Until recently (7), though, there has been no comparable information available for the juvenile hormones and their analogs. This present paper, which is particularly concerned with the determination of the chemical mechanism of inactivation of compound I in insects, therefore, constitutes one of the first detailed reports in the area.

Now, although compound I is one of two juvenile hormones which occur naturally in the silk moth *Hyalophora cecropia*, it constitutes the major (80-87%) one and is often referred to as Cecropia juvenile hormone or JH. It will be so referred to here.

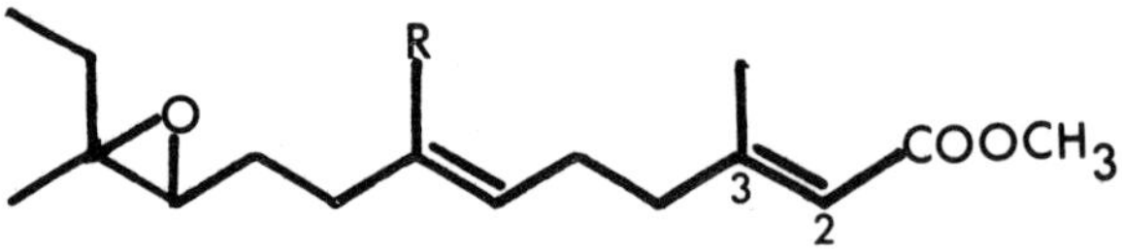

I : R=C$_2$H$_5$ (JH)

II : R=CH$_3$

Figure I. The natural juvenile hormones.

General Considerations and Materials

The hemolymph titer of juvenile hormone at different stages of the moult cycle has never really been measured directly in any insect. However, it has been generally inferred from biological experiments (involving corpus allatum extirpation and implantation, as well as JH injection) that juvenile hormone must be essentially absent from the body of holometabolous insects in order for pupation to occur. A very high rate of JH metabolism, possibly due to the presence of a high level of deactivating enzyme, just prior to pupation could be responsible for such a condition. Preliminary studies (8) with the lepidopteran, *Manduca sexta* have shown that this could be the case, as well as that the qualitative pattern of JH metabolism remains the same throughout the last larval instar and pupal stage. For these reasons, and because of the non-specificity of compounds I and II, JH metabolism was studied in detail in late fifth (i.e. last) instar larvae of *Manduca sexta*. Comparable studies have also been conducted with pupae of *Hyalophora cecropia*, fourth instar nymphs of *Schistocerca vaga*, and third instar larvae of *Sarcophaga bullata*.

Racemic juvenile hormone, labelled with ^{14}C in the 2-position and with a specific activity of 25mC/mM, was used in all of the studies. The compound was synthesized by the method of Hafferl and co-workers (9) outlined in figure 2.

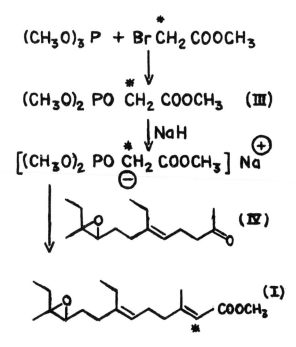

Figure 2. Synthesis of 2-^{14}C-Cecropia juvenile hormone.

Heating 2-^{14}C-methyl bromoacetate with trimethylphos-
phite under vacuum gave 2-^{14}C-trimethyl phosphonoacetate,
III, in nearly quantitative yield. Use of sodium hydride
generated the anion of III and this was allowed to react
with the epoxyketone IV, which was prepared by hydroxyla-
tion of 6-ethyl-10-methyldodeca-5,9-dien-2-one with osmium
tetroxide followed by tosylation and base catalyzed internal elimination. The desired labelled juvenile hormone,
which was more than 98% radiochemically pure, was formed in
23% yield.

Metabolism by *Manduca sexta*

In order to determine the nature of JH metabolism in
Manduca sexta, 0.5 μg of the racemic 2-^{14}C-juvenile hormone, dissolved in 60% aqueous acetone, was injected into
the abdomina of anesthetized prepupae. After being allowed
to incubate for 2.0 hrs at 27°C, the hornworms were worked
up in two separate portions, blood and carcass (excluding
the body wall). Each of these fractions was extracted
three times with 2:1 ether-ethanol buffered with ammonium
sulfate resulting in the recovery of all of the radiolabel
present. In the blood fraction this was 18% and in the
carcass fraction 67% of the injected ^{14}C.

The organic extracts of the blood and of the carcass
were examined by radio-thin-layer chromatography (TLC) on
silica chromatoplates. A 25% ethyl acetate in *n*-hexane
solvent system separated the radioactive components of each
fraction into three zones, designated A (the origin), B
(R_f0.25) and C (R_f0.8) in figure 3. Figure 3 shows the
radiochromatogram scan of the components present in the
blood. Essentially the same radiochromatographic pattern
was produced by the components present in the carcass. It
was apparent from these scans that zone A constitutes the
major, and zone C the minor, component in both the blood
and carcass. This contention is supported by the data in
table I, which was obtained, along with further analytical
information, by eluting each of the zones with tetrahydrofuran (THF) freshly distilled over potassium hydroxide.

Zone C, which was 3% of the injected ^{14}C in the case
of the blood and 5% in the case of the carcass, cochromatographed on silica TLC with Cecropia JH, an authentic
sample of which was synthesized using the method of Loew
and colleagues (10). The method is outlined in figure 4.

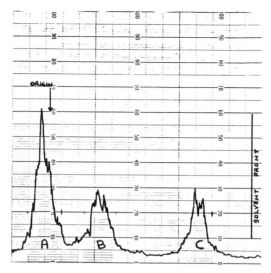

Figure 3.   Radiochromatogram showing the labelled
components present in the blood 2.0 hrs.
after injection of 2-^{14}C-Cecropia
juvenile hormone into *Manduca sexta*
prepupae.   The same radiochromatographic pattern is produced by the components present in the carcass.

Table I.   Radioactive components present in
blood and carcass, expressed as percentage of radiolabel injected, 2.0
hrs. after injection of 2-^{14}C-Cecro-
pia juvenile hormone into *Manduca
sexta* prepupae.

	A	B	C	TOTAL
BLOOD	10	5	3	18
CARCASS	50	12	5	67
TOTAL	60	17	8	85

Methyl 6-hydroxy-3-methyl-7-methylene-2-*trans*-
nonenoate, on treatment with the dimethyl ketal of 3-

chloro-3-methyl-2-pentanone and a catalytic amount of 2,4-dinitrophenol, was transformed into methyl 11-chloro-3,11-dimethyl-7-ethyl-10-oxo-2-*trans*,6-*trans*-tridecadienoate. Selective reduction with methanolic sodium borohydride gave a mixture of diastereoisomeric chlorohydrins separable by chromatography. The predominant *threo*-chlorohydrin, on exposure to methanolic potassium carbonate, was converted into pure racemic juvenile hormone.

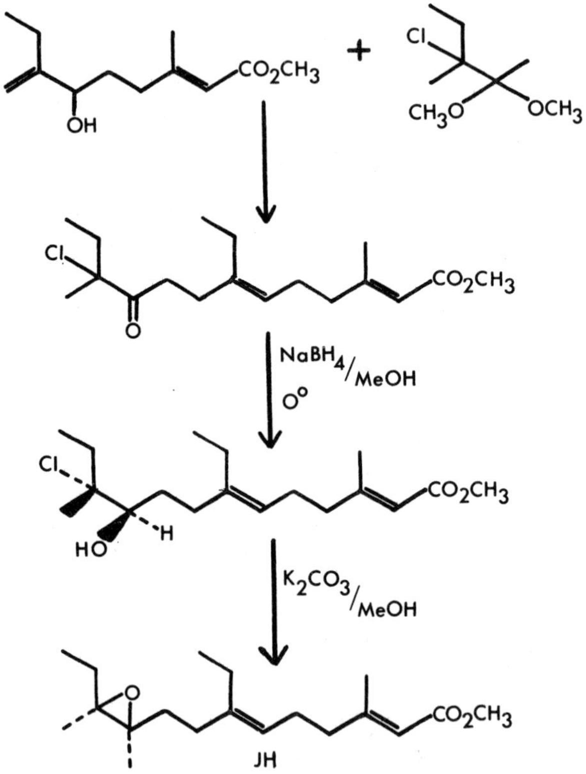

Figure 4.   Synthesis of Cecropia juvenile hormone.

Now, although zone C cochromatographed on TLC with authentic *trans, trans, cis*-JH, only 30% of it had the same retention time by radio-gas chromatography (GC). Only this portion of zone C was therefore assumed to be unchanged JH. The remainder of zone C was apparently a mixture of slightly less polar compounds, the structures of which are unknown. Since the retention times of these compounds did not correspond to those of any of the 8 possible stereoisomers of JH and since they were probably not metabolites, they could possibly have been either minor artifacts of the workup procedure for zone C or radio-impurities resulting from the method of radiochemical synthesis of Cecropia hormone.

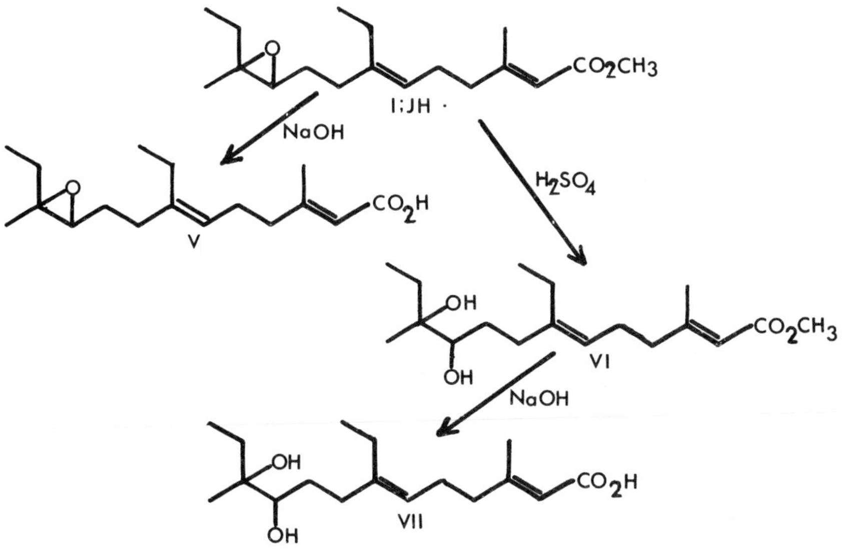

Figure 5. Synthesis of JH metabolites.

Zone B had the same R_f (0.25) as the acid V in figure 5. As indicated, this acid was prepared from authentic JH by hydrolysis with 0.5N sodium hydroxide in 50% aqueous ethanol for 23 hrs at 23°C (11). After methylation with diazomethane in ether, zone B cochromatographed with JH (compound I, figure 5) in both radio-TLC and GC systems, thus confirming its identity with the acid V.

Figure 6 shows that zone A, which was at the origin in the radiochromatogram scan illustrated in figure 3, was resolved into at least two components when chromatographed on silica TLC with 9:1 chloroform-ethanol. The major component, which had an R_f of 0.6 and constituted 80% of the mixture, cochromatographed with 10,11-dihydroxy-7-ethyl-11-methyltrideca-2,6-dienoic acid (VII, figure 5). Compound VII was synthesized by treating JH with 0.05N sulfuric acid in 40% aqueous tetrahydrofuran for 4.5 hrs at 25°C followed by alcoholic sodium hydroxide hydrolysis of the ester VI. The major component of zone A also was methylated with diazomethane, and the product was identified by both radio-TLC and GC with authentic ester VI. Further deriva-

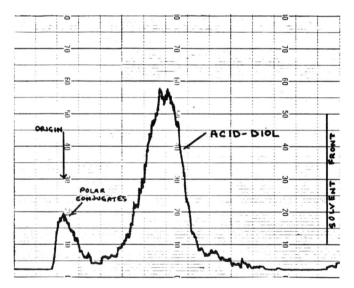

Figure 6.   Radiochromatogram of the components of zone A from *Manduca sexta*.

tization with bis-(trimethylsilyl)-trifluoroacetamide and subsequent radio-TLC and GC analyses confirmed the structure of this component as being compound VII. As indicated in figure 6, the minor component of zone A, which was the remaining 20% of the mixture, remained at the origin of the TLC plate in the chloroform-ethanol solvent system. However, use of more polar solvent systems showed this component to be a complex mixture. It could possibly consist of polar conjugates of acid V and/or diol VII.

The diol VI (figure 5) was not detected in any experiment with *Manduca* thereby demonstrating that the epoxide moiety was not hydrated during workup. This finding, together with studies on the dynamics of JH metabolism, indicates that ester hydrolysis precedes hydration of the epoxide. On being incubated for 5 minutes with blood *in vitro* in Weever's larval lepidopteran saline, JH was over 85% metabolized to acid V, without further conversion, as shown in figure 7(a). Virtually complete metabolism occurred within 30 minutes. Incubation with a body wall preparation scraped free of muscle and fat body tissue was also capable of metabolizing JH to the acid nearly quantitatively (figure 7(b)). This conversion occurred during 3.0 hours of incubation. In contrast, in 3.0 hours carefully rinsed fat body *in vitro* converted JH nearly completely to both the acid, which constituted 25% of the mixture and to diol VII, which represented the remaining 75% of the mixture. This is shown in figure 7(c). From these results it is

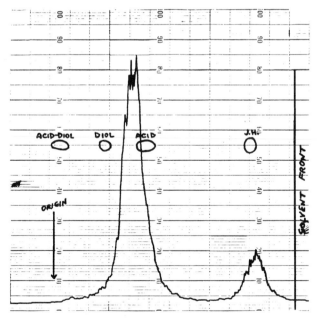

Figure 7(a)

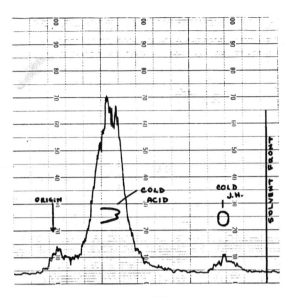

Figure 7(b)

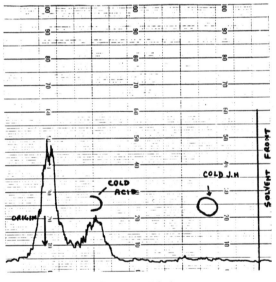

Figure 7(c)

Figure 7. Radiochromatograms of labelled compounds
present *in vitro* in (a) blood, (b) body
wall, and (c) fat body preparations from
Manduca sexta after incubation with
2-^{14}C-Cecropia juvenile hormone.

clear that carboxyesterase activity occurs in several of
the insect's tissues, whereas epoxide hydrolase activity is
found in the fat body; and evidently neither enzyme system
is enantiomer specific, because racemic ^{14}C-JH can be metabolized almost quantitatively.

Metabolism by *Hyalophora cecropia*

In contrast to *Manduca*, after *Hyalophora cecropia* pupae were incubated for 1.5 hrs at 27°C following injection
of 2-^{14}C-JH, the diol VI, formed directly from JH by cleavage of the epoxide ring, was established as being a metabolite as well. It is designated as A' (R_f 0.16) in the
radiochromatogram scan shown in figure 8. This scan is of
the radiolabelled compound from all the *Cecropia* pupal tis-

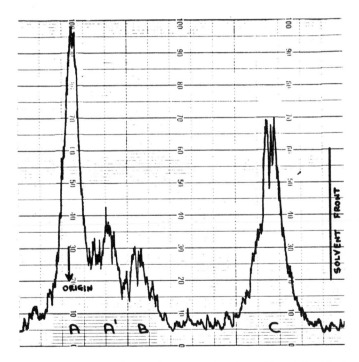

Figure 8. Radiochromatogram showing the labelled
compounds present in *Hyalophora cecropia* pupae 1.5 hrs. after injection of
2-^{14}C-Cecropia juvenile hormone.

165

sues after being extracted and analyzed by the same method
as that used for *Manduca*.

Freshly redistilled THF was used to elute each of the
zones shown, and subsequent cochromatography with authentic
compounds showed that, as with *Manduca*, the major portion
(92%) of zone A corresponded to the acid-diol VII (the rest
of this zone probably consisted of various polar conjugates), that zone B corresponded to the acid V, and that
zone C had the same R$_f$ as JH.

Metabolism by *Schistocerca vaga*

Fourth instar nymphs of *Schistocerca vaga*, a hemi-
metabolous insect, after being allowed to incubate for 2.0

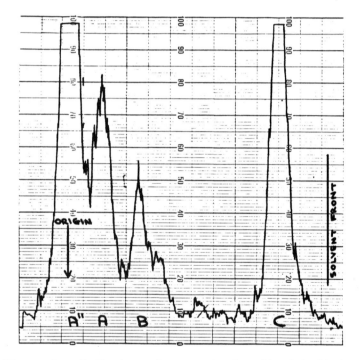

Figure 9.   Radiochromatogram showing the labelled
components present in the carcass 2.0
hrs. after injection of 2-^{14}C-Cecropia
juvenile hormone into fourth instar
nymphs of *Schistocerca vaga*.

hrs. following injection of 2-14C-JH, were shown to metabolize Cecropia juvenile hormone in a manner very similar
to that established for *Manduca*. Whilst the blood and carcass (excluding the exoskeleton) of the *Schistocerca* were
extracted and analyzed separately, each extract produced
the same radiochromatographic pattern after development of
the TLC plates with a 35% ethyl acetate in *n*-hexane solvent
system. Figure 9, which is the scan of the components present in the carcass, shows this pattern. Each of the zones
was eluted with THF and analyzed further.

Zone C cochromatographed with Cecropia JH. Zone B
cochromatographed with the acid V, and, after methylation
with diazomethane in ether, most of it was converted to JH.
This established that virtually all of zone B was indeed
the acid V. Some diol VI was also present following the
methylation of zone B, and, whilst it could have been a
metabolite, it is more likely to have arisen from the
break-down of acid V during workup. Zone A was converted
to the ester-diol VI by methylation with diazomethane.
This supported cochromatographic evidence that zone A was
the acid-diol VII. Zone A" consisted of a mixture of highly polar materials. These were probably conjugates of the
acid V and of the diol VII.

Metabolism by *Sarcophaga bullata*

Examination of the entire contents of third instar
larvae of *Sarcophaga bullata* 2.5 hrs. after injection of
labelled juvenile hormone revealed that Cecropia JH is
metabolized in this species in a manner different from that
established for *Manduca*. A 35% ethyl acetate in *n*-hexane
solvent system separated the labelled components of the
organic extract of the larval contents on a silica chromatoplate into the four zones shown in figure 10.

Zones A', B', and C were eluted with freshly redistilled THF. Subsequent cochromatography with authentic
materials showed that zone A' (R_f 0.30) corresponded to
ester-diol VI and that the R_f of zone C (0.88) was the
same as that of JH. The nature of zone B' (R_f 0.67) was
not investigated.

Zone A" (the origin) was eluted from the chromatoplate
with methanol. After evaporation of the methanol, A" was
incubated in air with glusulase (0 or 25 μl; 174,000 units
of glucuronidase and 46,000 units of sulfatase per ml.;

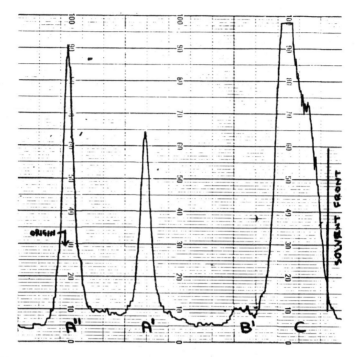

Figure 10. Radiochromatogram showing the labelled
compounds present in third instar larvae of *Sarcophaga bullata* 2.5 hrs.
after injection of 2-^{14}C-Cecropia
juvenile hormone.

Endo Laboratories, Inc.) in acetate buffer (1.0 ml.; pH
5.6) at 35°C overnight. Following incubation, brine was
added to the reaction mixture which was then extracted with
2:1 ether-ethanol. This resulted in the recovery of 64% of
the radiolabel present in the organic fraction. This fraction, when analyzed by radio-TLC using a 35% ethyl acetate
in *n*-hexane solvent system, was found to consist apparently
of three components, as shown in figure 11.

The component at the origin, which accounted for 50%
of the mixture was not analyzed further. It probably consisted of conjugates not cleaved by glusulase. The R_f
(0.48) of the minor component that was apparently present,
and constituted 6% of the mixture, corresponded to that of

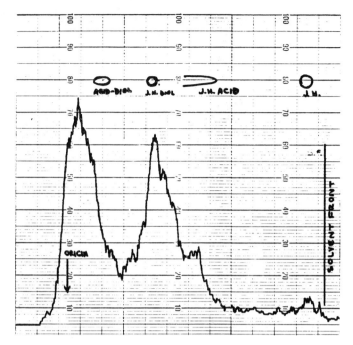

Figure II. Radiochromatogram of the labelled compounds present following incubation of
zone A" from *Sarcophaga bullata* with
glusulase.

epoxy-acid V. This is rather tentative evidence, though,
that acid V was formed as a metabolite and subsequently
conjugated in *Sarcophaga*. The component at R_f 0.35, which
was 44% of the mixture, was, however, firmly established by
cochromatography to be diol VI; and so this compound was
considered to be present in *Sarcophaga* in a conjugated
form, possibly as a sulfate. Dihydroxy-acid VII was not
detected at all in this experiment.

Discussion

Tentative pathways for the metabolism of Cecropia
juvenile hormone in (a) *Manduca sexta* (tobacco hormworm),
(b) *Hyalophora cecropia* (robin moth), (c) *Schistocerca vaga*
(vagrant grasshopper) and (d) *Sarcophaga bullata* (flesh-
fly) are outlined in figure 12. Letters without question-
marks represent established pathways. Where there are
question-marks, the pathways are experimentally indicated

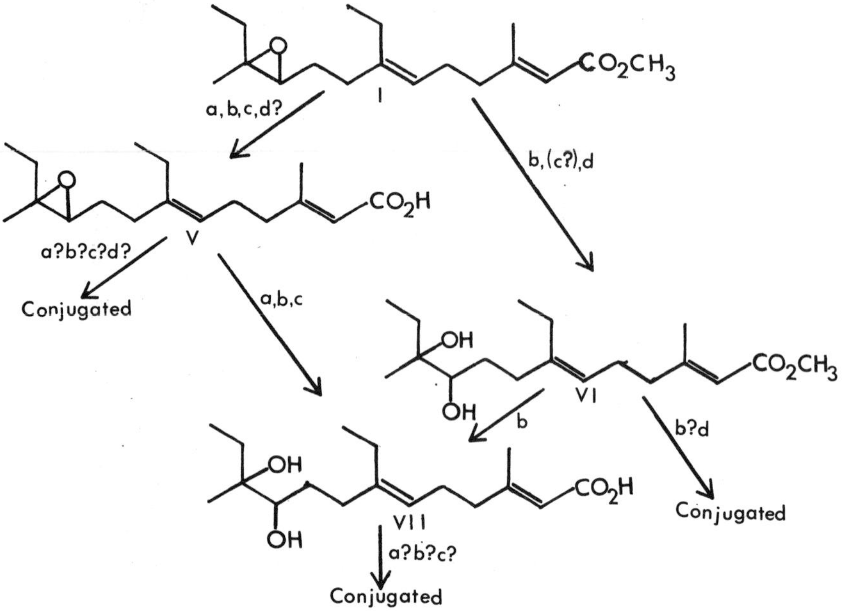

Figure 12. Tentative metabolic pathways for Cecropia juvenile hormone in (a) *Manduca sexta*, (b) *Hyalophora cecropia*,
(c) *Schistocerca vaga*, and (d) *Sarcophaga bullata*.

Letters only — established pathways. Letters and question-marks —
experimentally indicated, but not
established, pathways.

as probably occurring, but no conclusive evidence is currently available. The epoxy-acid V and the dihydroxy-acid
VII, which may be conjugated and excreted, and the dihydro-
xy-ester VI, which is certainly conjugated in *Sarcophaga*,
are all over 2,000 times less active than JH in the *Galleria* wax test for juvenile hormone activity (12), so these
pathways would appear to constitute the mechanisms of inactivation of Cecropia JH in many insects.

Within these pathways, though, much variation exists,

both qualitatively and quantitatively. The most clear qualitative difference amongst the insects studied is that *Sarcophaga* deactivate JH by hydrolyzing the epoxide ring almost exclusively. This is probably true of the higher Diptera in general, for preliminary experiments with a microsomal preparation from *Musca domestica* (housefly) have indicated that ester-diol formation is the major metabolic pathway *in vitro* in that genus. This, however, is just one possible pathway in *Hyalophora*, the evidence for its existence in *Schistocerca* is minimal at best, and it is not observed in *Manduca*. Ester hydrolysis followed by epoxide cleavage is the favored metabolic pathway in Lepidoptera and Orthoptera.

This difference in the manner of metabolizing JH probably reflects the fact that there are basic differences between Diptera and the other insects. For instance, development of adult structures of higher Diptera occurs from imaginal discs and these structures are quite different from those of the larvae. During the course of development, a juvenile hormone of the Cecropia-type to modify the expression of the moult is therefore not needed. Neither, also, presumably, is the mechanism for its metabolism. However, whilst this information is indicative, it is not conclusive, that if a hormone comparable to JH in being necessary for development is found in higher Diptera, it will be of a structure that is quite different from that of Cecropia juvenile hormone, whilst that of other Lepidoptera and Orthoptera may be very similar.

The difference between *Sarcophaga* and the other insect species studied is again apparent from the quantitative metabolic data given in table 2. Other quantitative differences are also reflected in these data, which are expressed as percentages of radiolabel recovered because, even though comparable extraction procedures were used in every case, a wide variation in total radiolabel recovery occurred — 85% from *Manduca*, 10% from *Hyalophora*, 56% from *Schistocerca*, and 99% from *Sarcophaga*. Clearly, though, Cecropia JH is metabolized relatively slowly in third instar larvae of *Sarcophaga bullata*, much more rapidly in pupae of *Hyalophora cecropia* and in fourth instar nymphs of *Schistocerca vaga*, where the metabolites appear to be quickly conjugated, and very rapidly in fifth instar larvae of *Manduca sexta*. This latter result was confirmed when all the radiolabel was recovered in the feces of *Manduca* following

171

	Inc. Time (Hrs)	A" Conjugates	A Acid-Diol	A' Ester-Diol	B Acid	B' ?	C JH Region
Manduca Sexta	2.0	14	57	-	20	-	9
Hyalophora Cecropia	1.5	3	32	19	11	-	35
Schistocerca Vaga	2.0	45	14	?	7	-	34
Sarcophaga Bullata	2.5	18	-	16	-	2	64

Table 2. Metabolites of $2\text{-}^{14}C$-Cecropia juvenile hormone, expressed as percentages of radiolabel recovered, after its injection into various insect species.

injection of 2-14C-JH into one-day old fifth instar larvae.
Essentially no unchanged JH was recovered. However, the
exact nature of the products has yet to be clearly defined.
Many are cleaved by the action of glusulase indicating that
conjugates are present.

The studies undertaken have thus established not only
the mechanisms of inactivation of Cecropia juvenile hormone
in a number of insects but also that the half-life of JH,
particularly in Lepidoptera, is short. From this it is
easy to understand why some species of insect seem to be
almost invulnerable to Cecropia juvenile hormone; and the
lack of response by Cecropia to exogenous JH should not be
unexpected. That insect undoubtedly has a very efficient
method of metabolizing its own hormone. Understanding
these things means that it should be possible to design
compounds that have the advantages of JH activity but which
are not as readily metabolized. Likewise, by knowing the
pathways of JH metabolism, it might be possible to enhance
the morphogenetic activity of JH itself by interfering
with those pathways. Use of enzyme inhibitors, such as an
esterase inhibitor, may well achieve this; and from the
point of view of pest control, these areas are certainly
worthy of more detailed investigation.

Now, the fact that exogenous JH has a short half-life,
especially in Lepidoptera, makes it seem unlikely that endogenous Cecropia juvenile hormone exists to any great extent in the free state; for, clearly, if it did, it would
be rapidly broken down. It is more probable that, in order for it to exert its biological action, endogenous JH
is protected in some manner such as being bound by a protein. In this form, it may well be transported to the site
of action and then, having acted, it will be metabolized,
most likely in the fat body, conjugated and excreted.

If endogenous juvenile hormone is in fact bound, then
the changes in hemolymph titer of JH at different stages of
the insect's life that have been generally inferred from
various biological experiments, may actually be reflecting
changes in availability of binding protein, and the secretion of juvenile hormone by the corpora allata may be a
continuous rather than a regulated process. This is because unbound JH is very quickly deactivitated in the
hemolymph, and only bound material, the level of which
would reflect the amount of binding protein available,
would be observed as being present. The level of the bind-

173

ing or carrier protein(s) may itself be regulated by a feed-back mechanism based on the relative levels of juvenile hormone and/or its metabolites; and, because of the dependence of insect development on the presence or absence of juvenile hormone, this process would be similarly controlled.

Gaining an adequate understanding of the nature of these control mechanisms is vital towards extending the concept of using insect hormones and disruption of the processes regulated by them as a means of pest control.

Metabolism by Mice

Of no less importance with regard to the practical application of insect juvenile hormones as pest control agents is the question of their effect upon other living systems, particularly mammals. The fact that one of the juvenile hormones occurring naturally in *Hyalophora cecropia* (compound II, figure I) and a simple analog, *trans, trans* ethyl 3,7,II-trimethyl-10,II-epoxydodeca-2,6-dienoate, have been shown (13) to produce no signs of toxicity when given to mice in a single oral dose of 5,000 mg/kg of body weight indicates only that large quantities of these compounds can be tolerated on acute ingestion by one mammalian species. More extensive toxicological studies, including metabolic evaluations, are required to demonstrate a complete absence of mammalian toxicities associated with juvenile hormones and their analogs.

With this in mind, male albino mice (20 g, Swiss-Webster strain) were treated orally, by stomach tube, with 3.0 μg of 2-^{14}C-JH. The administration vehicle was 50 μl of dimethylsulfoxide (DMSO) followed by a 50 μl DMSO rinse of the stomach tube. The treated mice were held for 72 hrs. while receiving food and water *ad libitum* in individual chambers designed for the collection of urine and feces. Expired CO_2 was not collected. Up to 30% of the administered radiocarbon was excreted in the urine in the first 24 hrs. following treatment. Virtually no radioactive material was detected in the urine after that time. Very little radiolabel was found in the feces at any time during the experiment.

In order to determine the nature of the excreted radiolabelled material, the residue from evaporation of the urine was incubated in air with glusulase (0 or 100 μl) in

174

acetate buffer (4.0 ml, 0.1 M, pH 4.8) at 37°C for 4 hrs.
After incubation, and following unsuccessful attempts to
extract it with ethyl acetate and ether-ethanol, all of the
radiolabel present was extracted into methanol. The radioactive components of the methanolic fraction were then analyzed by TLC.

All of the radiolabel remained at the origin when the
chromatoplate was developed in a 35% ethyl acetate in n-
hexane solvent system. Use of 10% methanol in chloroform,
a solvent system of greater polarity, produced a complex
mixture of products, all of which occurred in the region of
R_f 0.1 to 0.5. Some of these products had been liberated
on incubation with glusulase. Amongst these, it was possibly only to indicate that dihydroxy-acid VII might be present.

Because of the limited nature of these results, it is
not possible at this time to say that the initial sites of
metabolic attack on the Cecropia juvenile hormone are the
same in mice as in insects. Nor is it possible to say that
metabolism is necessarily a principal factor in the low
acute mammalian toxicity of juvenile hormones and their
analogs. However, the lack of appearance of metabolites
following the initial, relatively low level of excretion
might imply that storage is occurring within the animals.
From a chronic toxicity point of view, this could have interesting implications. Certainly, a lot more investigation in this and related areas is required before insect
hormones and related compounds will prove to be useful and
nontoxic pest control agents.

Acknowledgement

The invaluable technical assistance of Jean Wren during these studies is gratefully acknowledged.

References

1. Röller, H., Dahm, K.H., Sweeley, C.C., and Trost, B.M.,
   Angew. Chem. 79, 190 (1967).

2. Meyer, A.S., Schneiderman, H.A., Hanzmann, E., and Ko,
   J.H., *Proc. US Nat. Acad. Sci.* 60, 853 (1968).

3. Dahm, K.H., and Röller, H., *Life Sci.* 9, 1397 (1970).

4. Röller, H., and Dahm, K.H. in *Recent Progr. Hormone Res.* (edit. by Astwood, E.B.) 24, 651 (Academic Press, New York, 1968).

5. Williams, C.M., *Nature* 178, 212 (1956).

6. King, D.S., *Gen. Comp. Endocrinol. (Suppl.)*, in press.

7. Slade, M. and Zibitt, C.H., *Proc. 2nd. IUPAC Intl. Congr. Pest. Chem.* 3, in press.

8. Slade, M., and Zibitt, C.H., unpublished results, 1971.

9. Hafferl, W., Zurflüh, R., and Dunham, L., *J. Labelled Compounds*, in press.

10. Loew, P., Siddall, J.B., Spain, V.L., and Werthemann, L., *Proc. US Nat. Acad. Sci.* 67, 1824 (1970).

11. Cornforth, J.W., *J. Chromatog.* 4, 214 (1960).

12. Gilbert, L.I., and Schneiderman, H.A., *Trans. Am. Microscop. Soc.* 79, 38 (1960).

13. Siddall, J.B., and Slade, M., *Nature New Biol.* 229, 158 (1971).

PRELIMINARY CHROMATOGRAPHIC STUDIES ON THE METABOLITES
AND PHOTODECOMPOSITION PRODUCTS OF THE JUVENOID
1-(4'-ETHYLPHENOXY)-6,7-EPOXY-3,7-DIMETHYL-2-OCTENE

Sarjeet S. Gill, Bruce D. Hammock,
Izuru Yamamoto[*] and John E. Casida

Division of Entomology, University of California,
Berkeley, Calif. 94720

Abstract

Several metabolites and photodecomposition products of
the juvenoid, 1-(4'-ethylphenoxy)-6,7-epoxy-3,7-dimethyl-
2-octene, labeled with ^{14}C or ^{3}H in the phenyl group or
with ^{3}H in the 1-position of the octene moiety, were
tentatively identified by thin-layer chromatographic
comparison with 12 authentic, unlabeled compounds from
synthesis. On incubation with the rat liver microsome
or soluble fraction, the juvenoid is converted to two
metabolites, one of which is the diol formed by hydration
of the epoxide moiety. Addition of reduced nicotinamide-
adenine dinucleotide phosphate to the microsome incubation
mixture results in formation of: the diol; 1-(4'-ethyl-
phenoxy)-2,3,6,7-tetrahydroxy-3,7-dimethyloctane; 1-
[4'-(1-hydroxyethyl)-phenoxy]- and 1-(4'-acetophenoxy)-
6,7-epoxy-3,7-dimethyl-2-octenes; at least 9 other
metabolites retaining the ether linkage (detected with
both ^{3}H-phenyl and ^{3}H-octene preparations). Rats
administered the ^{3}H- or ^{14}C-juvenoid intraperitoneally
excrete almost all of the radioactivity within 54-96 hr,
about equally in urine and feces. The 6 or more ^{3}H-
phenyl-labeled metabolites in urine are not identified
but they are relatively polar compounds. The diol is one
of many metabolites excreted in rat and locust feces.
Photodecomposition of the juvenoid as a deposit on silica
gel chromatoplates occurs slowly in sunlight unless a
photosensitizer (xanthone, anthraquinone) is added in

*Present address: Department of Agricultural Chemistry,
Tokyo University of Agriculture, Setagaya, Tokyo, Japan.

which case it occurs rapidly forming 1-[4'-(1-hydroxy-ethyl)-phenoxy]- and 1-(4'-acetophenoxy)-6,7-epoxy-3,7-dimethyl-2-octenes and at least 6 other products retaining the ether linkage. The sites in this juvenoid most susceptible to degradation appear to be the epoxide moiety, the benzylic methylene group, and possibly the trans-olefin group.

Introduction

A wide variety of juvenile hormone analogs (juvenoids) have morphogenetic activity on certain insects under laboratory conditions. Juvenoids may be useful as ovicides, mosquito larvicides, in household pest control, and as protectants for livestock, stored grains, and agricultural crops. However, the effectiveness of juvenoids for control of agricultural insect pests under field conditions has been somewhat disappointing. This may be because the juvenoid, once applied to crops, fails to persist for the requisite time to contact most individuals of the population at sensitive stages of development. Since the use of juvenoids in insect control will potentially result in residues on or in food, feed and forage, it is important to understand the mechanisms and pathways for their metabolism and photodecomposition. Information of this type is being developed by several laboratories (1,2).

The juvenoid considered in this report is 1-(4'-ethylphenoxy)-6,7-epoxy-3,7-dimethyl-2-octene (Compound I of Fig. 1; R-20458 of Stauffer Chemical Co.; referred to in this communication as the juvenoid),a relatively simple but yet very potent morphogenetic agent (3). The degradation chemistry studies involved incubation of the juvenoid with rat liver enzymes, administration to rats and locusts to obtain excreted metabolites, and exposure to sunlight.

Materials and Methods

Chemicals. The structures for the chemicals used are given in Fig. 1. Although some of the compounds were cis- trans-mixtures, the trans isomer was predominant in each case.

Three radiolabeled preparations (A, B and C) of compound
I were used.

The ^{3}H-phenyl preparation (A, 654 mCi/mmole) was prepared
from ring-labeled ^{3}H-ethylphenol, obtained by an exchange
reaction under acidic conditions, and the ^{3}H-geranyl
preparation (B, 33 mCi/mmole) was made from ^{3}H-geraniol
containing some ^{3}H-nerol obtained by reducing citral with
NaB^{3}H$_4$ (4). Stauffer Chemical Co. (Mountain View, Calif.)
provided the ^{14}C-labeled preparation (C, 17 mCi/mmole).

Several unlabeled derivatives or possible degradation
products of compound I were prepared for use in cochromatographic comparisons with radiolabeled metabolites
and photodecomposition products. The corresponding diene
(II) (3,4) was converted to the diepoxide derivative(III)
by oxidizing it with 3 molar equivalents of m-chloro-
peroxybenzoic acid in chloroform solution. Three methods
were used to prepare diol IV: reacting the corresponding
diene (II) with equimolar osmium tetroxide in the
presence of 2 molar pyridine in benzene solution and
transesterification of the osmate ester with mannitol;
hydrolysis of the epoxide (I) in 0.5N H$_2$SO$_4$ in 40%
aqueous tetrahydrofuran at 25°C for 10 min; hydrolysis of
the epoxide (I) in 10% aqueous ethylene glycol containing
0.5% KOH at 120°C for 3 hr. The tetraol (V) was made
from the diepoxide (III) by hydrolysis in 0.5N H$_2$SO$_4$ in
40% aqueous tetrahydrofuran at 25°C for 10 min. Reduction of the epoxide (I) with NaBH$_4$ in ethanol yielded the
tertiary alcohol (VI). Titration of the diol (IV) with
lead tetraacetate in benzene converted it quantitatively
to the aldehyde (VII) which was oxidized with excess
silver nitrate and ammonium hydroxide (Tollens' reagent)
to form the acid (VIII). The diene resulting from
reaction of 4-hydroxyacetophenone with geranyl bromide
was either epoxidized to obtain compound IX (5) or
reduced with NaBH$_4$ and then epoxidized to obtain compound
X. Reaction of geranyl bromide with the methyl ester of
4-hydroxyphenylacetic acid, hydrolysis of the ester

group and epoxidation gave compound XI.   Compound XII was
made by reacting potassium 4-ethylphenylate with the
methyl ester of bromoacetic acid and subsequent hydrolysis
of the methoxycarbonyl group. The compounds were isolated
in pure form by preparative thin-layer chromatography
(TLC) on silica gel GF chromatoplates (2 mm gel thickness,
Analtech, Inc., Newark, Del.) or by column chromatography
on dry-packed Florisil (60/100 mesh, Floridin Co.,
Berkeley Springs, W. Va.) columns developed with hexane-
ether or ether-methanol gradients. In each case, infrared,
nuclear magnetic resonance and mass spectra confirmed the
identity of the synthesized products.

Analytical methods. Metabolites and photodecomposition products were separated by two-dimensional TLC on
silica gel F_{254} chromatoplates (0.25 mm gel thickness,
E. Merck, Darmstadt, Germany) developing with the following sequence of solvent systems: benzene-n-propanol
(20:1) (referred to as BP) in the first direction;
chloroform-dichloromethane-ethyl acetate-n-propanol
(10:10:1:1) (CDAP) in the second direction; carbon tetra-
chloride-ether (2:1) (TE) as a second development in the
first direction. Radioactive compounds were detected by
radioautography (6) and authentic unlabeled compounds
were detected with appropriate chromogenic reagents (7)
including: molybdophosphoric acid and heat yielding blue
spots on a yellow background; anisaldehyde, sulfuric
acid, acetic acid and heat, yielding spots of various
colors with different compounds, i.e. green for I and X,
blue for IX, violet for II, yellow for III, IV and V,
brown for VI and VII, and grey for XI; lead tetraacetate
in benzene giving white spots on a brown background
with much higher sensitivity for the 6,7-dihydroxy
compounds (IV and V) than for the other materials. The
labeled metabolites and photodecomposition products
derived from ^{3}H-compound A were subjected to cochromatographic comparisons with authentic unlabeled compounds
from synthesis for tentative identification of the
labeled compounds.

Enzyme studies. Livers of male albino rats were
homogenized at 20% (w/v) in potassium phosphate buffer
(0.1M, pH 7.4) and the homogenate was centrifuged at
15,000 g for 20 min. The supernatant was decanted

off and centrifuged at 105,000 g for 1 hr to separate the
microsomal and soluble fractions. The microsomal fraction
was resuspended in phosphate buffer while the soluble
fraction was further purified before use by passing it
through a Sephadex G-25 column.

Each incubation flask contained the following con-
stituents in a 2.0-ml total volume of phosphate buffer:
the microsome and/or the soluble fraction (approximately
10 mg total protein), $MgCl_2$ (21 μmoles), reduced nicotin-
amide-adenine dinucleotide phosphate (NADPH, 0 or 0.5
μmole), and the substrate (labeled compound A, B or C
mixed with some unlabeled material to give a total of
0.1 μmole; added in 10-25 μl ethanol). After incubation at $37°C$ for 2 hr, the reaction mixtures were frozen
and lyophilized, followed by extraction of the residue
with methanol. The methanol extract was concentrated
under nitrogen and analyzed for radioactive components
by TLC.

In vivo studies with rats and locusts. Male albino
rats (250 g) were treated intraperitoneally with the
labeled juvenoid (A, B or C) at 10-500 mg/kg administered
as a solution in corn oil. Urine and feces were collected
at 24 hr intervals for up to 96 hr. The level of radioactivity in the urine and feces was determined relative
to that in the administered dose. In another study, the
rats were treated with ^{3}H-compound A at 1 mg/kg, using
ethanol as the administration vehicle, and the urine and
feces were collected for 96 hr after treatment. The
urine was lyophilized and the residue extracted with
methanol. The feces were dried at reduced pressure over
phosphorus pentoxide and extracted with methanol. The
methanol extracts were analyzed by TLC.

Adult male desert locusts (Schistocerca americana)
were injected with the ^{3}H-labeled juvenoid (A, 1 μg in
1 μl ethanol), the feces collected for 48 hr after treatment were subjected to continuous Soxhlet extraction
with hexane, and the metabolites were then extracted
from the hexane into acetonitrile for analysis by TLC.

Photodecomposition. The labeled compound (A,B or C)
was applied at the origin of a silica gel F_{254} chromato-

plate to yield a residual deposit of 0.12 μmole/cm^2, in the presence or in the absence of a potential photo-sensitizing chemical (xanthone or anthraquinone, 0.06 μmole/cm^2). Following exposure in the dark or to direct sunlight for 8 hr, the chromatogram was developed to separate the products.

Results

Chromatographic separation of some of the possible metabolites and degradation products. The chromatographic positions of the various authentic compounds are shown in Fig. 1. The solvent systems are not appropriate for polar compounds such as V, XI and XII. Also, they fail to separate the aldehyde derivative (VII) from the parent compound (I).

Metabolites formed by rat liver enzymes. The epoxide (I) is converted, in small amount, by the microsomes without NADPH to two metabolites, one of which cochromatographs with the diol (IV) and the other, which is unidentified, chromatographs slightly above the diol. The soluble fraction also yields the diol (IV) and another metabolite which may be the same as the unidentified product formed by the microsomes alone. Addition of NADPH to the microsomal system results in the formation of at least 14 metabolites present in greater than 1% yield (Fig. 2). The same two metabolites are detected in the microsome- or soluble enzyme system and the same 14 metabolites are detected in the microsome-NADPH system using any one of the ^{3}H-phenyl- (A), ^{3}H-geranyl- (B), or ^{14}C-phenyl (C) preparations; so, each metabolite is an ether. The product of higher Rf than the parent compound (I) is not evident in all studies and so it is not known whether it is a metabolite or originates from other sources. The total radioactivity accounted for in the products separated by TLC was 62% of the amount used in the incubation mixture.

The metabolite of the juvenoid (I) formed most easily by the microsome system without NADPH and by the soluble fraction was found to cochromatograph with diol IV, as indicated above. When this metabolite derived from the ^{14}C-substrate (C) was isolated, by TLC, it was found to

cochromatograph with the diol (IV) on direct spotting,
with the corresponding aldehyde (VII) after oxidation with
lead tetraacetate, and with the corresponding acid (VIII)
after subsequent oxidation with Tollens' reagent. These
derivatives confirm the identity of the diol.

Other metabolites formed in the microsome-NADPH system
cochromatograph with the 1-[4'-(1-hydroxyethyl)-phenoxy]-

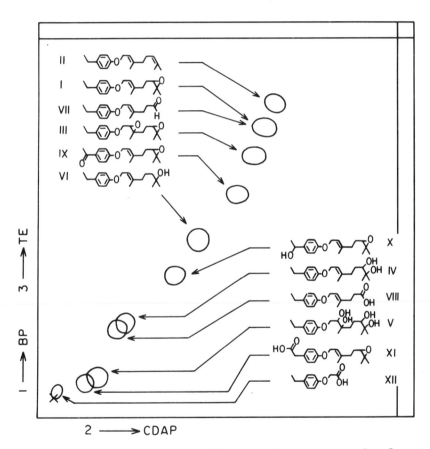

Fig. 1. Chromatographic positions and structures for 1-
(4'-ethylphenoxy)-6,7-epoxy-3,7-dimethyl-2-octene
(I) and related compounds (II-XII).

and 1-(4'-acetophenoxy)-6,7-epoxy-3,7-dimethyl-2-octenes
(X and IX, respectively) and possibly with the tetraol (V).

**Metabolites excreted by rats and locusts following
injection of the juvenoid.** Table 1 gives the data from

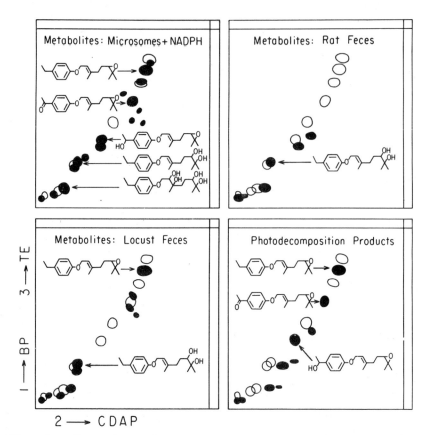

Fig. 2. Chromatographic positions for metabolites and
photodecomposition products of 1-(4'-ethylphen-^{3}H-oxy)-
6,7-epoxy-3,7-dimethyl-2-octene (darkened circles) and
the structures for compounds cochromatographing with
individual components. The positions for known
compounds not cochromatographing with metabolites and
photodecomposition products are shown as open circles
(see Fig. 1).

studies in which varying doses of labeled compounds A, B and C were administered intraperitoneally to rats and the level of radioactivity in the urine and feces was determined for up to 96 hr thereafter. The radioactivity of the ^{14}C- and ^{3}H-phenyl labeled compounds (C and A) is largely, if not completely, eliminated from the body within 54-96 hr, but a smaller amount of the radioactivity is accounted for in the excreta of rats treated with the ^{3}H-geranyl labeled preparation (B). The urine contains many metabolites, but none of these chromatograph with Rf values higher than that of the tetraol (V) under the standard conditions. Using repeated development with benzene-n-propanol (10:1) mixture in the same direction, the polar urinary metabolites are resolved into at least 6 components, no one of which is identified. The extracts of rat and locust feces contain many metabolites (Fig. 2) including one cochromatographing with the diol (IV) in each case and others chromatographing above and below this position.

There are preliminary indications of a specific tissue

TABLE 1

Balance study on excretion of radioactive compounds in the urine and feces of rats dosed intraperitoneally with ^{14}C- or ^{3}H-labeled 1-(4'—ethylphenoxy)-6,7-epoxy-3,7-dimethyl-2-octene[a]

Labeling position	Excreted radioactivity,%		
	Urine	Feces	Total
^{14}C-Phenyl (C)[b]	50	50	100
^{3}H-Phenyl (A)[c]	62	34	96
^{3}H-Geranyl (B)[c]	40	33	73

[a]Studies conducted by L. J. Hoffman and J. J. Menn.
[b]The dose was 46 mg/kg and the excreta were collected for 96 hr.
[c]The excretion results are averaged for administered doses of 10, 50, 250 and 500 mg/kg. The excreta were collected for 54 hr.

localization of the ^{3}H from labeled compound A in locusts
injected 3 weeks after allatectomy as newly-molted adults.
This localization, when it occurs, appears to be specific
for the testes and persists for several days; no comparable persisting ^{3}H levels appear in other tissues of the
males or in any tissues of the females. The chemical
basis for and significance of this localization are
unknown.

Photodecomposition. The juvenoid does not photodecom-
pose appreciably when exposed to sunlight for up to 8
hr (3) on a silica gel chromatoplate in the absence of a
photosensitizer, or in the dark in the presence of a
photosensitizer, but extensive degradation results when
xanthone or anthraquinone is added to the juvenoid and
it is then exposed to sunlight. At least 8 photodecomposition products are formed in the presence of
xanthone (Fig. 2) and two of these cochromatograph with
the 1-[4'-(1-hydroxyethyl)-phenoxy]- and 1-(4'-aceto-
phenoxy)-6,7-epoxy-3,7-dimethyl-2-octenes (X and IX,
respectively). The remaining photodecomposition products
are not identified but they do not include the diepoxide
(III) or any of the other authentic compounds available.
All of the major photodecomposition products are ethers
because they are detected with both the ^{3}H-phenyl (A)
and ^{3}H-geranyl (B) preparations. There are also other
photodecomposition products appearing after shorter
irradiation periods but these appear to be transient
materials leading to the formation of more stable
derivatives.

Discussion

The emphasis in the present study was placed on
relatively apolar metabolites and photodecomposition
products retaining the ether linkage. Thus, relatively
polar products such as glucuronide, glucoside, sulfate
and other conjugated metabolites and polar polymeric
photodecomposition products are not considered. The
cochromatographic technique employed is not adequate, by
itself, for identification of the metabolites and photodecomposition products. However, it does indicate that
the sites on the juvenoid most susceptible to attack,
depending on the conditions, include the epoxide moiety,

the benzylic methylene group, and possibly the trans-olefin group.

The ether group is not cleaved to an appreciable degree in the enzymatic systems studied; so, there is not extensive oxidation at C-1 of the geranyl-derived moiety. Epoxide cleavage by the liver soluble and microsomal fractions possibly results from the action of a "hydrase"; similar cleavage by insect enzyme preparations forms the corresponding diol from Cecropia juvenile hormone (2). The enzymatic conversion of the 4-ethylphenoxy moiety to the 4-acetophenoxy moiety via the corresponding alcohol is anticipated from studies on other 4-ethylphenoxy compounds (8). The reactions occurring in living rats and locusts seem to be similar, in part, to those encountered with the microsome-NADPH system. It is obvious from the number of metabolites that other sites on the molecule are also susceptible to attack or that some intramolecular rearrangements take place during the course of metabolism. However, many of the metabolites could be formed by combinations of attack at the sites already defined.

A specific inhibitor capable of blocking the enzymatic metabolism of this type of juvenoid would be potentially useful in prolonging the duration of juvenoid action in insects. It appears unlikely that a single compound would be adequate to block all of the enzymes involved in juvenoid breakdown by the liver system investigated. However, an inhibitor for the most rapid reaction in a particular enzyme system (or species in vivo) might extend the persistence of the juvenoid and the epoxide cleavage reaction is a candidate for this purpose. The imino analog of the epoxide is of potential interest in this respect (9).

The methylene position of the ethylphenoxy moiety undergoes sensitized photochemical oxidation and this occurs, in part, without other modification of the molecule. The diepoxide is not detected among the photo-decomposition products of compound I (this report) but it is with a related compound (1).

The activities of several of the possible metabolites

and degradation products of juvenoid I in producing 50% pupal-adult intermediates when applied topically to Tenebrio molitor pupae are as follows, as µg/pupa: I-0.007; II and IX - 0.3-0.5; III - 10; VII - 80; IV, V, VIII and XII - > 100. The activities found for compounds I, II, and IX are in general agreement with earlier reports (3, 5). Within the limitations of this test, the products are all of reduced biological activity. It is of interest to test these compounds for potency on phytoplankton because compound I at 10 ppm inhibits the growth of Chlamydomonas sp.

The juvenoid investigated (compound I) represents a class of many related compounds with high morphogenetic activity (3,5). The reactions noted with this compound should therefore be applicable, in part, to other 1-(substituted-phenoxy)-6,7-epoxy-3,7-dialkyl-2-octenes where the alkyl substituents are methyl or ethyl.

Acknowledgement

Aided by PHS grant ES 00049, AEC Contract No. AT(04-3)-34, project agreement No. 113, and The Rockefeller Foundation. For advice and assistance we thank H. Kamimura, formerly of this laboratory; W. J. Loher of the Division of Entomology and J. A. West of the Department of Botany, University of California, Berkeley; J. J. Menn and L. J. Hoffman of Stauffer Chemical Co., Mountain View, Calif.; F. M. Pallos of Stauffer Chemical Co., Richmond, Calif.

References

1. B. A. Pawson, F. Scheidl, and F. Vane, this volume.
2. M. Slade and C. H. Zibitt, this volume.
3. F. M. Pallos, J. J. Menn, P. E. Letchworth and J. B. Miaullis, Nature 232, 486 (1971).
4. H. Kamimura, B. D. Hammock, I. Yamamoto and J. E. Casida, J. Agr. Food Chem., in press.
5. W. S. Bowers, Science 164, 323 (1969).
6. M. Elliott and J. E. Casida, J. Agr. Food Chem., in press.
7. E. Stahl, "Thin-Layer Chromatography", Springer-Verlag, New York, 1969.

8. M. Eto and M. Abe, _Biochem. Pharmacol._ 20, 967 (1971).
9. E. J. Corey, First Swiss Symposium on Juvenile Hormones, Basle, October 17, 1970.

ENVIRONMENTAL STABILITY
OF
JUVENILE HORMONE MIMICKING AGENTS

B. A. Pawson, F. Scheidl and F. Vane

Hoffmann-La Roche Inc.
Nutley, N. J.   07110

The isolation and structure determination of
the two insect juvenile hormones (Figure 1)[*]from
the Cecropia moth by Röller, Dahm and Trost (1967)
and by Meyer and co-workers (1968) has led a number of research groups to synthesize these compounds. Recently, the synthesis of the natural
optically active Cecropia juvenile hormone, the
optical activity of which was determined by Meyer
and Hanzmann (1970), and the assignment of absolute configuration as 10R, 11S have been reported
by the Loew and Johnson group (1971) and by Faulkner and
Petersen (1971). Other groups have synthesized
numerous insect juvenile hormone mimicking agents.
This has resulted in a great many active compounds
from laboratory screening. The potential use of
any of these compounds in the control of economically important pests has led to a number of questions which must be answered before commercializa-
tion. Many of these questions are considered elsewhere in these symposium proceedings. These include greenhouse and field evaluation, and metabolism and residue studies. Another factor of importance is the environmental stability of these
materials.   *Figures follow text

One possible method of application of these
materials would be spraying which would leave a
thin film on the plant foliage. Thus, the com-

pounds would be exposed to heat, sunlight and oxygen from the air as well as climatic conditions. They could also be adsorbed on the plant surfaces and absorbed through the cell wall. Therefore it was important to study the effects of some of these environmental factors on two representative compounds: the synthetic insect juvenile hormone, compound I, and compound II, one of the juvenile-hormone mimicking agents developed at the U.S.D.A. by Dr. W.S.Bowers (1969)(Figure 2).

Compound I as prepared by our procedures is a mixture of cis/trans isomers: hence it contains all eight isomers (Figure 3). Isomer mixture A consists of the 2-cis,6-cis,10,11-cis/trans compounds; B,the 2-cis, 6-trans,10,11-cis,trans; C, 2-trans,6-cis,10,11-cis/trans; and D, 2-trans,6-trans,10,11-cis/trans. The liquid phase used for this chromatogram (SE 30) did not separate the 10,11-epoxy isomers. However, through the use of other liquid phases such as XF-1150, separation of the 10,11-cis,trans isomers can be achieved. Similarly, II is a cis/trans mixture and contains all four isomers (Figure 3). The major portion of the material has the trans-orientation for the double bond. Again, the 6,7-epoxy isomers are not separated under the chromatographic conditions employed.

In laboratory studies of the stability of these materials, no attempt was made to duplicate closely field conditions. The absorption and adsorption phenomena previously mentioned and meteorological conditions found in field application were lacking. In the laboratory procedure, a thin film of pure active compound was placed on a glass surface and this was exposed to ultraviolet light. A weighed amount of material (equivalent to 4 mg/cm^2) was placed on the glass surface

and a small amount of hexane was added to facili-
tate coating of the entire surface. The hexane
was allowed to evaporate and the resulting film
was exposed to ultraviolet light supplied by a
275-watt Hanovia sun lamp at a distance of 20 cm.
from the film surface. After a given time, the
decomposition mixture was removed from the glass
surface by washing with chloroform and diluting
to give a 1% solution. The extent of decomposition was followed visually by thin layer chromatography.

In this way the stability of the insect juvenile hormone I under these conditions was studied with respect to time. The results, shown in
Figure 4, demonstrate that under the ultraviolet
light conditions, more than 95% of the starting
material has disappeared after 24 hours. For comparative purposes, a similar time study was carried out using a visible heat lamp set at a distance to achieve 40°C, the temperature which was
reached under the ultraviolet light conditions.
As shown in Figure 4, under these conditions, decomposition occurs at a lower rate. Eighty-five
percent of the starting material remains after 24
hours and 65% after 96 hours. Since it was found
that this material had a considerable breakdown
after 16 hours under ultraviolet conditions, it
was also of interest to determine the effect of
this exposure on the juvenile hormone activity.

Unless otherwise described, the insect juvenile hormone assay used was a topical test on
Tenebrio molitor pupae less than 24 hours old.
One microliter, containing the desired amount of
the candidate compound in acetone solution, is
placed on the abdomen of each pupa. The pupae
are held for 10-14 days at which time pupal
changes are recorded. The results are expressed

as percent Adult Formation Inhibition; that is the percent of treated pupae retaining pupal characteristics.

As shown in Figure 5, the activity of the synthetic juvenile hormone I after exposure to sunlight for 16 hours is approximately 1/10 that of material which had not been subjected to these decomposition conditions. In this experiment, no starting material was detected in the decomposition mixture by thin layer chromatography.

Thin layer chromatography of the decomposition mixture obtained in the experiments using ultraviolet light showed that in addition to material, presumably polymeric in nature, which remained at the origin of the chromatogram, a product was formed which was more polar than the starting juvenile hormone I. This material was isolated by preparative thin layer chromatography for analysis by gas chromatography, mass spectroscopy and nuclear magnetic resonance spectroscopy (Figure 6). In the high resolution mass spectrum, the molecular ion was observed at m/e 310, which corresponded to a molecular formula of $C_{18}H_{30}O_4$. NMR showed the presence on only 1 vinyl proton, that one associated with the α, β-unsaturated ester moiety. The lack of any other type of vinyl proton ruled out the possibility of the product being any of the allylic alcohols one might expect from photolytic attack of singlet oxygen on the double bond followed by reduction.

The structure was solved when a sample of the bis-epoxide of the starting material was obtained by peracid oxidation of the synthetic juvenile hormone I (Figure 7). Comparison of this material with the product isolated from the decomposition mixture by gas chromatography, mass spectroscopy, nmr, and thin layer chromatography showed the two materials to be compatible.

These results encouraged the investigation of the decomposition of the pure synthetic juvenile hormone III, the trans, trans, cis-isomer, isolated from Cecropia moth and found to have the highest juvenile hormone activity of all the possible geometrical isomers (Figure 8). This material, when subjected to the decomposition conditions, that is, exposure of the material in a thin film on a glass surface to ultraviolet light for 6 and 24 hours, was found to decompose at a slower rate than the mixture of isomers I. However, gas chromatographic analysis of the decomposition showed that isomerization of the double bonds was occurring under the conditions of the decomposition (Figure 9). The major isomerization product was the 2-cis, 6-trans, 10-cis/trans isomer formed by isomerization of the C-2, C-3 double bond. The 2-cis, 6-cis, 10-cis/trans, and the 2-trans, 6-cis, 10-cis/trans isomers were also formed but to a lesser degree. By integration of the gas chromatograms using an internal standard, it was found that 59% of the pure isomer III remained after six hours exposure to ultraviolet light and an additional 26% of isomerized product was present (Figure 10). No volatile decomposition products of III were detected after this time of exposure. In contrast, with isomer mixture I, only 53% of the starting material was present after six hours exposure to the ultraviolet light conditions, and only 7% after 24 hours. The same decomposition product was formed from the pure synthetic isomer as was found with the mixture of isomers; that is the bis-epoxide.

For a comparison of their juvenile hormone activity, the mixture of isomers I and the pure trans, trans, cis-isomer III were subjected to the

decomposition conditions for 24 hours. The resulting mixtures without removal of any undecomposed
starting material were assayed for juvenile hormone activity against the Tenebrio. The results
are shown in Figure 11.

Similar decomposition studies were carried
out on the juvenile hormone mimicking agent II developed by Dr. Bowers at the U.S.D.A. (Figure 2).

Under the ultraviolet light conditions described previously, the stability of this material
was studied with time. As shown in Figure 12, 50%
of the starting material had disappeared after 16
hours; 70% after 48 hours and 90% after 96 hours.
For comparison purposes, the decomposition of this
material under conditions utilizing a visible heat
lamp at 40° was also studied. As was the case
with the juvenile hormone mixture I referred to
earlier, in the absence of ultraviolet light an
increase in stability was found: 85% of the starting material remained after 24 hours and 65%
after 96 hours.

The juvenile hormone activity of the decomposition product mixture was assayed in the Tenebrio screen and compared with material which had
not been subjected to the decomposition conditions.
For this experiment, the juvenile hormone mimicking agent II was exposed to the ultraviolet light
conditions for 40 hours. The starting material
remaining after this time was removed by preparative thin layer chromatography, so that only the
mixture of products resulting from decomposition
was assayed. The results of this evaluation,
shown in Figure 13, demonstrate that the activity
of the decomposition mixture is <1/10 that of the
original material.

The four pure isomers (Figure 14) of this
juvenile hormone mimicking agent were synthesized

in our laboratories for comparative studies of
stabilities and activities of the individual isomers.

The synthesis of these materials is outlined
in Figures 15 and 16. Horner reaction of methyl
ethyl ketone with trimethylphosphonoacetate afforded the mixture of esters which were separated by
distillation. Reduction with sodium aluminum
(bis-2-methoxyethoxy)hydride, conversion to the
bromide with phosphorus tribromide and alkylation
with the anion of ethyl acetoacetate afforded the
cis ketone A and the trans ketone B. Horner reaction with trimethylphosphonoacetate again afforded the mixture of cis and trans esters from each
of the ketones. These esters were separated by
distillation or by chromatography. Reduction,
conversion to the bromide, alkylation of the potassium salt of sesamol and epoxidation with per
acid afforded the final products.

When these isomers were subjected to the conditions of ultraviolet light on a thin film on the
glass surface, as previously described, the four
isomers were found to have similar stabilities, as
shown in Figure 17.

The insect juvenile hormone activities of
these four isomers were evaluated against four insects: Tenebrio, Mexican bean beetle, housefly,
and milkweed bug. These results are shown in Figures 18 and 19. In Figure 18 a comparison of the
activities of the four isomers in the topical
Tenebrio molitor assay is shown.

As these data show, the isomer with the cis
orientation at the epoxide and the trans orientation at the double bond is the most active in
this test, followed by the trans, trans isomer.

The results found for these four isomers in
a modified topical test on <u>Tenebrio</u>, Mexican bean
beetle, housefly and milkweed bug egg are shown in
Figure 19. The modified topical test consists of
topical treatment of the insect specimens on filter paper with aqueous solutions of the candidate
compound. The insects are held until all controls
have matured and then are rated.

In summary, the more active compounds are
those with the <u>trans</u> orientation of the double
bond, and the less active compounds are those with
the <u>cis</u> orientation.

Another factor of utmost importance in as-
sessing the potential use of a juvenile hormone
mimicking agent in the field is the effect of the
material on the plant itself. Any plant damage
as a result of these materials would make them un-
acceptable. Therefore the phytotoxic properties
of these four isomers and the mixture were evaluated on sugar beets, corn, wheat, soybean, cotton
and tomato. The materials were applied by post-
emergence procedures at 8, 2 and 1/2 lb/A active
material in an acetone, methanol, dimethyl forma-
mide solvent mixture. Observations for phytotoxicity were made 8 days after treatment. No significant differences between the isomers and the
mixture were observed. Plant injury was the same
in all cases, typified by slight necrosis.

The authors wish to acknowledge the contri-
butions of the following persons, all of Hoffmann-
La Roche Inc., to this work: Drs. T. Williams and
W. Benz for nuclear magnetic resonance and mass
spectroscopic analyses; Dr. M. Rosenberger and
Drs. E. Broger and A. Pfiffner (Hoffmann-La Roche,
Basel, Switzerland) for providing synthetic material; Dr. M.Mitrovic and Miss A. Popick for biological evaluation, and Miss T. Clemente, Mrs. B.

Tytla and Mr. Y. Doumato for technical assistance.

References

W. S. Bowers, Science, 164, 323 (1969).

D. J. Faulkner and M. R. Petersen, J.Amer. Chem.Soc., 93, 3766 (1971).

P. Loew and W.S. Johnson, ibid., 93, 3765 (1971).

A. S. Meyer, H. A. Schneiderman, E. Hanzmann, and J. H. Ko, Proc. Nat. Acad. Sci., U.S.A., 60, 853 (1968).

A. S. Meyer and E. Hanzmann, Biochem. Biophys. Res. Comm., 41, 891 (1970).

H. Röller, K. H. Dahm, C. C. Sweeley, and B. M. Trost, Angew. Chem., 79, 190 (1967).

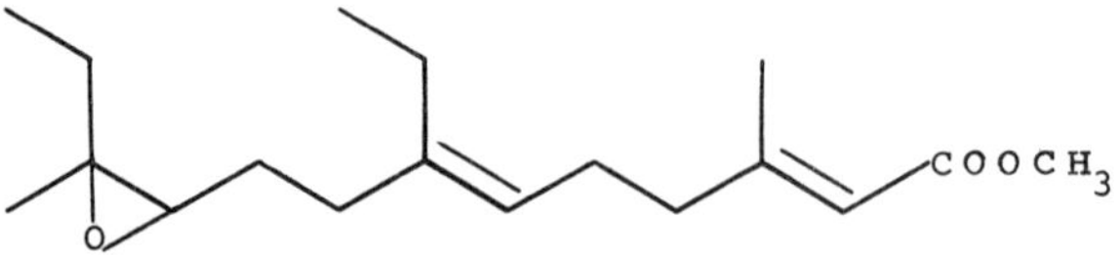

H. Röller, K. H. Dahm, C. C. Sweeley, and B. M. Trost
Angew. Chem., 79, 190 (1967).

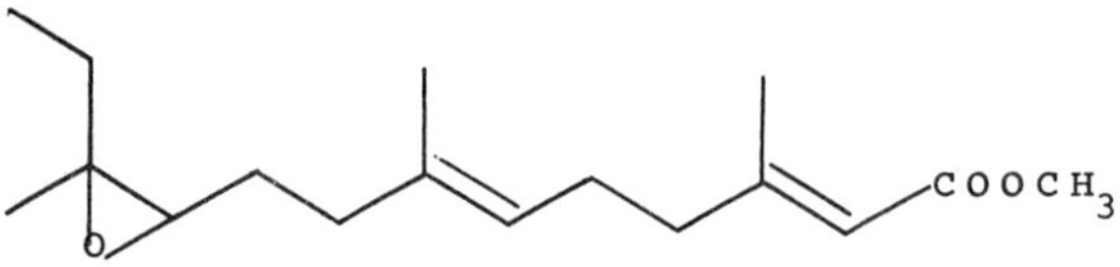

A. S. Meyer, H. A. Schneiderman, E. Hanzmann, and J. H. Ko,
Proc. Nat. Acad. Sci., U.S.A., 60, 853 (1968).

Fig. 1

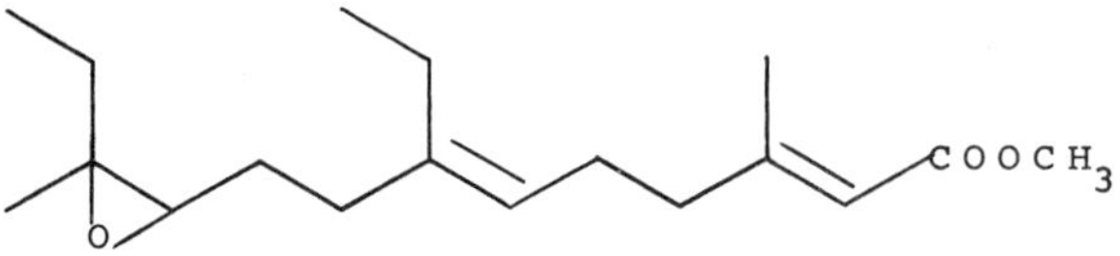

I

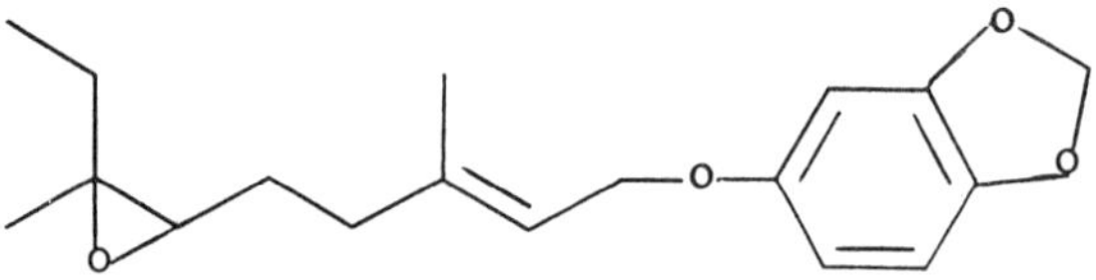

II

Fig. 2

200

ISOMER COMPOSITION OF INSECT JUVENILE HORMONE COMPOUNDS

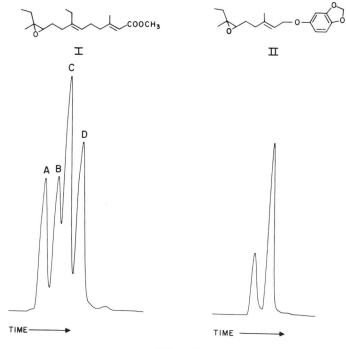

Fig. 3

STABILITY OF SYNTHETIC INSECT
JUVENILE HORMONE I TO ULTRA-
VIOLET AND VISIBLE LIGHT AT 40°c

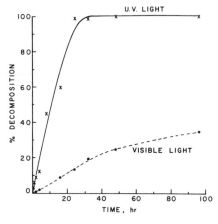

Fig. 4

JUVENILE HORMONE ACTIVITY OF I
(TENEBRIO TEST)

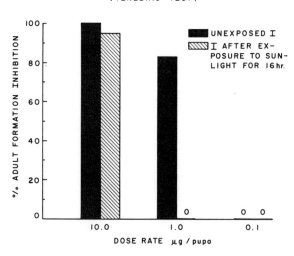

Fig. 5

Physical-Chemical Analysis Of Product From Decomposition Of Insect Juvenile Hormone I by Ultraviolet Light

Thin Layer Chromatography	More Polar Than I
Mass Spectroscopy	Molecular Ion $^{m}/_{e}$ 310
NMR Spectroscopy	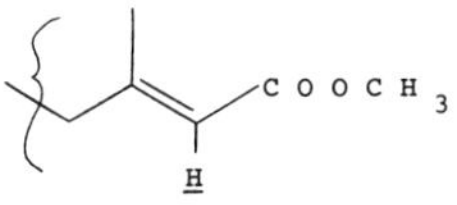 Present
	No other Vinyl Protons Present

$COOCH_3$
H

Fig. 6

STRUCTURE OF DECOMPOSITION PRODUCT FROM JUVENILE HORMONE I

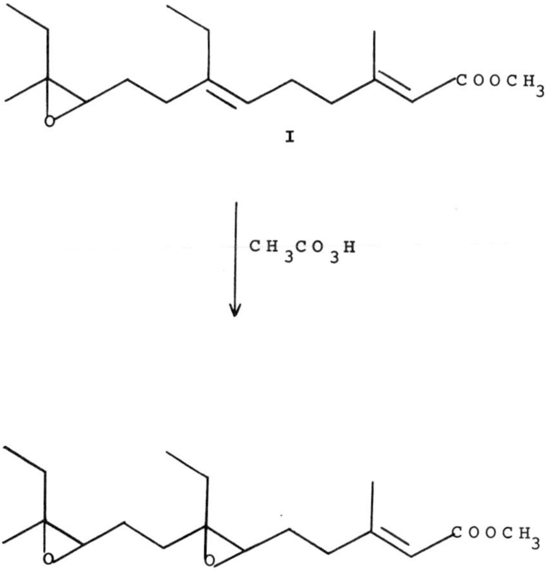

$COOCH_3$
I
CH_3CO_3H
$COOCH_3$

Fig. 7

B. A. PAWSON, F. SCHEIDL, AND F. VANE

SYNTHETIC JUVENILE HORMONE III

(CECROPIA JUVENILE HORMONE)

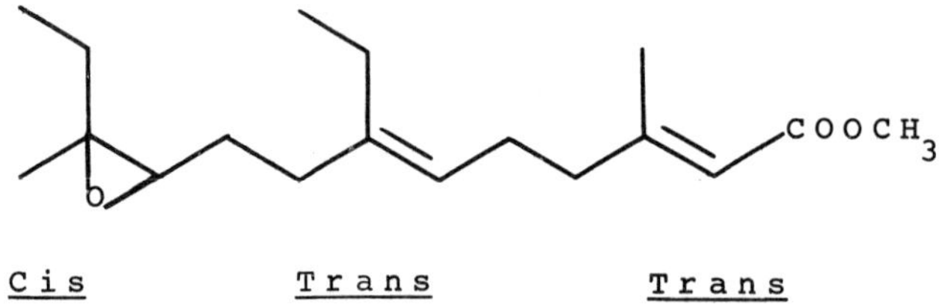

Cis   Trans   Trans

III

Fig. 8

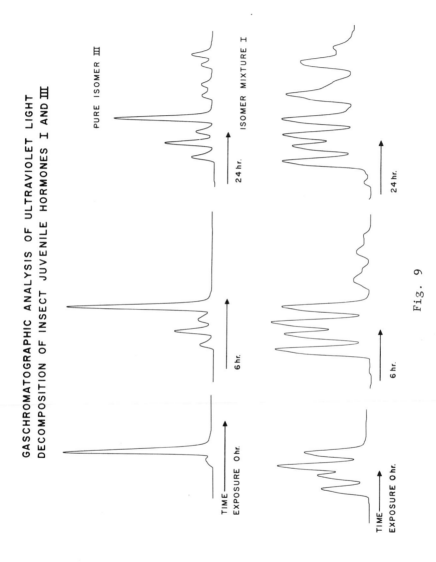

GASCHROMATOGRAPHIC ANALYSIS OF ULTRAVIOLET LIGHT
DECOMPOSITION OF INSECT JUVENILE HORMONES I AND III

PURE ISOMER III

ISOMER MIXTURE I

Fig. 9

ULTRAVIOLET LIGHT INDUCED DECOMPOSITION OF JUVENILE

HORMONE COMPOUNDS I AND III

(ANALYSIS BY GAS CHROMATOGRAPHY)

Compound	Dec. Time, Hr:	% Compound Remaining[a]		
		0	6	24
III		95	59	9
III + Isomers		100	85	18
Decomposition Products of III (+Isomers)		0	0	8
I		100	53	7
Decomposition Products of I		0	12	11

a - Material unaccounted for is non-volatile and presumably polymeric.

Fig. 10

INSECT JUVENILE HORMONE ACTIVITIES
OF COMPOUNDS I AND III AFTER 24 HR.
EXPOSURE TO ULTRAVIOLET LIGHT
(TENEBRIO TEST)

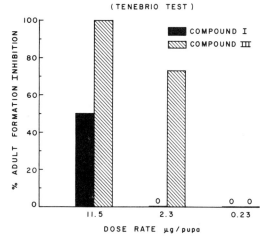

Fig. 11

STABILITY OF INSECT JUVENILE
HORMONE MIMICKING AGENT II TO
ULTRAVIOLET AND VISIBLE LIGHT
AT 40°c

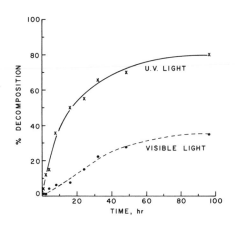

Fig. 12

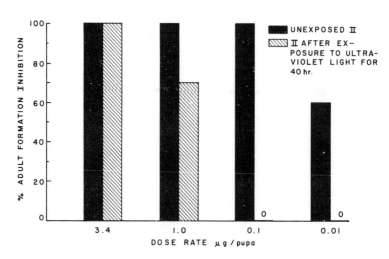

Fig. 13

STEREOISOMERS OF INSECT JUVENILE HORMONE MIMICKING AGENT II

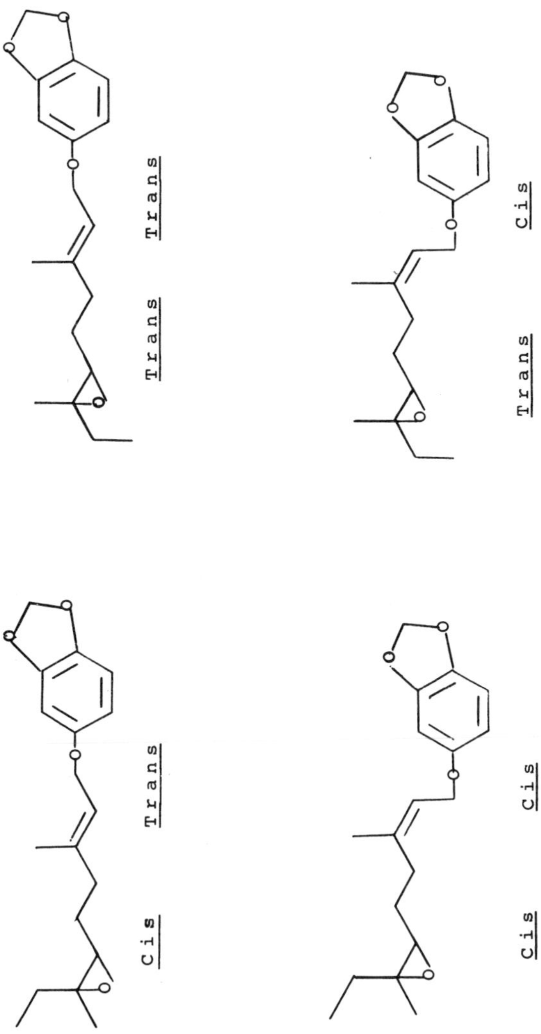

Fig. 14

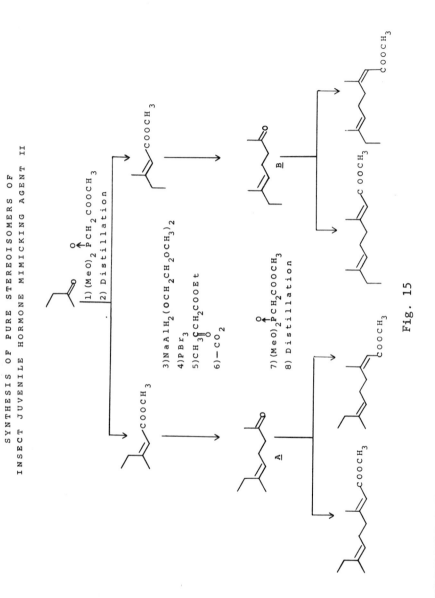

SYNTHESIS OF PURE STEREOISOMERS OF
INSECT JUVENILE HORMONE MIMICKING AGENT II

Fig. 15

SYNTHESIS OF STEREOISOMERS (Cont'd)

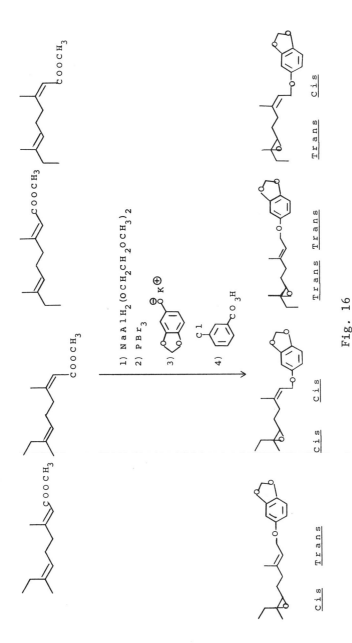

Fig. 16

211

COMPARATIVE STABILITIES OF
STEREOISOMERS OF INSECT JUVEN-
ILE HORMONE MIMICKING AGENT II
(ULTRAVIOLET LIGHT EXPOSURE)

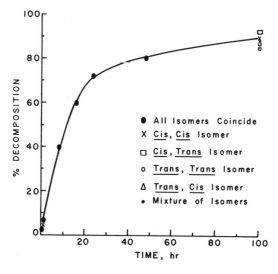

Fig. 17

ACTIVITY OF STEREOISOMERS OF INSECT JUVENILE
HORMONE MIMICKING AGENT II (TENEBRIO TEST)

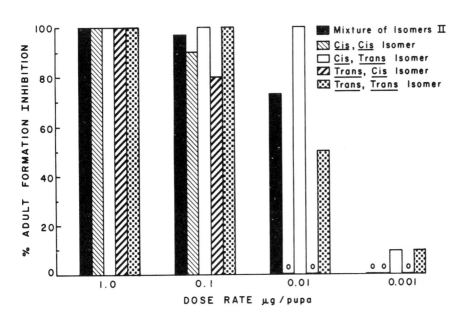

Fig. 18

ACTIVITY OF STEREOISOMERS OF INSECT JUVENILE HORMONE
MIMICKING AGENT II AGAINST 4 INSECTS (MODIFIED TOPICAL TEST)

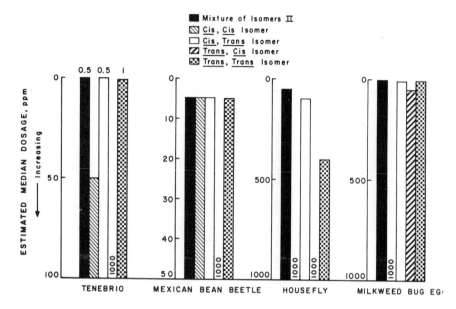

Fig. 19

PART III
CHEMICAL ASPECTS

THE ORIGIN OF JUVENILE HORMONE CHEMISTRY

Barry M. Trost

Department of Chemistry, University of Wisconsin
Madison, Wisconsin 53706

The general interest in developing alternative methods
to existing chemical insect control agents has led to detailed studies of the chemical basis of insect development.[1]
Insect physiologists outline a control system for insect
metamorphosis comprising three "hormones."[2] The brain
hormone, released by neurosecretory cells, acts on the prothoracic gland to stimulate production of the prothoracic
gland hormone, better known as ecdysone. In one instance,
it can be demonstrated that the prothoracic gland need not
be the site of hormonal synthesis.[3] Its function may mainly be the synthesis of the enzyme or enzyme system responsible for ecdysone biosynthesis. Ecdysone has been identified as a pentahydroxycholestenone derivative by x-ray
crystallography.[2a,b,4,5] Molting hormones from other sources
have closely related structures, mainly differing in the
number and pattern of hydroxyl groups as well as the nature
of the acyclic sidechain. Indeed, it appears that all
arthropods employ essentially the same compound as their
molting hormones.[3]

$2\beta,3\beta,14\alpha,22\beta_F,25$-pentahydroxy-5$\beta$,$\Delta^7$-cholesten-6-one

The third member of the trio, the juvenile hormone, plays several roles during the life span of an insect.[6] During metamorphosis its presence opposes adult differentiation. Thus, the relative concentrations of juvenile hormone and ecdysone determine the nature of the insect molt. For an insect to molt from a larval to a pupal or a pupal to an adult stage, juvenile hormone must be absent. The profound effects on the insect when juvenile hormone is present at the "wrong" times during metamorphosis make it a key substance in the search for a "third generation" pesticide.[1] The search for the chemical identity of juvenile hormone was hampered by its exceedingly low titer in almost all insects at most stages of development. During various searches for a source of juvenile hormone, active substances, subsequently identified as farnesol and farnesal, were found in insect fecal material.[7] Such a find led to a

farnesol   farnesal

general testing of various naturally occurring compounds of the terpene family in the hopes of gaining insight into the structure of JH.[2a,8] As the data in Table I indicate the

Table I. Activity of Selected Terpenes

Compound	Activity TU/mg	Compound	Activity TU/mg
farnesol	50 (25.0)	geraniol	12
farnesal	170	citral	0
nerolidol	50	β-ionone	2
squalene	1.5	N,N-diethyl	
phytol	10	farnesylamine	2300
citronellol	3	farnesylmethyl ether	10,000 (170,000)
		Cecropia juvenile hormone	(5,000,000)

TU = Tenebrio Unit = minimum amount of juvenile hormone active substance capable of producing a positive response in 40% of total pupae injected.

activity of most of the compounds are many orders of magnitude less than the natural material. Most significant is
the observed high activity of the farnesyl derivatives
farnesylmethyl ether and N,N-diethylfarnesylamine. Bowers
discovered that methyl 10,11-epoxyfarnesoate   had excep-
tional activity (about 200 TU/mg).[9] Its extraordinary activity led Bowers to speculate that the naturally occurring
hormone, when isolated, would have a quite similar structure. The high activity of this family of compounds was
also reflected in the preparation of a highly active complex mixture of products upon passing dry hydrogen chloride
through an ethanolic solution of farnesoic acid.[10]   Although the mixture contains more than twenty compounds, one
of these possesses only 1/5 less activity than the
Cecropia hormone. An active substance was isolated and
identified as methyl 7,11-dichloro-7,11-dimethyldodeca-2-
enoate (2) from a similarly prepared mixture.[11]

Juvabione 3 and dehydrojuvabione 4 have been identified as the active ingredients of the extracts of balsam
fir trees that possessed high JH activity for Pyrrhocoris
apterus.[12] These compounds are approximately five powers
of ten less active than Cecropia juvenile hormone in the
Tenebrio test. Several methylenedioxyphenyl derivatives,

such as sesoxane 5 and piperonylfarnesyl ether epoxide 6,
possessed JH activity as well as serving as synergists for

other JH active substances.[15]

Cecropia Hormone Isolation and Structure

The discovery that the adult males of Hyalophora
cecropia possessed a reasonably high titer of the precious
hormone (subsequently estimated to be about 1-2 μg per
animal) provided the impetus to undertake chemical investigations.[16] Williams and coworkers identified methyl 9,10-
epoxyhexadecanoate 7 as the active substance.[17] However,
synthetic derived samples of the cis and trans isomers
were devoid of all biological activity. The close similar-

cis or
trans   7

ity of the chromatographic properties of this substance
with the natural Cecropia hormone led to speculation that
it served as a carrier for the active substance. However,
other investigators failed to find either isomer in their
crude extracts. Meyer and coworkers also failed to achieve
isolation of a chemically homogeneous substance.[18] Roeller,
Bjerke, Norgard, and McShan developed a five-step isolation
scheme that achieved approximately a 10^5 purification.[19]
Gas chromatography indicated a single component was present.

Mass spectrometry established a molecular formula of
$C_{18}H_{30}O_3$.[6a,20] Catalytic hydrogenation led to the uptake of
three equivalents of hydrogen and loss of an oxygen. The
mass spectrum of this substance, especially in comparison
with the mass spectrum of a model compound, methyl 3,7,11-
trimethyldodecanoate 8, established the placement of two
branches at C-3 and C-7. Strong peaks at m/e 101 and 69
suggest a methyl branch at C-3. The twin pair of peaks at
143-111 and 185-153 suggest a two-carbon branch at C-7.
That this branch is in fact an ethyl group, rather than a
gem dimethyl grouping, arises from the nmr spectrum (see
Fig. 1). The presence of a triplet for six hydrogens at
δ0.96 (A) suggests two ethyl units. The absorptions at
δ5.46 (1H,bs,L), 3.59 (3H,s,G) and 2.12 (3H,d,E) clearly
establishes a crotonate unit 9; whereas a trisubstituted

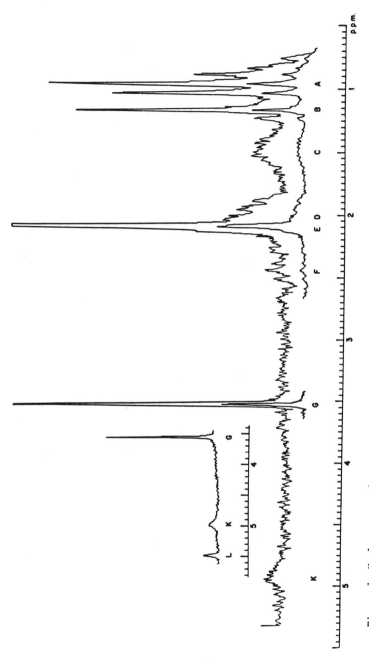

Figure 1. Nuclear magnetic resonance spectrum of Cecropia juvenile hormone.

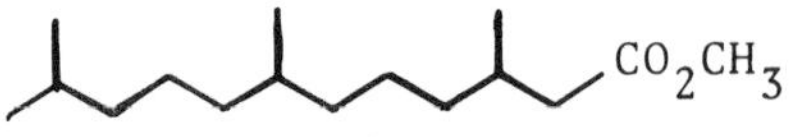
CO_2CH_3

8

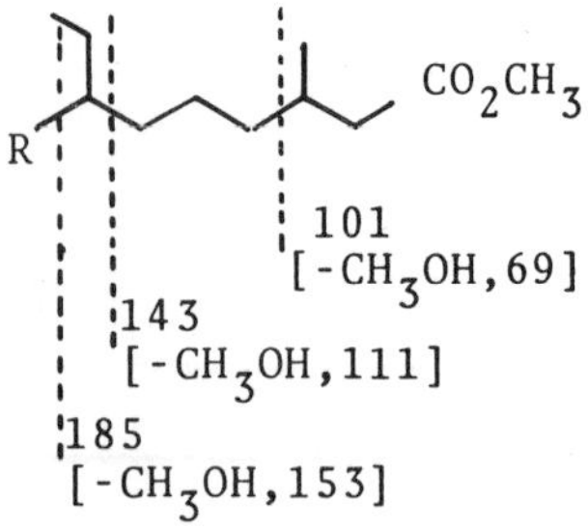
CO_2CH_3
R
101
[-CH_3OH,69]
143
[-CH_3OH,111]
185
[-CH_3OH,153]

epoxide unit 10 derives from the absorptions at δ2.50 (1H, t,F) and 1.16 (1H,s,B). The presence of a second trisub-

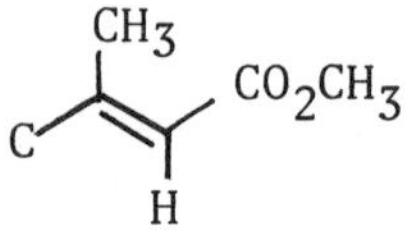
CH_3
CO_2CH_3
C
H

9

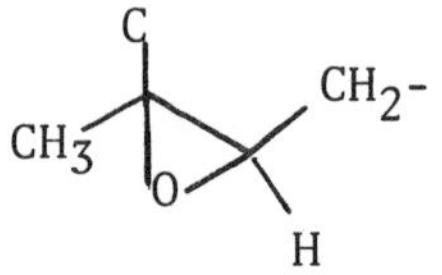
C
CH_2-
CH_3
O
H

10

stituted double bond is indicated by the complex absorption at δ4.96 (K). In combination with an oxidative cleavage utilizing osmium tetroxide and sodium metaperiodate in which levulinaldehyde was obtained the partial structure 11 was deduced. The final gross molecular features derived from

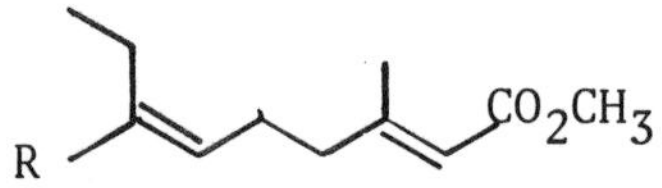
CO_2CH_3
R

11

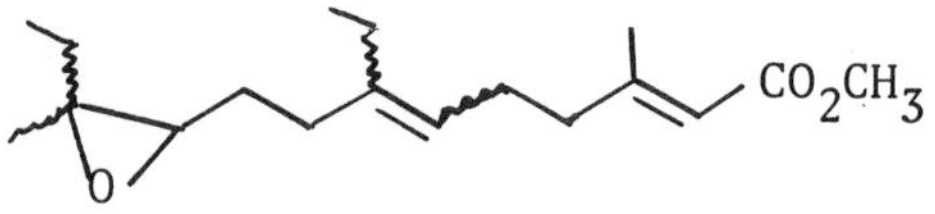
O
CO_2CH_3

12

the mass spectrum of juvenile hormone itself which led to the structure 12. Although the stereochemistry of the 2,3 double bond was secure from the nmr data, the stereochemistry of the remaining sites of unsaturation was uncertain.

Nonselective Chemical Syntheses

Confirmation of the structural deductions mainly based

on spectroscopic data was essential. Initial work focussed
on confirmation of the carbon skeleton with lesser attention
paid to the problem of stereochemistry. On the hypothesis
that the thermodynamically more stable all trans isomer
constituted the correct geometrical assignment, construction
of the proper skeleton was undertaken. The basis of the
approach evolved from the known ring opening of cyclo-
propylcarbinyl alcohols to homoallylic halides (see Scheme
1).[21,22] The geometry of the resultant olefin should be
determined mainly by the eclipsing interactions developing
in the transition state for ring cleavage assuming the
reaction requires a trans coplanar arrangement (eq. 1).
Thus, for the case of 2-cyclopropyl-2-butanol, conformer 13

$$(R^1 = CH_3, \quad R^2 = C_2H_5, \quad R^3 = H)$$ eclipses the two bulkier
groups (ethyl and cyclopropylmethylene); whereas, conformer
14 ($R^1 = CH_3$, $R^2 = C_2H_5$, $R^3 = H$) minimizes eclipsing interactions. Thus, 1-bromo-4-methyl-trans-3-butene 15 should
be the major product; indeed, it comprises 85% of the mixture. By proper choice of R^1, R^2, and R^3 the stereospec-
ificity can be increased to greater than 95% one isomer as
has been achieved in the total synthesis of juvenile
hormone by Johnson and his collaborators.[23] Repetition of
the process with 3-cyclopropyl-7-methyl-trans-6-nonen-3-ol
(16), obtainable by addition of the Grignard reagent from
homoallylic bromide 15, generated the C_{13} homoallylic
bromide 17 with an equal and inseparable mixture of
geometric isomers. Chain extension by Grignard addition of
the organometallic corresponding to 17 to acetaldehyde
followed by oxidation gave the key C_{15} ketone 18 as a mixture of four isomers in which the $\Delta^{9,10}$ double bond was
predominantly trans.   The final chain extension utilized
the Emmons-Wadsworth modification of the Wittig olefin
reaction to produce triene 19 as a mixture of all eight
isomers. Catalytic hydrogenation generated methyl 3,11-
dimethyl-7-ethyltridecanoate 20 identical by vpc chromatographic and mass spectroscopic comparisons with authentic
deoxyhexahydrojuvenile hormone.

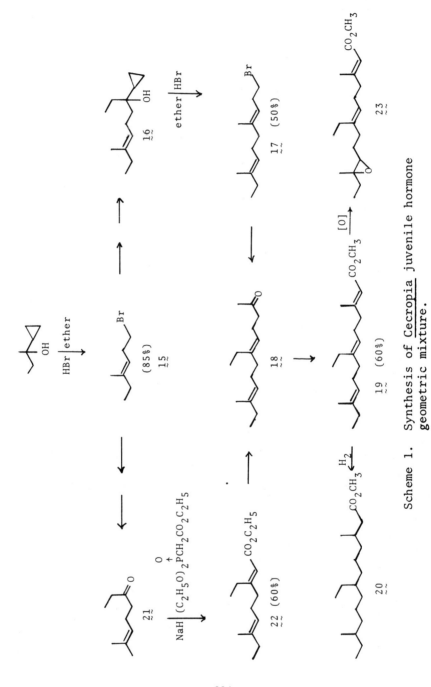

Scheme 1. Synthesis of Cecropia juvenile hormone geometric mixture.

The inseparability of the geometric isomers led to the development of an alternative synthesis of the C_{15} ketone.[24] Predominantly trans-C_{10} ketone 21, available from homoallylic bromide 15, was condensed with the anion of triethyl phosphonoacetate. The 60/40 trans/cis mixture of ester 22 was readily separable by column chromatography. Conversion of the corresponding allylic alcohol of the trans,trans isomer, obtained by lithium aluminum hydride reduction to the bromide with phosphorus tribromide, followed by ethyl acetoacetate chain extension generated 6-ethyl-10-methyl-trans,trans-5,9-dodecadien-2-one 18 contaminated with only 10-15% of the trans,cis isomer. Repetition of the Emmons-Wadsworth procedure with trimethyl phosphonoacetate and separation of the resultant 3:2 mixture of cis,trans,trans and trans,trans,trans triene esters 19 yielded methyl 3,11-dimethyl-7-ethyl-trans,trans-trans-2,6,10-tridecatrienoate. m-Chloroperbenzoic acid predominantly epoxidized the unconjugated terminal double bond to give a material, 23, that was extremely similar but nonidentical to natural juvenile hormone. The exceedingly close properties of the synthetic compound and natural juvenile hormone suggested the trans,trans,cis stereochemistry of the natural product.

The Emmons-Wadsworth procedure provides an ideal solution to confirmation of the structure of juvenile hormone (eq. 2). It proceeds readily and in high yield even

$$\underset{R'}{\overset{R}{>}}{=}0 \quad + \quad >\overset{+}{P}-\overset{-}{C}HCO_2CH_3 \quad \longrightarrow \quad \underset{R'}{\overset{R}{\diagup}}CO_2CH_3 \quad + \quad \underset{R}{\overset{R'}{\diagup}}CO_2CH_3 \quad (2)$$

with rather unreactive ketones. More importantly, the resultant α,β-unsaturated esters can be readily separated either by distillation or chromatography due to the substantial differences in properties between olefin isomers when one of the substituents is a highly polarized group. The ester functionality also facilitates assignment of olefin geometry. Thus, substituents cis to the ester experience 0.2-0.7 ppm downfield shift relative to their trans isomers. Utilizing this approach (see Scheme 2) as the key reaction and traditional chain extension reactions allowed unambiguous generation of all eight geometrical

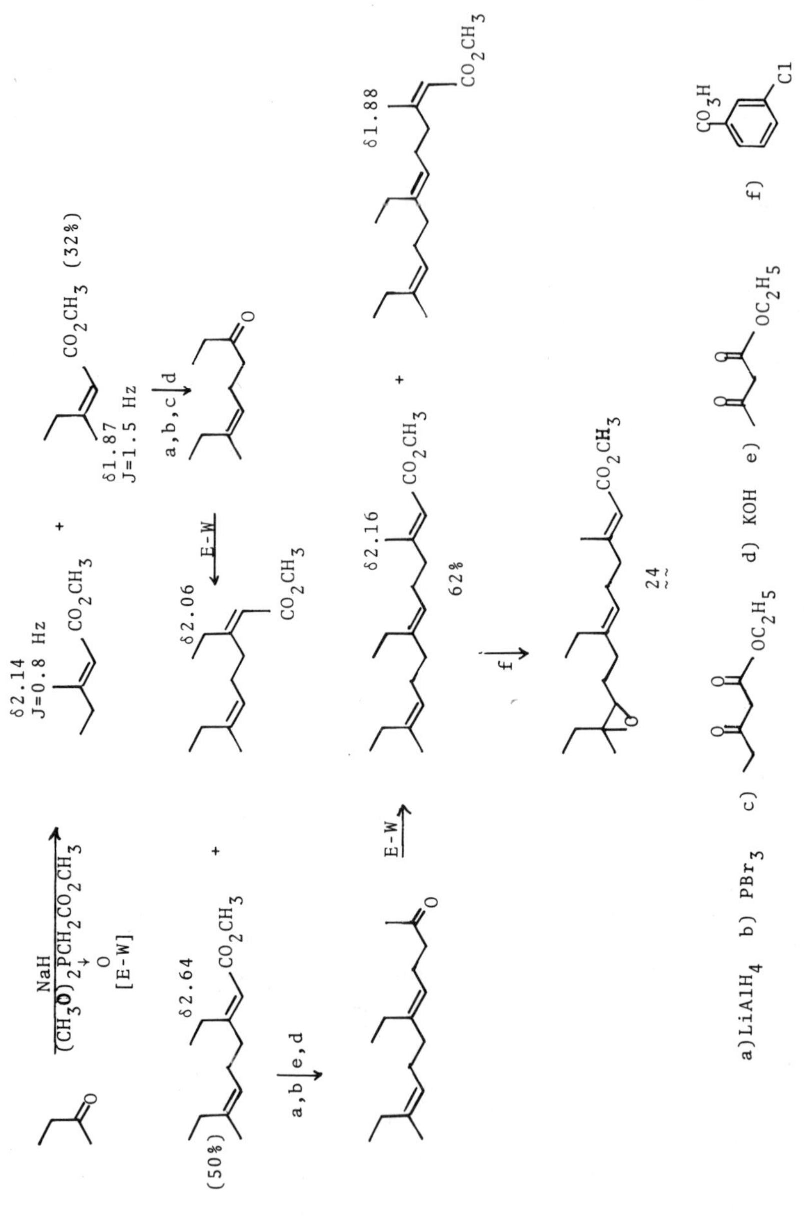

CO_2CH_3 (32%)

$\delta 1.87$
J=1.5 Hz

a,b,c | d

$\delta 2.14$
J=0.8 Hz

CO_2CH_3

CO_2CH_3

E-W

$\delta 2.06$

CO_2CH_3

$\delta 1.88$ CO_2CH_3

CO_2CH_3 +

$\delta 2.16$ CO_2CH_3

62%

CO_2CH_3

24

$\underset{[E-W]}{\overset{NaH}{\xrightarrow{(CH_3O)_2PCH_2CO_2CH_3}}}$

$\delta 2.64$ CO_2CH_3

(50%)

a,b | e,d

E-W

f

CO_3H Cl

OC_2H_5 d) KOH   e) OC_2H_5 f)

a) LiAlH$_4$ b) PBr$_3$ c) OC_2H_5

Scheme 2.   Synthesis of each geometrical isomer of Cecropia juvenile hormone.

isomers of juvenile hormone.[25] Comparison of the chemical
and biological properties of methyl 3,11-dimethyl-7-ethyl-
cis-10,11-epoxy-trans,trans-2,6-tridecadienoate 24 with
Cecropia juvenile hormone indicated their identity. The
wrong stereochemistry at either the $\Delta^{2,3}$ or $\Delta^{6,7}$ double
bonds essentially destroys activity (see Table 2).

Table 2. Activities of geometrical isomers

Compound	Activity [TU/µg]
methyl 3,11-dimethyl-7-ethyltrideca-2,6,10-trienoate	
trans,trans,cis	500
trans,trans,trans	200
trans,cis,cis	<10
trans,cis,trans	<33
cis,trans,cis	<10
cis,trans,trans	<10
cis,cis,cis	<10
cis,cis,trans	<10
methyl 3,11-dimethyl-7-ethyl-10,11-epoxytrideca-2,6-dienoate	
trans,trans,cis	5000
trans,trans,trans	2000
trans,cis,cis	<10
trans,cis,trans	<20
cis,trans,cis	<10
cis,trans,trans	<10
cis,cis,cis	<10
cis,cis,trans	<10

Many additional nonselective approaches have been
employed utilizing as the key reaction other Wittig type
condensations,[26] Claisen rearrangements,[27] and organocopper
additions to allylic halides.[28]

Stereospecific and Stereoselective Synthetic Approaches

With the establishment of the correct structure for

racemic Cecropia juvenile hormone, the stage was set for its
selective synthesis. Several approaches have been employed
by a variety of workers. Corey and coworkers developed
approaches based upon the Wittig condensation of the ylide
derived from a phosphorus betaine and formaldehyde, addition
of aluminum hydrides to propargyl alcohols, and the thermal
isomerization of cis-2-alkyl-1-vinylcyclopropanes.[29]
Johnson and his collaborators employed the Claisen rearrangement[30] and the cleavage of cyclopropyl carbinols[23]
as the key reactions in several approaches.

Our interest focused on the conversion of ring geometry
into olefin geometry. It had been known that monoderiv-
atives of 1,3-glycols undergo base induced fragmentation
to ketoolefins (eq. 3). Extension of this concept suggests

$$\qquad\qquad\qquad (3)$$

the trans fused perhydroindane 25 would generate the key C_{15}
ketone with proper olefin geometry; whereas, the cis fused
compound 26 would produce the cis,cis-C_{15} ketone.

25

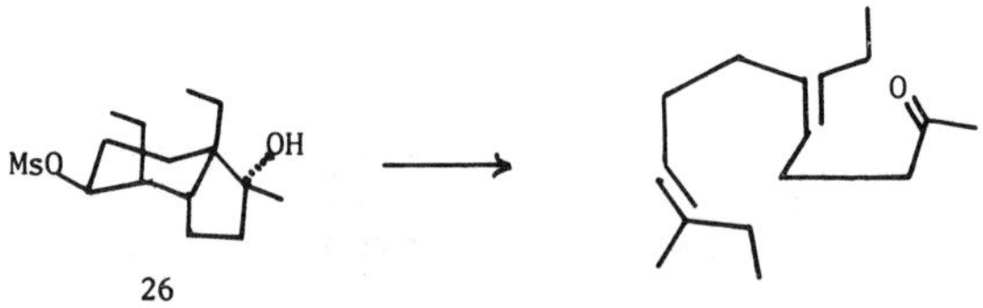

26

Scheme 3 sketches the synthetic route. The aldol
condensation step in the Robinson annelation procedure has
led to production of either the desired perhydroindendione
27 or the bicyclo[3.2.1]octandione 28. The latter appears

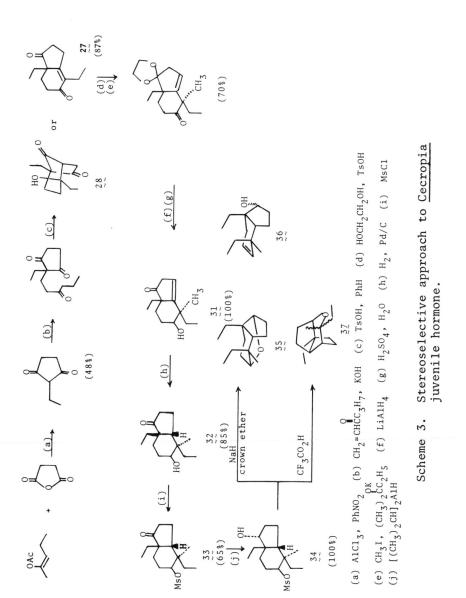

Scheme 3. Stereoselective approach to Cecropia juvenile hormone.

(a) AlCl$_3$, PhNO$_2$ (b) CH$_2$=CHCC$_3$H$_7$, KOH (c) TsOH, PhH (d) HOCH$_2$CH$_2$OH, TsOH

(e) CH$_3$I, (CH$_3$)$_2$CC$_2$H$_5$ (f) LiAlH$_4$ (g) H$_2$SO$_4$, H$_2$O (h) H$_2$, Pd/C (i) MsCl

(j) [(CH$_3$)$_2$CH]$_2$AlH

229

to be the kinetic product; whereas the former is the thermodynamic product. Ketalization of the unconjugated ketone followed by methyl iodide alkylation utilizing potassium t-amyloxide in benzene to generate the enolate led to a 70% yield of almost exclusively a single isomer. Carrying through the sequence employing ethylvinyl ketone in the Robinson annelation step and ethyl iodide in the alkylation step generated the alternate isomer. The geometry of alkylation was proven by comparison of the nuclear Overhauser effects (NOE) between the methyl group

29　　　　　　　　30

protons and the vinyl proton in the tetrahydropyranyl ether derivatives 29 and 30. Irradiation of the methyl group caused a 24% increase in the integrated intensity of the vinyl proton in 29 and only an 11% increase in 30. Although catalytic hydrogenation over Pd/C led to a 3:2 mixture of the cis and trans isomers at the ring fusion; only capillary vapor phase chromatography achieved their separation. Alternatively, a single isomer 32 was obtained by reduction of the unsaturated ketol 31--obtained by lithium aluminum hydride reduction followed by aqueous acid hydrolysis of the ketal. Mesylation with methanesulfonyl chloride generated a crystalline mesylate 33 in 55% overall yield from 27. That it is cis is established by subsequent cyclizations. Although the wrong isomer was obtained pure, the synthetic scheme proceeded with this compound to examine the validity of the approach. Diisobutylaluminum hydride reduction generated a quantitative yield of a single hydroxymesylate 34.

Attempts to fragment this hydroxymesylate to a keto-diene failed. Base treatment in tetrahydrofuran led to recovered starting material. Use of dicyclohexyl-18-crown-6 ether in conjunction with sodium hydride led to only the products of intramolecular O-alkylation and elimination, 35 and 36, respectively. Alternatively, attempts to generate the equivalent of carbonium ion 38, which could fragment in a 1,3-fashion also only led to products of skeletal rearrangement, i.e., 37. Thus, four-bond fragmentations of diols cannot be extended to six-bond fragmentations.

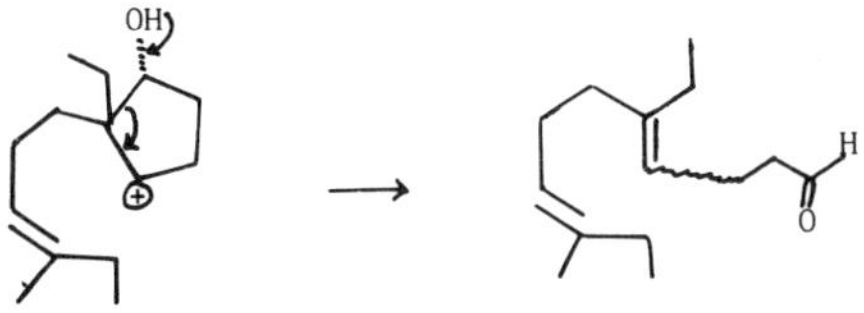

38

The elegant work of the Zoecon group under the leadership of Siddall successfully employed the four-bond fragmentation approach to the key C_{15} ketone (see eq 4).[32]

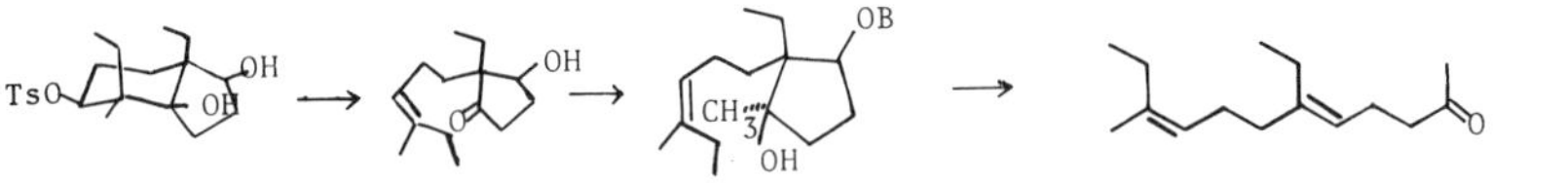

(4).

The Second Cecropia Hormone

Meyer, Schneiderman, Hanzmann, and Ko established the presence of a second substance with juvenile hormonal activity in their Cecropia oil extracts.[33] The ratio of this substance to the major active component (the latter shown to be identical to the above identified hormone) varied in each preparation from 1:4 to 1:10. By a combination of spectral techniques similar to the above, the minor component has been identified as methyl cis-10,11-epoxy-3,7,11-trimethyl-2,6-tridecadienoate 39. Its synthesis by techniques similar to the synthesis of the major component confirmed the spectral interpretation.[27a,29,34]

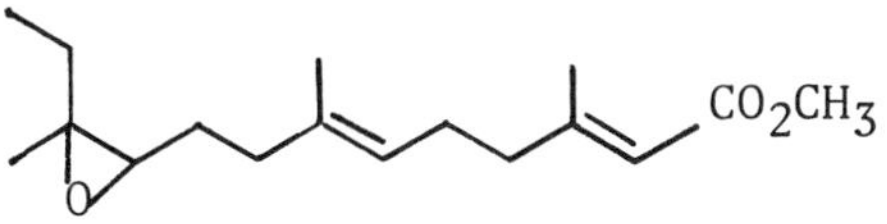

39

Absolute Configuration of Cecropia Hormone

Although the size of the original samples of pure
Cecropia juvenile hormone precluded determination of
optical activity, the similar biological activity of the
synthetic racemate to the natural material suggested
similar biological activity of both enantiomers. Meyer
and Hanzmann isolated over 1 mg of a 10:1 mixture of the
two Cecropia hormones 24 and 39. With this quantity
available they determined a normal positive dispersion
curve with $[\alpha]_D \simeq + 7°$.[35] Utilizing Brewster's rules for
the relationship of absolute configuration with the sign
of the dispersion curve, they suggested a 10R, 11S
configuration (i.e., structure 40).

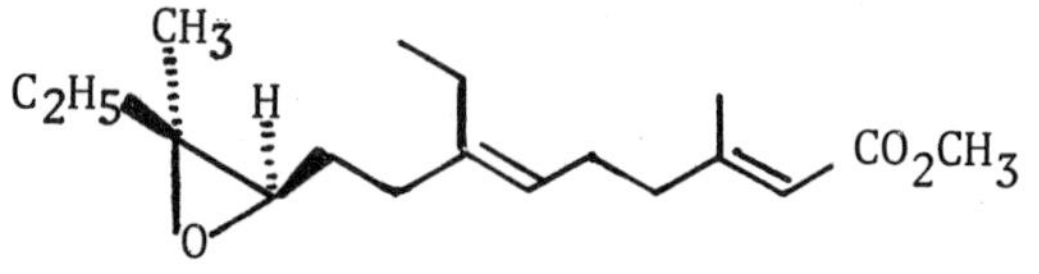

40

Utilizing a Claisen rearrangement approach, Loew and
Johnson[36] starting with optically active chloroketal 41
and Faulkner and Petersen[37] starting with optically active
hydroxyketal 42 synthesized optically active juvenile

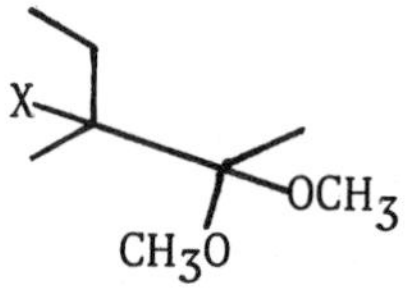

41 X = Cl

42 X = OH

hormone. Faulkner and Petersen determined the absolute
configuration of their hydroxyketal by converting it to
2-hydroxy-2-methylbutyric acid, a compound of known
absolute configuration. Thus, their synthetic juvenile
hormone possessing $[\alpha]_D^{23}$ +4.8° was assigned the 10R, 11S
configuration. Nakanishi and coworkers[38] converted the
synthetic juvenile hormone of Loew and Johnson into the
corresponding diol whose absolute configuration was
determined by a CD method. In this way, synthetic JH of

232

$[\alpha]_D^{20}$ +12.2° was assigned the 10R, 11S configuration. This sample of JH had 6-8 times higher biological activity than its enantiomer. The possibility that the biological activity of the enantiomer having $[\alpha]_D^{20}$ -11.7° may be due to up to 10% of (+)JH impurity was not discounted.

References

1. C. M. Williams, Sci. Am., 217, 12 (1967); Chem. Ecol., 103 (1970).
2. (a) P. Karlson, Angew. Chem. Intern. Ed. Engl., 2, 175 (1963); (b) P. Karlson, Pure Appl. Chem., 14, 75 (1967); (c) N. A. Tamarina, Usp. Soorum. Biol., 62, 415 (1966); (d) K. D.Highnam, J. Endocrinol., 39, 115 (1967); (e) C. E. Berkoff, Quart. Rev. (London), 23, 372 (1969).
3. K. Nakanishi, "7th International Symposium on the Chemistry of Natural Products," Riga (USSR), June 1970; Pure Appl. Chem., to be published.
4. a) R. Huber and W. Hoppe, Chem. Ber., 98, 2403 (1965); b) W. Hoppe, Angew. Chem., 77, 484 (1965).
5. a) V. Kerb, P. Hocks, R. Wiechert, A. Furlenmeier, A. Furst, A. Tangemann, and G. Waldvogel, Tetrahedron Letters, 1387 (1966); b) J. G. Siddall, J. P. Marshall, A. Bomers, A. D. Cross, J. A. Edward, and J. H. Fried, J. Amer. Chem. Soc., 88, 379 (1966); c) J. B. Siddall, A. D. Cross, and J. H. Fried, ibid., 88, 862 (1966).
6. For reviews, see a) B. M. Trost, Accounts Chem. Res., 3, 120 (1970); b) K. Slama, Ann. Rev. Biochem., 40, 781 (1971); c) V.J.A. Novak, "Insect Hormones," Methuen Press, London, 1966, p. 478.
7. P. Schmialek, Z. Naturforsch, 16b, 461 (1961); 18b, 513, 516 (1963).
8. a) M. Gabe, P. Karlson, and J. Roche, Comp. Biochem., 6, 246 (1964); b) V. B. Wigglesworth, J. Insect Physiol., 9, 105 (1963); c) H. A. Schneidermann, A. Krishnakumaran, V. G. Kulkarni, L. Friedmann, ibid., 11, 1641 (1965); d) V. B. Wigglesworth, J. Insect Physiol., 15, 73 (1969); e) V. Jarolim, K. Hejno, F. Sehnal, and F. Sorm, Life Sci., Part II, 8, 831 (1969).
9. W. S. Bowers, M. J. Thompson, and E. C. Uebel, Life Sci., 4, 2323 (1965).

10. J. H. Law, C. Yuan, and C. M. Williams, Proc. Natl. Acad. Sci., U.S., 55, 576 (1966).
11. M. Romanuk, S. Slama, and F. Sorm, ibid., 57, 349 (1967).
12. K. Slama and C. M. Williams, Proc. Natl. Acad. Sci. U.S., 54, 411 (1965); Biol. Bull., 130, 235, 247 (1966)
13. W. S. Bowers, H.M. Fales, M. J. Thompson, and E. C. Uebel, Science, 154, 1020 (1966); V. Cerny, L. Dolejs, L. Labler, F. Sorm, and K. Slama, Collection Czech. Chem. Commun., 32, 3926 (1967); J. F. Blount, B. A. Pawson, and G. Saury, Chem. Commun., 715 (1969).
14. B. A. Pawson, H. C. Cheung, S. Gurbaxani, and G. Saucy, J. Amer. Chem. Soc., 92, 336 (1970); K.Mori, M. Matsui, I. Yoshimura, and K. Saeki, Agr. Biol. Chem., 34, 1204 (1970); A. J. Birch, P. L. MacDonald, and W. H. Powell, Tetrahedron Lett., 351 (1969); K. Mori and M. Matsui, Tetrahedron, 24, 3127 (1968); K. S. Ayyar and G.S.K. Rao, Tetrahedron Lett., 4677 (1967).
15. W. S. Bowers, Science, 161, 895 (1968). For related structures see W. S. Bowers, ibid., 164, 323 (1969).
16. C. M. Williams, Nature, 178, 212 (1956).
17. C. M. Williams and J. H. Law, J. Insect Physiol., 11, 569 (1965).
18. A. S. Meyer, H. A. Schneidermann, and L. J. Gilbert, Nature, 206, 272 (1965).
19. H. Roeller and J. S. Bjerke, Life Sci., 4, 1617 (1965); H. Roeller, J. S. Bjerke, and W. H. McShan, J. Insect. Physiol., 11, 1185 (1965); H. Roeller, J. S. Bjerke, D. W. Norgard, and W. H. McShan, "Proceedings of the International Symposium on Insect Endocrinology, Brno, Czech., 1966," Academic Press, New York, 1967.
20. H. Roeller, K. H. Dahm, C. C. Sweeley, and B. M. Trost, Angew. Chem. Internat. Ed., Engl., 6, 179 (1967).
21. M. Julia, J. Julia, and R. Guegan, Bull. Soc. Chim. Fr., 1072 (1960).
22. K. H. Dahm, B. M. Trost, and H. Roeller, unpublished results.
23. W. S. Johnson, T. Ti, D. J. Faulkner, and S. F. Campbell, J. Amer. Chem. Soc., 90, 6225 (1968); S. F. Brady, M. A. Ilton, and W. S. Johnson, ibid., 90, 2882 (1968).

24. K. H. Dahm, H. Roeller, and B. M. Trost, *Life Sci.*, Part II, 7, 129 (1968).

25. K. H. Dahm, B. M. Trost, and H. Roeller, *J. Amer. Chem. Soc.*, 89, 5292 (1967).

26. H. Schulz and I. Sprung, *Angew. Chem.*, 81, 258 (1969); J. A. Findlay and W. D. MacKay, *Chem. Commun.*, 733 (1969); G.W.K. Cavill, D. G. Laing, and P. J. Williams, *Aust. J. Chem.*, 22, 2145 (1969).

27. a) K. Mori, B. Stalla-Bourdillon, M. Ohki, M. Matsui, and W. S. Bowers, *Tetrahedron*, 25, 1667 (1969); b) W. Hoffmann, H. Pasedach, and H. Pommer, *Ann.*, 729, 52 (1969).

28. E. E. van Tamelen and J. P. McCormick, *J. Amer. Chem. Soc.*, 92, 737 (1970); R. J. Anderson, C. A. Henrick, and J. B. Siddall, *ibid.*, 92, 735 (1970).

29. E. J. Corey, J. A. Katzenellenbogen, S. A. Roman, and N. W. Gilman, *Tetrahedron Lett.*, 1821 (1971); E. J. Corey and H. Yamamoto, *J. Amer. Chem. Soc.*, 92, 6636 (1970); E. J. Corey, H. Yamamoto, D. K. Herron, and K. Achiwa, *ibid.*, 92, 6635 (1970); E. J. Corey, J. A. Katzenellenbogen, N. W. Gilman, S. A. Roman, and B. W. Erickson, *J. Amer. Chem. Soc.*, 90, 5618 (1968).

30. W. S. Johnson, T. J. Biocksom, P. Loew, D. H. Rich, L. Werthemann, R. A. Arnold, T.-t. Li, and D. J. Faulkner, *J. Amer. Chem. Soc.*, 92, 4463 (1970); P. Loew, J. B. Siddall, V. L. Spain, and L. Werthemann, *Proc. Natl. Acad. Sci. U.S.*, 67, 1462, 1824 (1970).

31. For a review see J. A. Marshall, *Rec. Chem. Progr.*, 30, 3 (1969).

32. R. Zurfluh, E. N. Wall, J. P. Siddall, and J. Edwards, *J. Amer. Chem. Soc.*, 90, 6224 (1968).

33. A. S. Meyer, H. A. Schneiderman, E. Hanzmann, and J. H. Ko, *Proc. Natl. Acad. Sci.*, 60, 1853 (1968).

34. W. S. Johnson, S. F. Campbell, A. Krishnakumaran, and A. S. Meyer, *Proc. Natl. Acad. Sci. U.S.*, 62, 1005 (1969).

35. A. S. Meyer, E. Hanzmann, and R. C. Murphy, *ibid.* 68, 2312 (1971).

36. P. Loew and W. S. Johnson, *J. Amer. Chem. Soc.*, 93, 3765 (1971).

37. D. J. Faulkner and M. R. Peterson, *ibid.*, 93, 3766 (1971).

38. K. Nakanishi, D. A. Schooley, M. Koreeda, and J. Dillon, *Chem. Commun.*, 1235 (1971).

TERPENOID ROUTES TO THE SYNTHESIS OF HOMOJUVENATES

Patrick M. McCurry Jr.

Department of Chemistry, Carnegie-Mellon University
Pittsburgh, Pennsylvania 15213

Abstract

The Cecropia juvenile hormone, methyl-12,14-dihomo-juvenate (methyl cis-10,11-epoxy-3,11-dimethyl-7-ethyl-trans, trans-2,6-tridecadienoate) can be conveniently pre-pared from the readily available terpenoids isoprene, geraniol or trans, trans-farnesol.

Introduction

The structural similarities shared by the terminal epoxide of methyl farnesate[1] (1), and the two naturally occurring[2,3] juvenile hormones 2 and 3 are not without potential synthetic utility.

Because of the longstanding interest in the bio-organic chemistry of terpenoid terminal epoxides in the laboratories of Professor E. E. van Tamelen,[4] studies directed toward the synthesis of the hormone from <u>Hyalophora cecropia</u>, $\underset{\sim}{3}$ (JH), were undertaken. Out of these studies two new approaches to the synthesis of JH have recently been reported.[5,6] One of these pathways[5] involves the coupling of isoprenoid-like units and begins with either isoprene itself $(\underset{\sim}{4})$ or the C_{10} terpenoid, geraniol $(\underset{\sim}{5})$ while the other approach[6] entails the use of the C_{15} terpenoid <u>trans</u>, <u>trans</u>-farnesol $(\underset{\sim}{6})$ as the starting material.

The conversion of isoprene $(\underset{\sim}{4})$ into the ester C_5 moiety of JH required the introduction of (i) an oxygen at C_1, (ii) a <u>trans</u> double bond between C_2 and C_3, and (iii) synthetically useful functionality at C_4. All of these requirements were nicely fulfilled by extension of a reaction[7] first reported by Oroshinik and Mallory in 1950. The oxidation of isoprene $(\underset{\sim}{4})$ with t-butyl hypochlorite in the presence of protic solvents had been shown[7] to yield compounds of type $\underset{\sim}{7}$.

The choice of R was simplified by knowledge of an earlier[8] bio-organic approach to JH. It was found that a free primary allylic alcohol was not stable to conditions required to cleave other allylic groups. Specifically, attempted reductive hydrogenolysis of 8 gave a mixture of olefin migrated products, farnesol (6) and deoxyfarnesol.

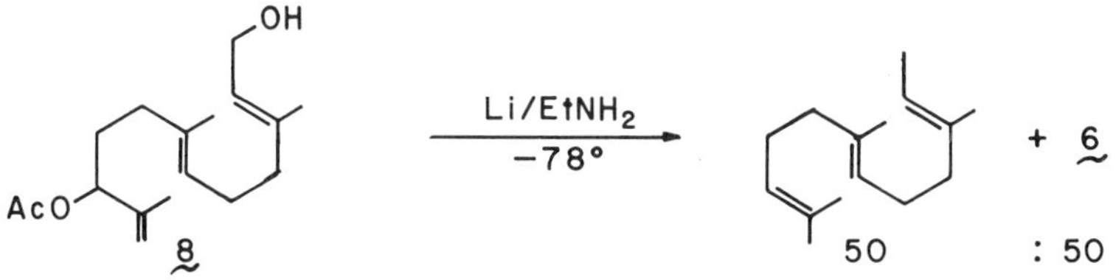

However, this difficulty could be overcome. Thus, geraniol could be quantitatively recovered under these conditions when protected initially as either its trityl or benzyl ether. An explanation for this difference is advanced below:

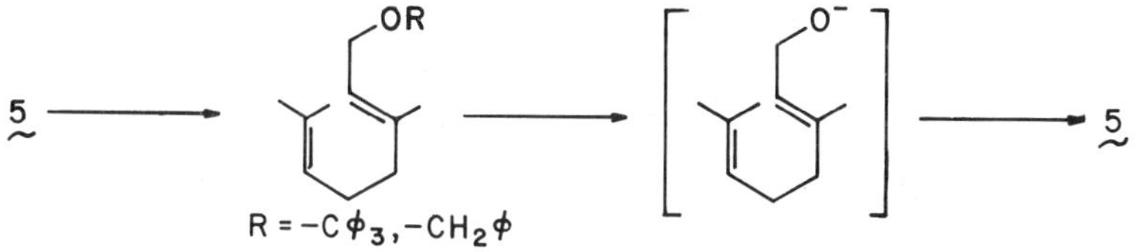

Operationally, it is seen that an allylic alcohol can be protected against reductive cleavage when exposed to the action of Li/RNH$_2$ in the form of its benzyl ether. The benzyl moiety was especially suitable for our future plans, and using benzyl alcohol as solvent, we were able to obtain the benzyl ether of trans-1,4-chlorohydrin 7a.

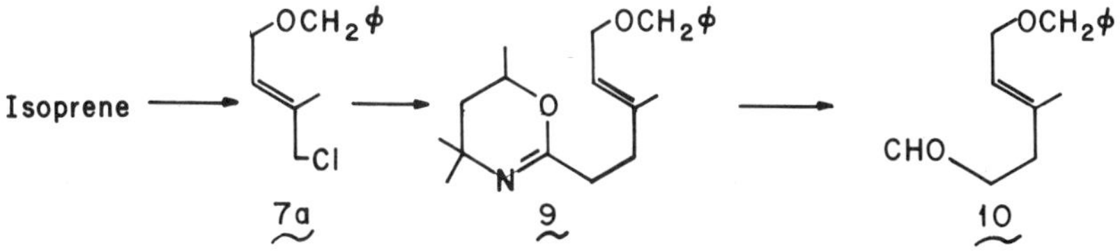

Conversion of 7a to the known aldehyde 10 was accomplished by using it to alkylate 2,4,4,6-tetramethyl-5,6-dihydro-1,3-(4H)-oxazine. The intermediate 9 was successively reduced and hydrolyzed to yield 10.

It was at this point that the preparations of JH from isoprene and geraniol merged.

The aldehyde $\underset{\sim}{10}$ is readily recognized as being tris-norgeranyl benzyl ether, and had been prepared[10] by the now standard sequence for the oxidative cleavage of isopropylidine groups.

However the normal procedure involves chromatography of both the bromohydrin and the vicinal glycol. Although we were able to modify this approach to allow preparation of $\underset{\sim}{10}$ from the benzyl ether of geraniol without isolation of intermediates, its efficiency left room for improvement. A much simpler method involved selective ozonolysis[11] of the apparently more nucleophilic C6–C7 double bond to produce $\underset{\sim}{10}$ directly.

Addition of aldehyde $\underset{\sim}{10}$ to the Grignard reagent from 2-bromo-1-butene produced the butenylcarbinol $\underset{\sim}{11}$ in high yield.

This type of compound had been encountered before in the Stanford laboratories. van Tamelen and McCormick had reported[5] the stereospecific homologation of geraniol via the following sequence:

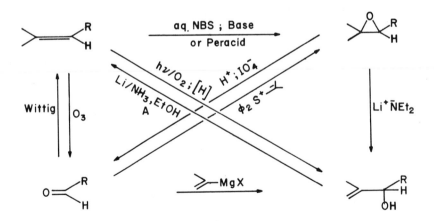

In this case the secondary allylic alcohol was produced by a Hofmann-like elimination[12] involving the epoxide group, in contrast to the Grignard addition.

The following scheme illustrates the methods available for interconverting these compounds.

Reaction A, the reductive cleavage of free allylic
alcohols, has been reported by Birch[13] and requires the
presence of ethanol and that one of the termini of the
allylic system be either primary or benzylic. The migration of the double bond is again observed, as in the
analogous cleavage of the allylic acetate.[8] This reaction
has also been carried out with ketones, i.e.,

and should prove useful as a general method for the
conversion of a carbonyl entity to an isopropylidine
function.

The $S_N i$ reaction of allylic alcohols used for the
conversion of the secondary allylic alcohol 12 to the
trans primary allylic chloride 13 constituted a novel trisubstituted olefin synthesis. This stereospecific reaction
has been postulated[6] to proceed via a six-membered chair-
like transition state, having the alkyl substituent R_1 in
the equatorial position.

When compound 11 was submitted to this reaction, the
primary allylic chloride 14 was obtained.

For the completion of the synthesis of JH, we considered two recent methods[14,15] available for the stereospecific head-to-head coupling of two allylic units. The preparations of the terminal C_6 units are shown below.

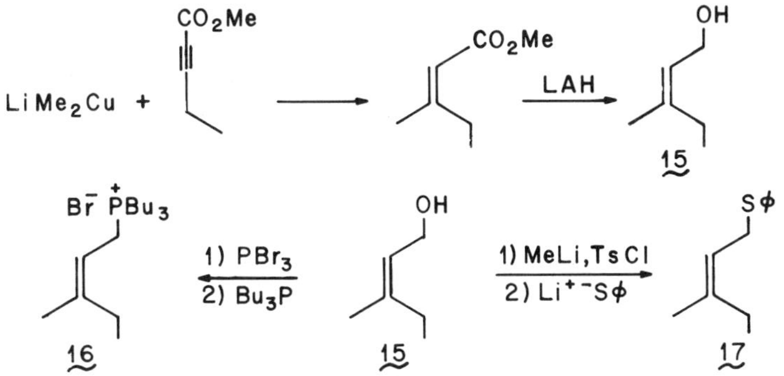

The allylic alcohol 15 was converted to both the phosphonium salt 16 and the phenylthioether 17. However, the ylid derived from the phosphonium salt 16 was, in our hands, not sufficiently nucleophilic to react with the allylic chloride 14 under conditions which avoided iso-merization of the olefinic linkage to produce a mixture of 16 and 16a.

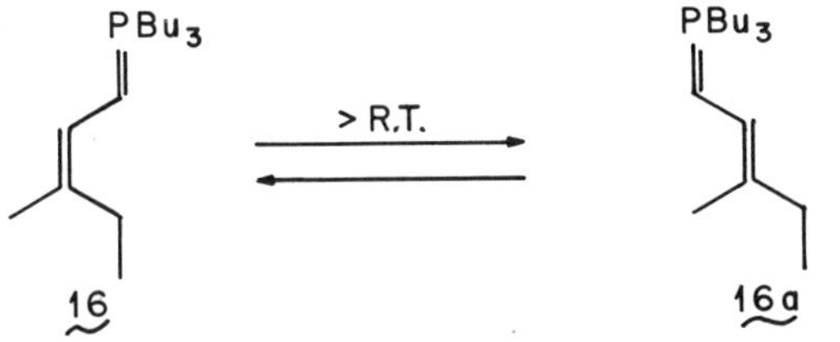

243

The sulfur-substituted anion derived from 17, on the other hand, smoothly reacted with chloride 14 to yield 18.

With compound 18 in hand, the basic carbon skeleton of JH was complete, and simultaneous reductive cleavage of the thiophenyl and benzyl linkages was accomplished using lithium in ethylamine at low temperatures.

The previously reported[16] oxidation (a,b) of the allylic alcohol 19, to the corresponding methyl ester and selective terminal epoxidation (c,d) completed this highly stereospecific synthesis of JH.

The conversion of trans, trans-farnesol (6) to JH requires i) bis homologation of both the C_7 and C_{11} methyl groups, ii) oxidation of the C_1 allylic alcohol function to a methyl ester, and iii) terminal epoxidation.

244

Steps ii) and iii) are precisely those described above and so the problem could be defined as the introduction of two methyl groups.

The homologation was achieved, albeit non stereo-specifically, by the following route

Farnesol, protected as its acetate, was selectively epoxidized at the two isolated double bonds, and after hydrolysis, the bis-epoxy alcohol 21 was obtained. This material underwent the double Hofmann-like elimination[12] when treated with excess lithium diethylamide in refluxing benzene. The primary alcohol function of 22 was then protected as its trityl ether in preparation for methylation. When 23 was acetylated and treated with lithium dimethyl-copper,[17] the undesired **trans**, **cis**, **trans** isomer corresponding to 19 was obtained.

t,c,t 19
(trityl ether)

This result is probably a consequence of a cyclic transition state, similar to that suggested[6] for the thionyl chloride rearrangement.

When 23 was converted to the unrearranged[18] dichloride 24, and then coupled with lithium dimethylcopper, a mixture of the isomers of 19 was obtained.

Cleavage of the trityl group and oxidation to the methyl esters permitted glpc separation of the desired trans, trans, cis isomer from the t,c,c: t,c,t: t,t,c: t,t,t geometrical isomers (1:2:1:1 ratio). Completion of this synthesis once again used the well-established terpenoid terminal epoxidation procedure.

1) Separate   1) MnO$_2$ 2) MnO$_2$,CN$^-$
                 ───────────────────────────── 3
                 3) aq. NBS 4) Base

Acknowledgment. The author thanks Professor E. E. van Tamelen for the opportunity to participate in this work and the National Institutes of Health for a Post-doctoral Fellowship to support his part of the work described herein, all of which was completed at Stanford University.

References and Footnotes

1. E. E. van Tamelen, A. Storni, E. J. Hessler, and M. Schwartz, J. Amer. Chem. Soc. 85, 3295 (1963).
2. A. S. Meyer, H. A. Schneiderman, E. Hanzman, and J. H. Ko, Proc. Nat. Acad. Sci. USA, 60, 853 (1968).
3. H. Röller, K. H. Dahm, C. C. Sweely, and B. M. Trost, Angew. Chem. Intern. Ed. Eng. 6, 179 (1967).
4. E. E. van Tamelen, Accounts Chem. Res. 1, 111 (1968).
5. E. E. van Tamelen and J. P. McCormick, J. Amer. Chem. Soc. 92, 737 (1970).
6. E. E. van Tamelen, P. McCurry, and H. Huber, Proc. Nat. Acad. Sci. USA, 68, 1294 (1971).
7. W. Oroshinik and R. A. Mallory, J. Amer. Chem. Soc. 72, 4608 (1950).
8. Unpublished work by the author at Stanford University.
9. A. I. Meyers, A. Nabeya, H. W. Adickes, and I. R.

Politzer, J. Amer. Chem. Soc. 91, 763 (1969).

10. K. B. Sharpless, R. P. Hanzlik, and E. E. van Tamelen, J. Amer. Chem. Soc. 90, 209 (1968).

11. G. Stork, M. Gregson, and P. A. Grieco, Tetrahedron Lett. 1391 (1969).

12. J. K. Crandall and L. H. Chang, J. Org. Chem. 32 435 (1967).

13. A. J. Birch, Quarterly Reviews (London) 4, 69 (1950).

14. J. F. Biellman and J. B. Ducep, Tetrahedron Lett. 3707 (1969).

15. A. H. Axelrod, G. M. Milne, and E. E. van Tamelen, J. Amer. Chem. Soc. 92, 2139 (1970).

16. E. J. Corey, N. W. Gilman, and B. E. Ganem, J. Amer. Chem. Soc. 90, 5616 (1968).

17. P. Rona, L. Tökes, J. Tremble, and P. Crabbé, J. Chem. Soc., D, 43 (1969).

18. G. Stork, P. A. Grieco, and M. Gregson, Tetrahedron Lett. 1393 (1969).

JUVENILE HORMONE ACTIVITY OF A VARIETY OF STRUCTURAL TYPES AGAINST SEVERAL INSECT SPECIES

M. Jacobson,[a] M. Beroza,[a] D. L. Bull,[b] H. R. Bullock,[c]
W. F. Chamberlain,[d] T. P. McGovern,[a] R. E. Redfern,[a]
R. Sarmiento,[a] M. Schwarz,[a] P. E. Sonnet,[a]
N. Wakabayashi,[a] R. M. Waters,[a] and J. E. Wright[b]

U.S. Department of Agriculture,
Agricultural Research Service

Abstract

Series of compounds were prepared and tested for juvenile hormone activity against Tenebrio molitor, Oncopeltus fasciatus, and a number of other species of insects. Included were aryl esters of citronellylcarbamic acid, alkyl and aryl esters of methylcitronellylcarbamic, ethylcitronellylcarbamic, citronellylcarbonic, 3-(citronelloxy)crotonic, citronellylthionocarbamic, citronellyldithiocarbamic, and β-substituted aminocrotonic acids, compounds related to sesamex (acetaldehyde 2-(2-ethoxyethoxy)ethyl 3,4-methylenedioxyphenyl acetal), and phenyl terpenoid ethers. The sesamex structures were varied by replacing the methylenedioxy group with other substituents and by modifying the side chain. The terpenoid moiety of the phenyl ethers included geranyl, 3,7-dimethyl-2,6-nonadienyl, citronellyl, 3,7-dimethyl-6-nonenyl, 3,7,9-trimethyl-2,6-decadienyl, and their 6,7-epoxides. Bioassays are described, data on activity are presented, and structure-activity relationships are discussed.

Introduction

The possibility that compounds exhibiting juvenile hormone (JH) activity might be useful in controlling insect

[a]Beltsville, Maryland   [c]Baton Rouge, Louisiana
[b]College Station, Texas   [d]Kerrville, Texas

pests led scientists in the USDA to synthesize and test
compounds for JH activity against a variety of insect species. This paper, which presents the results of these trials, includes a description of the bioassay methods and the
test results on more than 450 compounds. Compounds both
unrelated and related to cecropia juvenile hormone were
prepared for these studies.

Bioassay Methods

Tenebrio molitor (Yellow mealworm)   R. E. Redfern

Activity was determined by using newly-molted (2-24
hours)* pupae. Compounds were formulated to contain 10 µg/
µl in acetone, unless otherwise specified. Topical application was with a microapplicator fitted with a tuberculin
syringe and a 27-gauge needle. One µl of the solution was
administered to each pupa (10 pupae/compound) on the venter
of the last three abdominal segments. Vapor action was
determined by applying an acetone solution of 100 µg of the
candidate compound to the lower 1/3 of a 1-pint freezer
type fruit jar, evaporating the solvent, and then inverting
the jar into a 1/2-pint ice cream container holding 10 pupae. All pupae were held until the following molt (usually
ca. 5-7 days) to determine JH activity, signaled by the
presence of immature characters. Activity was rated from
0-4 as follows:

0 = Perfect adult, no JH activity
1 = Retention of gin traps or urogomphi
2 = Retention of both gin traps and urogomphi
3 = Intermediate—retention of both gin traps and
    urogomphi plus retention of pupal cuticle around
    area of treatment.
4 = 2nd pupa—retention of all pupal characters

The average rating (or activity) was calculated by
multiplying the number of pupae by their numerical activity
ratings and dividing the sum by the number of insects tested (the dead being excluded). For example, if 3 pupae
rated 3 and 7 rated 4, then $\dfrac{3 \times 3 + 7 \times 4}{10} = 3.7$

Compounds active in initial tests were diluted progressively and were tested until the average rating dropped
below 2.0.

Farnesyl methyl ether (methyl 3,7,11-trimethyl-2,6,10-dodecatrienyl ether) at 6.25 µg/µl** in acetone was used as the standard throughout. Controls (no treatment with chemical) were treated with 1 µl of the acetone solvent only.

* Pupae 2-8 hours old presently being used.
** FME at 10 µg/µl presently being used.

Oncopeltus fasciatus (Large milkweed bug)   R. E. Redfern

Activity was determined by using newly-molted (2-8 hours) 5th instar nymphs. Compounds were formulated to contain 10 µg/µl in acetone unless otherwise specified. Topical application was with a microapplicator fitted with a tuberculin syringe and a 27-gauge needle. One µl of the solution was administered to each nymph on the venter of the last three abdominal segments. Treated nymphs were confined to a 1/2-pint ice cream carton (containing food and water) by a plastic Petri dish top. All nymphs were held until the following molt to determine JH activity, signaled by the presence of immature characters. Activity was rated from 0-3 as follows:

0 = Perfect adult, no JH activity
1 = Perfect adult except retention of nymphal coloration in abdomen
2 = Adult with reduced wings and nymphal coloration in abdomen
3 = 2nd (supernumerary) nymph

The standard was sesamex.

Spodoptera frugiperda (Fall armyworm)   R. E. Redfern

Candidate materials were coated on the dry ingredients of larval rearing medium using methylene chloride. The solvent was evaporated and the dry ingredients were then blended with the remaining media, poured into plastic 5/8-ounce jelly cups, and allowed to cool. One 3rd or 4th instar larva was placed in each cup. JH activity was determined by the number of adults that emerged and was recorded as the minimum dose in parts per million (ppm) of the diet that gave a 50% reduction in adult emergence.

Bovicola bovis (cattle biting louse)   W. F. Chamberlain

Late 2nd instars were placed on diet coated with 50 ppm of the candidate material that had been dissolved in acetone at 0.001% active ingredient; 200 µl was used to coat 40 mg of diet. The diets were dried at 36–37°C for 1–2 hr, and lice were added. JH activity was signaled by the retention of immature characters in the normally adult 4th instar; e.g., absence of adult melanization in the abdomen or the absence or alteration of parameres in the male or gonapophyses in the female. Activity was rated I to IV as follows:

I. Typical melanization, typical parameres or gonapophyses.
II. Degree of melanization less than typical but observable on both sternites and tergites, parameres or gonapophyses present.
III. Melanization absent on sternites (may appear on tergites), parameres or gonapophyses typical.
IV. Melanization absent and parameres or gonapophyses absent or rudimentary.

Stomoxys calcitrans (Stable fly)   J. E. Wright

One µl containing 10 µg of chemical in acetone was applied topically to each pupa (less than 1 hr old), and the pupae were held at 27°C and 90% RH for 10 days. The treated pupae (25) were examined for pupal-adult intermediates (abdomen is pupal, head and thorax are adult), which do not eclose. Final evaluation was based on percent inhibition of adult eclosion. The percent hatching of eggs from treated insects that eclosed was determined.

Anthonomus grandis (Boll weevil)   Howard R. Bullock

Pupae less than 8 hours old were treated on their dorsal surface with several concentrations of the candidate chemical in 1 µl of acetone and then held for a week at 27° $\pm$ 1°C on moist filter paper in Petri dishes with a daily exposure to a 14-hour photoperiod. Chemicals were tested on 3 separate occasions. Retention of immature characteristics (e.g. urogomphi) in adults was considered unequivocal evidence of JH-like activity. Compounds were rated as follows:

++ active -- stopped growth and development in at
　　　　least 50% of the insects at 1 µg/pupa.

+ moderately active -- stopped growth and develop-
　　　　ment in at least 50% of the insects at
　　　　10 µg/pupa.

- less than moderately active.

Lygus lineolaris (Tarnished plant bug)　　D. L. Bull
Geocoris punctipes (Big-eyed bug)　　　　D. L. Bull

Activity was determined by using newly molted 5th instar nymphs.　Test compounds were formulated to contain 1
µg/µl of acetone, and 1 µl was applied topically with a
tuberculin syringe, fitted with a 27-gauge needle, to the
dorsum.　Treated nymphs were held individually at 27°C in
2-ounce ventilated plastic cups until the molt and surviving adults were held to detect possible sterility or development of latent effects.　JH activity was signaled by
deformation of adult appendages, development of nymphal-
adult intermediates that died soon after formation, death
while attempting to molt, and sterilization of surviving
adults.　Activity was rated from 0.3, as follows:

0 = Perfect adult, no apparent JH activity
1 = Adults with minor deformation of appendages
2 = Adults with major deformation of wings, legs, or
　　mouthparts; locomation and feeding seriously
　　impaired
3 = Insects do not survive or cannot reproduce due to
　　death of nymphs while attempting to molt, formation
　　of nymphal-adult intermediates that soon die, or
　　sterilization of surviving adults.

Aphis gossypii (Cotton aphid)　　　D. L. Bull

Second instar nymphs were held on cotton seedlings
that were treated by dipping in a solution of the test compound (1000 ppm).　The JH effect measured was the reduction
in the populations that developed over a 6-day test period.

Chrysopa carnea (Green lacewing)   D. L. Bull

Third instar larvae were exposed continuously to filter papers impregnated with 1 mg of the test compound. JH activity was signaled by failure to pupate and eventual death.

Preparation and Activities of Test Compounds

Since changes in the system of rating JH activity were made as the bioassay procedures evolved, the rating systems used in early comparisons differ somewhat from those described above. The comparisons of activity of the different structures are believed to be correct despite the lack of uniformity in the rating system.

Following the publication by Röller and coworkers (1) of the structure of the C_{18} cecropia juvenile hormone, we carried out a convenient nonstereoselective synthesis of this compound (mixed isomers) (2). We then decided to direct our efforts to preparing minor modifications of the JH structure to find out what structural features are necessary for activity.

The effect of ethyl branching on the activity of the methyl juvenate skeleton (formula of Table 1, $R_1R_2R_3 = CH_3$) was first investigated using the yellow mealworm (3). Table 1 gives the dose (μg/pupa) necessary to cause juvenilization (activity rating 1.0). It was concluded that the increased activity of ethyl branching as opposed to methyl branching at the C_7 position (R_2) was about 3 to 10 for this insect.

TABLE 1

Effect of Ethyl Branching on JH Activity in T. molitor

Compound			
R_1	R_2	R_3	Activity (μg)[a]
C_2H_5	C_2H_5	CH_3	0.03
C_2H_5	CH_3	C_2H_5	0.3
C_2H_5	CH_3	CH_3	0.3
CH_3	C_2H_5	CH_3	0.1
C_2H_5	C_2H_5	C_2H_5	0.3
CH_3	CH_3	CH_3	0.06

[a]
Dose required to give activity rating 1.0.

We then systematically eliminated double bonds and/or the epoxide group from methyl juvenate. The results are shown in Table 2, which lists the compounds and the minimum weight (μg) causing detectable retention of juvenile characteristics (4). The cecropia JH (mixed isomers) and methyl 10,11-epoxy-3,7,11-trimethyl-2,6-dodecadienoate are included as references. The removal of unsaturation in either type molecule drastically reduced activity. However, on Rhodnius prolixus, Wigglesworth (5) has reported that ethyl 6,7-dihydrojuvenate was one of the two most active compounds tested; it was four times as active as ethyl juvenate, which can be explained only by species specificity (assuming no difference between ethyl and methyl esters).

TABLE 2

Effect of Modifying Methyl Juvenate Unsaturation on
JH Activity in T. molitor

Compound	Activity (μg)[a]
Methyl laurate	>10
Methyl 10,11-epoxyundecanoate	>10
Methyl 10,11-epoxy-11-methyl-tridecanoate	>10
Methyl 10,11-epoxy-11-methyl-dodecanoate	>10
Methyl 3,7,11-trimethyldodecanoate	10
Methyl 10,11-epoxy-3,7,11-trimethyl-dodecanoate	>10
Methyl 10,11-epoxy-3,7,11-trimethyl-2-dodecenoate	>10
Methyl 10,11-epoxy-3,7,11-trimethyl-6-dodecenoate	>10
Methyl farnesate 10,11-epoxide	0.031
Cecropia JH (mixed isomers)	0.01

[a]Dose required to give activity rating 1.0.

Previous cyclization of the mixed isomers of cecropia
JH and of methyl farnesate 10,11-epoxide under acid conditions had given both monocyclic and bicyclic acids whose
esters were completely devoid of activity in Tenebrio;
this was additional proof that unsaturation was necessary
for significant activity in this insect (4,6). The effect
of modification of the epoxide end of methyl juvenate on
activity is illustrated in Table 3; again activity was
greatly reduced.

Since overwhelming evidence supported the idea that a
prerequisite for compounds to display high juvenile hormone
activity, at least in Tenebrio, was the possession of an
acyclic terpenoid skeleton, we prepared a number of

TABLE 3

Effect on JH Activity in I. molitor of Modification
of the Epoxide End of Methyl Juvenate

Compound	Activity (µg)[a]
	10
	25
	10
	15
	0.06

[a]Dose required to give activity rating 1.0

compounds (Table 4) with terpenoid backbones to which
various functional groups were attached. The compounds
were prepared by standard chemical methods (7). The activity of the carbamates (2nd-6th cpds.) was of considerable
interest since these were the first instances of compounds
with JH activity containing nitrogen as part of the chain.
The lack of significant difference in activity between
compounds 2 and 3 was in contrast with our previous findings (4), wherein saturation of any double bond in methyl
farnesate destroyed activity. Replacement of the epoxy
group with an aziridine diminished activity (compare
compounds 5 and 6). The most interesting finding was the
outstanding activity of compounds 9-11; compounds 10 and 11
showed a 30-fold increase in activity over our JH mixture
(compound 1). Compound 11 is also quite active on B.
limbata.

A number of terpenoid-aromatic hybrid compounds were
prepared and tested for JH activity on Tenebrio and
Oncopeltus (8). The unsaturated compounds are listed in
Table 5 and the saturated compounds in Table 6. Compounds
in Table 5 were prepared by epoxidizing the Wittig reaction
products between citronellal and the phosphorane derived
from the appropriate substituted benzyltriphenylphosphonium
halide and butyllithium in tetrahydrofuran; all compounds
were cis-trans mixtures, but compounds 1 and 2 were obtained as the pure trans and cis isomers by preparative gas
chromatography. Both of these compounds, which were active
on Oncopeltus, also gave 85% reduction in cotton aphid
populations at 1000 ppm. Compounds listed in Table 6 were
prepared by hydrogenation at atmospheric pressure, with
PtO_2 catalyst, of the appropriate precursors listed in
Table 5. All of the compounds but one showed greater activity in Oncopeltus than in Tenebrio; the average activity
in Tenebrio was generally unchanged or reduced when the
double bond was reduced, whereas in Oncopeltus the activity
was enhanced in several cases by saturation. In all cases
in Table 6, the most active compounds were para-substituted,
except when the substituent was methyl. Attempts to corre-
late activity with substitution in the aromatic portion of
the molecule showed no relationship between the electron-
donating or electron-withdrawing ability of the substituents and JH activity.

TABLE 4

JH Activity of Various Compounds With Terpenoid
Backbones on T. molitor

Compound	Activity (μg)[a]
	0.03
	3.0
	3.0
	3.0
	0.1
	1.0
	.1.0
	0.1
	0.03
	0.001
	0.001

[a]Dose required to give activity rating 1.0

TABLE 5

JH Activity of Unsaturated Arylterpenoid Compounds

| No. | R | Activity (μg)[a] | |
		Tenebrio	Oncopeltus
1	H (trans)	5.0	0.01
2	H (cis)	>10	0.1
3	o-chloro	>10	0.1
4	m-chloro	10.0	0.01
5	p-chloro	5.0	0.01
6	2-methyl	>10	0.1
7	3-methyl	10.0	1.0
8	4-methyl	1.0	1.0
9	2-methoxy	10.0	10.0
10	4-methoxy	5.0	1.0
11	2-cyano	10.0	1.0
12	4-cyano	10.0	0.1

a
Dose required to give activity rating 2.0.

TABLE 6

JH Activity of Saturated Arylterpenoid Compounds

| No. | R | Activity (μg)[a] | |
		Tenebrio	Oncopeltus
1	H	>10	0.01
2	o-chloro	10.0	0.1
3	m-chloro	5.0	0.01
4	p-chloro	1.0	0.001
5	2-methyl	10.0	0.1
6	3-methyl	10.0	1.0
7	4-methyl	>10	1.0
8	2-methoxy	>10	10.0
9	4-methoxy	5.0	0.1
10	2-cyano	>10	1.0
11	4-cyano	10.0	0.01

[a] Dose required to give activity rating 2.0.

The relationship of JH activity to position of the double bond was investigated with the compounds listed in Table 7; the compound having a double bond in a position beta to the ring was most active on Oncopeltus.

Since considerable JH activity had been demonstrated by at least one of the carbamates (compound 5) in Table 4, numerous alkyl and unsubstituted aryl carbamates and other amine derivatives were prepared by standard methods and tested (9). The carbamates, sulfonamides, amides, and amines prepared are listed in Table 8, together with their activity ratings on Tenebrio treated topically with 300 μg of the test compound. Compounds showing an activity rating equal to or greater than 2.0 were then tested at lower concentrations, and these results are reported in Table 9. The ethyl carbamates were slightly more active than the methyl carbamates, but the phenyl carbamates showed considerably greater activity. The methanesulfonamide derivatives of the amines (compounds 12-14) had very high activities; however, replacement of the methyl group by phenyl reduced the activity rather than enhancing it. The amides were practically devoid of activity. Among the anilines, the activity of the parent compound (compound 21) was not altered much by introducing chlorine atoms on the phenyl ring, even though the electron donating ability of the latter compounds is drastically reduced. The 2,3- and 2,5-dichloroanilines of R_1, not listed in Table 8, showed considerable activity against tarnished plant bugs and big-eyed bugs; the corresponding 2,4- and 2,6-dichloroanilines were inactive in these species but were very active against cotton aphids.

The activity of several thiono- and dithiocarbamates on Tenebrio is shown in Table 10. Replacement of both oxygens with sulfur appeared to enhance the activity.

Our lead with the phenylcarbamates was followed up by preparing 51 citronellylcarbamates of the more readily available phenols and testing them on both Tenebrio and Oncopeltus (10). Citronellyl- and geranylamines were prepared by reducing the appropriate oximes with lithium aluminum hydride. The phenols were treated with phosgene and triethylamine to convert them to phenyl chloroformates and these were then allowed to react with the appropriate

262

TABLE 7

Effect of Double Bond Position on JH Activity of
Arylterpenoid Compounds

Compound	Activity (μg)[a]	
	Tenebrio	Oncopeltus
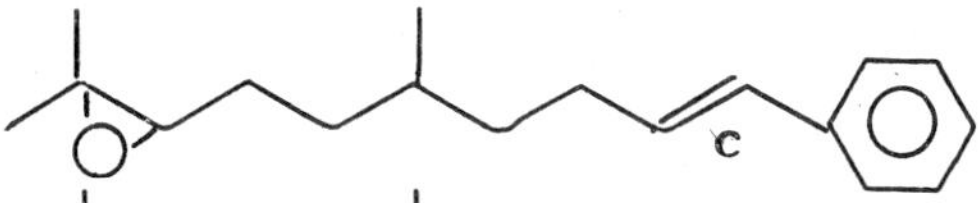	0.1	1.0
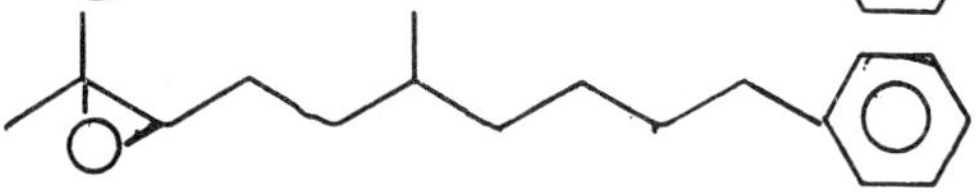	>10	1.0
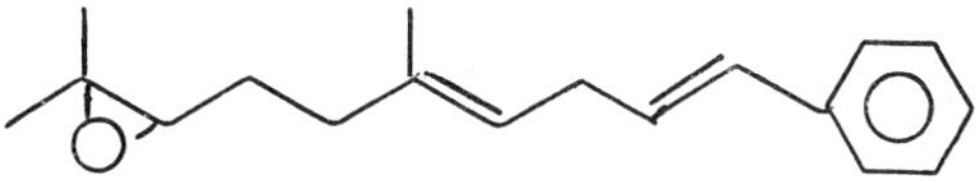	10.0	1.0
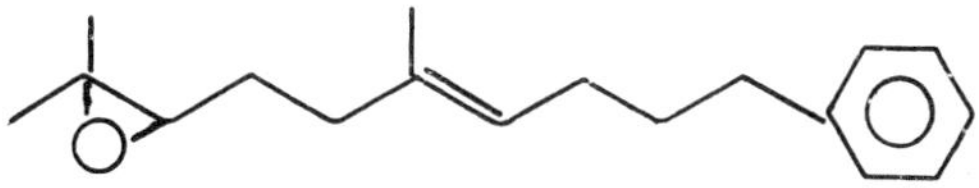	>10	0.1
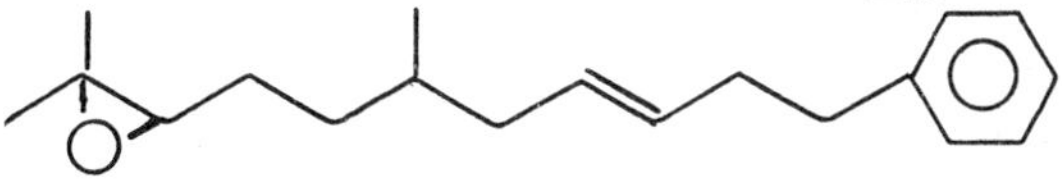	>10	10.0
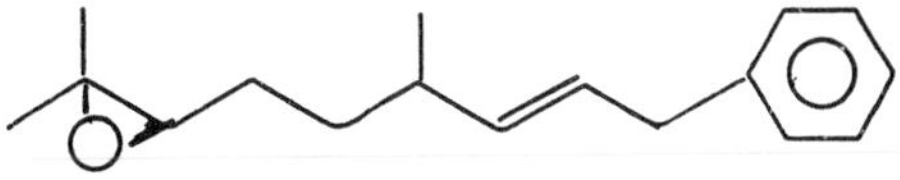	10.0	0.01
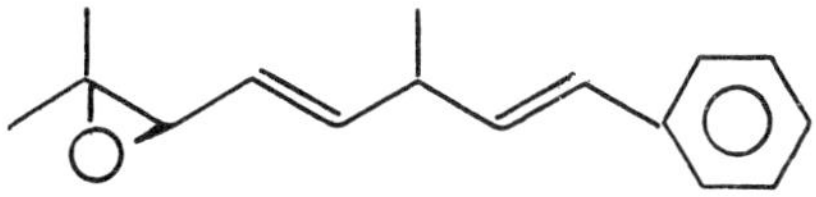	>10	>10

[a]Dose required to give activity rating 2.0

263

TABLE 8

JH Activity Ratings of Derivatives of Terpenoid
Amines on <u>T. molitor</u>

No.	Compound	Activity Rating[a]
1	$R_1NHCO_2CH_3$	4.0
2	$R_2NHCO_2CH_3$	4.0
3	$R_1N(CH_3)CO_2C_2H_5$	3.1
4	$R_1NHCO_2C_6H_5$	3.0
5	$R_2NHCO_2C_6H_5$	3.8
6	$R_5NHCO_2C_2H_5$	4.0
7	$R_4NHCO_2C_6H_5$	3.6
8	$R_5NHCO_2C_6H_5$	3.0
9	$R_1NHCO_2(CH_2)_2Cl$	2.8
10	R_1NCOO	0.6
11	$R_2NHSO_2CH_3$	2.0
12	$R_4NHSO_2CH_3$	4.0
13	$R_5NHSO_2CH_3$	4.0
14	$R_6NHSO_2CH_3$	3.8
15	$R_2NHSO_2C_6H_5$	0.0
16	$R_2NHCOCH_3$	0.0
17	$R_2NHCOC_2H_5$	0.0
18	$R_2NHCOC(CH_3)_3$	0.0
19	$R_2NHCOC_6H_5$	0.0
20	$R_3NHCOCH_3$	0.6

TABLE 8 (cont'd)

No.	Compound	Activity Rating[a]
21	$R_1NHC_6H_5$	3.2
22	$R_1NH-2-ClC_6H_4$	4.0
23	$R_1NH-4-ClC_6H_4$	3.2
24	$R_1NH-3-ClC_6H_4$	2.6
25	$R_1NH-2,4-Cl_2C_6H_3$	3.2
26	$R_1NH-2,3-Cl_2C_6H_3$	2.6
27	$R_1NH(CH_3)C_6H_5$	3.4
28	$R_1N(COCH_3)C_6H_5$	1.2
29	$R_1N(CH_3)CH_2C_6H_5$	1.4
30	$R_1N=CHC_6H_5$	4.0
31	$R_2N=CHC_6H_5$	4.0
32	$R_3N=C(CH_3)_2$	2.4
33	Farnesyl methyl ether	4.0
34	Acetone (control)	0.0

[a]All compounds applied at 300 $\mu g/\mu l$/pupa except compound 33, which was applied at 10 $\mu g/\mu l$/pupa.

TABLE 9

JH Activity Ratings of the Most Effective Compounds of Table 8 on T. molitor

No. in Table 8	Activity Rating at Dose (μg)				
	300	30	3	0.3	0.03
5	3.8	3.8	3.6	3.0	1.0
6	4.0	4.0	2.8	0.4	0.0
7	3.6	3.4	3.0	2.4	–
8	3.0	3.0	3.0	3.0	1.8
9	3.0	3.0	2.0	–	–
12	4.0	4.0	3.8	3.2	0.5
13	4.0	3.6	2.4	2.0	0.0
14	3.8	3.2	2.0	0.0	–
21	3.2	3.0	2.6	0.2	–
22	4.0	3.5	2.0	–	–
25	3.4	3.0	1.0	–	–
26	2.6	2.4	1.2	–	–

TABLE 10

JH Activity of Several Thiono- and Dithiocarbamates
on T. molitor

Compound	Dose (µg)	Activity Rating
	10.0 5.0 1.0 0.1	4.0 3.8 3.0 0.2
	10.0	1.6
	10.0 5.0 1.0 0.1	4.0 3.8 3.0 1.2
	10.0	0.2
Farnesyl methyl ether	10.0	4.0

amine in the presence of triethylamine to give the car-
bamate. The purity of all carbamates was determined by
thin layer chromatography, infrared, and NMR spectroscopy.
The activity ratings with 10-µg doses are shown in Table 11.
Only a few compounds were as active as the unsubstituted
phenyl ester (compound 3). The o-chlorophenyl ester (compound 37) was somewhat more active than the p-tolyl (compound 7) and the 3,4-(methylenedioxy)phenyl ester (compound
36). Only those carbamates showing considerable activity
against Tenebrio were even weakly active on Oncopeltus.
No striking increase in activity was obtained by adding
substituents to the phenyl ring, unlike the observations of
Bowers (11), Pallos and Menn (this Volume), and subsequent results reported here with geranyl phenyl ethers.

A series of 48 alkyl and aryl esters of citronellyl-,
methylcitronellyl-, and ethylcitronellylcarbamic acids and
the analogous β-substituted aminocrotonic acids were prepared and tested for JH activity on Tenebrio and Oncopeltus
(12). The same esters of citronellylcarbonic and β-
(citronelloxy)-crotonic acids were also prepared and tested.
The compounds and their activity ratings at 10-µg doses are
listed in Table 12. Citronellylamine reacted with alkyl
and phenyl chloroformates in the presence of triethylamine
to produce the corresponding carbamates (compounds 1, 3, 5,
7, and 9); the chloroformates had been synthesized from the
alcohols and phenols with phosgene and triethylamine. In
similar manner, the reaction between citronellol and these
same chloroformates produced the carbonates (compounds 35,
37, and 38). Lithium aluminum hydride reduction of 3 gave
N-methylcitronellylamine. Acetylation of the citronellylamine followed by reduction gave the N-ethylcitronellyl-
amines. The amines were converted to carbamates 16, 18,
20, 22, 24, and 26. Condensation of the amines with alkyl
and phenyl acetoacetates produced β-aminocrotonates 11-15
and 28-33. β-Alkoxycrotonates 41, 43, and 45 were prepared
by heating the sodium salt of β-chlorocrotonic acid with
sodium citronelloxide; the resulting acid was converted to
the acid halide with oxalyl chloride and then to the ester
by treatment with the appropriate alcohol.

TABLE II

JH Activity Ratings of Aryl Citronellylcarbamates and Related Esters

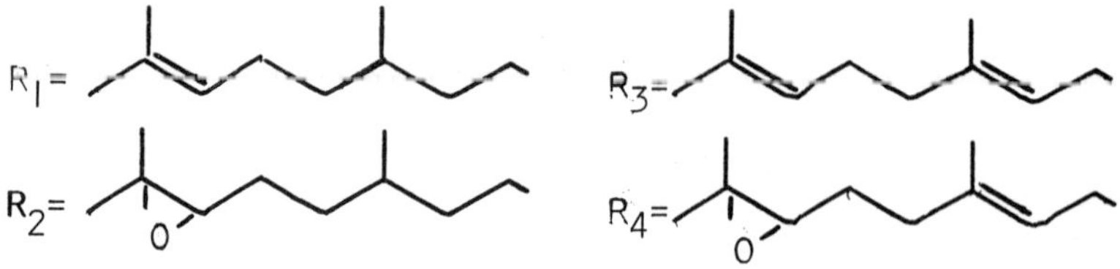

$R_1 =$

$R_2 =$

$R_3 =$

$R_4 =$

No.	Compound	Activity Rating[a] Tenebrio	Oncopeltus
1	$R_1NHCO_2C_2H_5$	4.0[b]	2.6[b]
2	$R_2NHCO_2C_2H_5$	4.0	3.0
3	$R_1NHCO_2C_6H_5$	3.6	2.8
4	$R_2NHCO_2C_6H_5$	4.0	3.0
5	$R_1NHCO_2-2-CH_3C_6H_4$	3.0	0.0
6	$R_1NHCO_2-3-CH_3C_6H_4$	2.6	0.0
7	$R_1NHCO_2-4-CH_3C_6H_4$	3.4	0.0
8	$R_1NHCO_2-2,3-(CH_3)_2C_6H_3$	0.4	0.0
9	$R_1NHCO_2-2,4-(CH_3)_2C_6H_3$	2.8	0.0
10	$R_1NHCO_2-2,5-(CH_3)_2C_6H_3$	0.0	0.0
11	$R_1NHCO_2-3,4-(CH_3)_2C_6H_3$	0.0	0.0
12	$R_1NHCO_2-4-(iso-C_3H_7)C_6H_4$	0.2	0.0
13	$R_1NHCO_2-2,6-(iso-C_3H_7)_2C_6H_3$	0.0	0.0
14	$R_1NHCO_2-4-C_2H_5C_6H_4$	3.0	0.0
15	$R_1NHCO_2-3-C_2H_5C_6H_4$	1.2	0.6
16	$R_1NHCO_2-4-(t-C_4H_9)C_6H_4$	0.0	0.0
17	$R_1NHCO_2-2,6-(t-C_4H_9)_2C_6H_3$	0.0	0.2
18	$R_1NHCO_2-2-OCH_3-4-(CH_2CH=CH_2)C_6H_3$	0.8	0.0
19	$R_1NHCO_2-4-(CH_2CH_2COCH_3)C_6H_4$	0.0	0.0
20	$R_1NHCO_2-2-(C_6H_5)C_6H_4$	0.0	0.0
21	$R_1NHCO_2-4-(C_6H_5)C_6H_4$	0.0	0.0
22	$R_1NHCO_2-1-naphthyl$	0.0	0.0

TABLE II (cont'd.)

No.	Compound	Activity Rating[a] Tenebrio	Oncopeltus
23	R_1NHCO_2-2-naphthyl	0.0	0.0
24	R_1NHCO_2-4-$(OCH_2C_6H_5)C_6H_4$	0.0	0.0
25	$R_1NHCO_2CH_2C_6H_5$	0.0	0.0
26	$R_1NHCO_2CH_2$-4-ClC_6H_4	0.0	0.0
27	R_1NHCO_2 cyclopentyl	3.0	0.0
28	R_1NHCO_2-4-$(COC_2H_5)C_6H_4$	2.5	0.0
29	R_1NHCO_2-4-$(CO_2C_2H_5)C_6H_4$	1.2	0.0
30	R_1NHCO_2-4-$(COCH_3)C_6H_4$	1.7	0.0
31	R_1NHCO_2-3-$(CO_2C_2H_5)C_6H_4$	1.0	0.0
32	R_1NHCO_2-2-$(OCH_3)C_6H_4$	1.4	0.0
33	R_1NHCO_2-3-$(OCH_3)C_6H_4$	1.7	0.3
34	R_1NHCO_2-4-$(OCH_3)C_6H_4$	1.6	0.0
35	R_1NHCO_2-2,6-$(OCH_3)_2C_6H_3$	2.0	0.0
36	R_1NHCO_2-3,4-$(OCH_2O)_2C_6H_3$	3.0	3.0
37	R_1NHCO_2-2-ClC_6H_4	4.0	3.0
38	R_1NHCO_2-3-ClC_6H_4	3.0	0.0
39	R_1NHCO_2-4-ClC_6H_4	2.8	0.0
40	R_1NHCO_2-2,4-$Cl_2C_6H_3$	1.8	0.0
41	R_1NHCO_2-4-BrC_6H_4	3.0	0.4
42	R_1NHCO_2-4-$NO_2C_6H_4$	3.0	0.0
43	R_2NHCO_2-4-$CH_3C_6H_4$	4.0	3.0
44	R_2NHCO_2-2-ClC_6H_4	3.0	3.0
45	R_2NHCO_2-3,4-$(OCH_2O)C_6H_3$	3.8	3.0
46	$R_3NHCO_2C_6H_5$	3.0[b]	–
47	R_3NHCO_2-4-$CH_3C_6H_4$	2.0	0.0
48	R_3NHCO_2-3,4-$(OCH_2O)C_6H_3$	2.8	3.0
49	$R_4NHCO_2C_6H_5$	3.0[b]	–
50	R_4NHCO_2-4-$CH_3C_6H_4$	3.0	2.0
51	R_4NHCO_2-3,4-$(OCH_2O)C_6H_3$	3.0	3.0

[a]Compounds applied at 10 µg/µl unless noted otherwise.
[b]Compounds applied at 30 µg/µl.

TABLE 12

JH Activity Ratings of Citronellylamine and Citronellol Derivatives

$R_1 =$ $R_2 =$

No.	Compound	Activity Rating[a]	
		Tenebrio	Oncopeltus
1	$R_1NHCO_2CH_3$	2.6^b	0.0
2	$R_2NHCO_2CH_3$	4.0	3.0
3	$R_1NHCO_2C_2H_5$	4.0	2.6^b
4	$R_2NHCO_2C_2H_5$	4.0	3.0
5	$R_1NHCO_2C_3H_7$	4.0	1.4
6	$R_2NHCO_2C_3H_7$	4.0	3.0
7	$R_1NHCO_2CH_2C\equiv CH$	4.0	2.6
8	$R_2NHCO_2CH_2C\equiv CH$	4.0	3.0
9	$R_1NHCO_2C_6H_5$	3.6	2.8
10	$R_2NHCO_2C_6H_5$	4.0	3.0
11	$R_1NHC(CH_3)=CHCO_2CH_3$	4.0	0.3
12	$R_1NHC(CH_3)=CHCO_2C_2H_5$	3.0	2.0
13	$R_1NHC(CH_3)=CHCO_2C_3H_7$	3.0	0.0
14	$R_1NHC(CH_3)=CHCO_2CH_2C\equiv CH$	3.0	2.4
15	$R_1NHC(CH_3)=CHCO_2C_6H_5$	0.4	0.2
16	$R_1N(CH_3)CO_2CH_3$	0.0	0.0
17	$R_2N(CH_3)CO_2CH_3$	1.3	3.0
18	$R_1N(CH_3)CO_2C_2H_5$	3.1^b	3.0
19	$R_2N(CH_3)CO_2C_2H_5$	0.0	3.0
20	$R_1N(CH_3)CO_2C_6H_5$	0.8	0.0
21	$R_2N(CH_3)CO_2C_6H_5$	3.0	1.8
22	$R_1N(C_2H_5)CO_2CH_3$	0.2	0.7
23	$R_2N(C_2H_5)CO_2CH_3$	3.4	2.5
24	$R_1N(C_2H_5)CO_2C_2H_5$	0.0	0.8

TABLE 12 (cont'd.)

No.	Compound	Activity Rating[a]	
		Tenebrio	Oncopeltus
25	$R_2N(C_2H_5)CO_2C_2H_5$	3.8	3.0
26	$R_1N(C_2H_5)CO_2C_6H_5$	3.0	2.0
27	$R_2N(C_2H_5)CO_2C_6H_5$	4.0	3.0
28	$R_1N(CH_3)C(CH_3)=CHCO_2CH_3$	0.2	0.0
29	$R_1N(CH_3)C(CH_3)=CHCO_2C_2H_5$	0.0	0.0
30	$R_1N(CH_3)C(CH_3)=CHCO_2C_6H_5$	0.0	0.0
31	$R_1N(C_2H_5)C(CH_3)=CHCO_2CH_3$	3.8	0.0
32	$R_1N(C_2H_5)C(CH_3)=CHCO_2C_2H_5$	3.0	1.2
33	$R_1N(C_2H_5)C(CH_3)=CHCO_2C_6H_5$	0.0	0.0
34	R_1N ⌬—$CO_2C_2H_5$	0.8	3.0
35	$R_1OCO_2CH_3$	0.0	0.0
36	$R_2OCO_2CH_3$	0.0	0.0
37	$R_1OCO_2C_2H_5$	0.2	0.4
38	$R_2OCO_2C_2H_5$	0.0	0.0
39	$R_1OCO_2C_6H_5$	0.0	0.0
40	$R_2OCO_2C_6H_5$	0.0	0.0
41	$R_1OC(CH_3)=CHCO_2CH_3$	3.0	1.2
42	$R_2OC(CH_3)=CHCO_2CH_3$	3.0	3.0
43	$R_1OC(CH_3)=CHCO_2C_2H_5$	3.7	2.8
44	$R_2OC(CH_3)=CHCO_2C_2H_5$	3.0	3.0
45	$R_1OC(CH_3)=CHCO_2C_6H_5$	1.3	2.0
46	$R_2OC(CH_3)=CHCO_2C_6H_5$	0.2	2.0
47	$R_1CH_2C(CH_3)=CHCO_2CH_3$	0.2	2.0
48	$R_2CH_2C(CH_3)=CHCO_2CH_3$	1.6	3.0

[a]Compounds applied at 10 μg/μl unless otherwise noted.
[b]Compounds applied at 30 μg/μl.

In Table 12 the carbamates and β-aminocrotonates with
the citronellyl radical and an alkyl group were roughly
equivalent in JH activity against <u>Tenebrio</u>. Replacement
of NH by NCH_3 or NC_2H_5 drastically reduced the activity.
Replacement of NH by NCH_3 or NC_2H_5 in the phenyl esters,
on the other hand, did not affect activity. The carbamates
and aryl carbamates were not significantly enhanced in activity against either of the test species when the citronellyl group was replaced by geranyl. However, a similar
substitution in the aminocrotonates did increase activity.
Perhaps a relationship exists between chain length and
requirement for internal stereoregulation. The longer
chain makes better use of an internal olefinic link while
the somewhat less flexible shorter chain experiences no
real advantage from it. In general, the unepoxidized
compounds (R_1) were more effective on <u>Tenebrio</u> than on
<u>Oncopeltus</u>. Epoxidation usually increased the activity on
both species, and the nitrogen-containing compounds were
more active than the oxygen analogs.

Following the report by Bowers (13) in 1968 that the
pyrethrum synergist "sesamex" (14) increased the JH action
of methyl juvenate and also produced morphogenetic changes
associated with JH activity by itself, we prepared and
tested a long series of related compounds (15). Since
sesamex had been selected from a variety of compounds on
the basis of its synergistic action with pyrethroids and
not because of its JH activity, it appeared probable that
related compounds might be more active, more stable, or
less expensive.

Compounds containing a (methylenedioxy)phenyl group
and their JH activity ratings against <u>Tenebrio</u> are listed
in Table 13. Modifications of the structure of sesamex
(compound no. 14) included variations in the number of
ethoxy units and end alkyl groups in the side chain of the
aromatic ring, replacement of the acetal group $-OCH(CH_3)O-$
by an ether, and the preparation of piperonyl acetals with
alkylethoxy groups, sulfonates, heterocylics, and a number
of other types of structure. Compounds with substitutions
on the phenyl ring in the 6 position (propyl, propenyl or
allyl group) were also tested.

TABLE 13

Juvenile hormone activity rating of chemicals containing
a 3,4-(methylenedioxy)phenyl moiety applied topically (10 μg
in 1 μl of acetone) to <u>Tenebrio</u> pupae.

No.	R	Avg. rating	No.	R	Avg. rating
1.		0.0	15.		3.4
2.		2.4	16.		2.4
3.		2.4	17.		2.4
4.		2.4	18.		1.4
5.		2.9	19.		1.3
6.		.0	20.		.0
7.		1.3	21.		1.9
8.		.0	22.		.6
9.		.0	23.		.2
10.		1.0	24.		1.0
11.		.0	25.		.3
12.		1.2	26.		.3
13.		3.6	27.		.3
14.		3.6[b]	28.		.5

TABLE 13 (cont'd.)

No.	R	Avg rating	No.	R	Avg rating
29.		.0	45.		1.6
30.		.0	46.		2.1
31.		.0	47.		.2
32.		.5	48.		.2
33.		1.7	49.		.1
34.		.0	50.		.1
35.		.9	51.		.6
36.		2.1	52.		2.3
37.		1.4	53.		2.3
38.		.0	54.		2.4
39.		.0	55.		3.1
40.		2.0	56.		.0
41.		.0	57.		.0
42.		.3	58.		3.5
43.		2.2		(Standard)	
44.		.0	59.	Control (acetone)	0.5

TABLE 13 (cont'd.)

No.	R	R'	Avg rating
60.			0.0
61.			2.7
62.			1.5
63.			2.3
64.			3.0

[a]See Bioassay Methods for description of rating system.

[b]Sesamex.

Sesamex was the most active of the series, rating
3.6 out of a 4.0 maximum. Of the two next best compounds,
no. 13 had a methylene group less than sesamex, and no. 15
had a methylene group more. The sesamex side chain therefore appeared to provide optimum activity. Compounds with
an ether grouping at the aryl-side-chain juncture (no. 1-5)
did not rate as high as the corresponding acetals (those
with $-OCH(CH_3)O-$); the best ether (no. 5) rated 2.9.
Benzyloxy structures (no. 38-48, 52), piperonyl acetals
(no. 32-37), the heterocyclics, and sulfonates varied in
activity between zero and 2.3. Compounds substituted on
the phenyl ring at the 6-position (no. 60-64) did not
achieve an activity high enough to encourage further study.
Interestingly, some compounds that were highly active as
pyrethrum synergists exhibited very little or no JH
activity.

In one test trial to determine effective means of
using JH-active chemicals, sesamex was applied to Tenebrio
at the rate of 10 µg/insect at four stages of its growth
(16). As shown in Table 14, the activity of sesamex varied
from no effect (0.0 out of 4.0), when applied to the last-
instar, to complete juvenilization (4.0 out of 4.0) when
applied to 0- to 4-hour-old pupae. These results demonstrate the criticality of timing in the application of
sesamex to Tenebrio (and very likely in the application of
other JH chemicals to insects). From a practical stand-
point, the data show that a JH compound should be long-
lasting because insects do not usually mature at the same
rate, and the chemical must be on hand in sufficient amount
when the stage of maximum sensitivity to the chemical is
reached if control is to be effected. Increasing the
number of applications could help, but there is a limit to
the number of applications that can be made economically.

Another obvious modification of the sesamex molecule
is the replacement of the methylenedioxy group on the
aromatic ring with other substituents. Compounds of this
type are apt to be less costly than sesamex since most of
the phenol and vinyl polyalkoxy ether intermediates used
in their synthesis (14) are potentially inexpensive. Table
15 lists compounds of this type (all containing the sesamex
side chain) with their JH activity ratings against Tenebrio

TABLE 14

JH activity of sesamex administered at 10 µg/µl/insect at 4 stages of development of Tenebrio

Stage of development	Avg. rating
Last-instar larvae	0.0
Pre-pupae	1.8
Pupae 0-4 hr old	4.0
Pupae 8-24 hr old	3.2

when the compounds were applied topically as well as in vapor form (15, 16). In the topical tests five of these compounds (no. 1-5) achieved the maximum rating of 4.0, and eight others rated 3.0 or better. Where comparisons could be made, meta or para substitution appeared to be superior to ortho substitution for high JH activity.

In the vapor tests two compounds (no. 1 and 10) rated 4.0, and three others rated 3.0 or better. The data indicated that vapor-phase application of JH compounds might be effective for some applications, e.g., protection of products stored within containers.

As part of our effort to develop the vapor-phase bioassay (see bioassay methods for Tenebrio), candidate chemicals plated out in the bioassay jar both above and below the pupae were tested (16). The results, given in Table 16, show that placement of the chemical above the pupae was superior to placement below in all but one instance. These results were not unexpected. Vapors of the organic molecules, being much heavier than air, tend to sink; the heavy vapors, when below the pupae, would have little tendency to rise (except by diffusion) and would therefore not be apt to contact the pupae to as great a degree. Should the application of JH compounds in vapor form eventually prove useful, placement of the chemical and the tendency of vapors to sink should be considered.

The compounds in Tables 13 and 15 most effective by topical application were evaluated against Tenebrio further by testing them at 10, 1, 0.1 µg/pupa (15, 16). Results are given in Table 17. Sesamex (no. 14 of Table 13) and

TABLE 15

Juvenile hormone activity rating [a] of candidate chemicals containing no (methylenedioxy)-phenyl group applied topically (10 µg in 1 µl of acetone) and as a vapor to Tenebrio pupae.

$$R-\text{C}_6\text{H}_4-\overset{\overset{\text{CH}_3}{|}}{\text{OCHOCH}_2\text{OCH}_2\text{CH}_2\text{OCH}_2\text{CH}_3}$$

No.	R	Avg. rating Topical	Vapor	No.	R	Avg. rating Topical	Vapor
1.	3,4-di-Cl	4.0	4.0	16.	2,4-di-Cl	2.2	0.0
2.	3-CH$_3$,4-SCH$_3$	4.0	2.0	17.	p-$\overset{\overset{\text{O}}{\|}}{\text{C}}CH_3$	2.2	0.0
3.	3,4-di-CH$_3$	4.0	2.5	18.	2-OCH$_3$,4-CH=CHCH$_3$	2.0	0.0
4.	p-SCH$_3$	4.0	3.0	19.	2-CH$_3$,4-Cl	2.0	0.0
5.	p-Br	4.0	2.2	20.	p-C$_8$H$_{17}$	2.0	0.0
6.	p-Cl	3.8	3.8	21.	m-$\overset{\overset{\text{O}}{\|}}{\text{C}}CH_3$	2.0	0.2
7.	p-CH(CH$_3$)$_2$	3.8	2.0	22.	2-OCH$_3$,4-CH$_2$CH=CH$_2$	1.8	0.0

No.	Substituent		
8.	m-Cl	3.6	3.6
9.	p-OCH$_3$	3.4	2.0
10.	p-CH$_3$	3.2	4.0
11.	m-OCH$_3$	3.2	2.0
12.	3-CH$_3$,4-S$\overset{O}{C}$H$_3$	3.0	0.0
13.	p-$\overset{O}{S}$CH$_3$	3.0	0.0
14.	p-C$_9$H$_{19}$	2.8	0.0
15.	H	2.3	0.2
23.	p-$\overset{O}{C}$OCH$_3$	1.1	0.0
24.	m-$\overset{O}{C}$OC$_2$H$_5$	1.1	0.0
25.	p-$\overset{O}{C}$OC$_2$H$_5$	0.9	0.0
26.	o-OCH$_3$	0.6	0.0
27.	2,3-di-CH$_3$	0.2	0.0
28.	2,5-di-OCH$_3$	0.2	0.0
29.	FME [b] (Standard)	4.0	2.8
30.	Control-(acetone)	0.0	0.0

[a] See Bioassay Methods for description of rating system.

[b] Farnesyl methyl ether used at a concn. of 6.25 µg/µl acetone.

TABLE 16

JH-Ratings of topically active acetals in vapor tests against <u>Tenebrio</u> (20 µg/pupa of test chemical placed above or below the insect; 10 pupae/treatment).

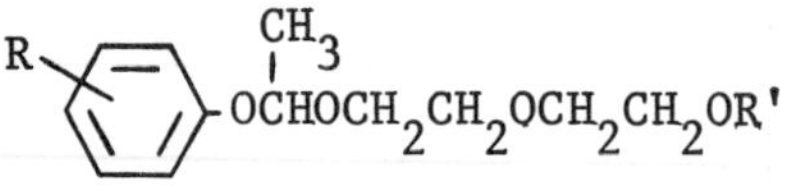

$R-\text{C}_6\text{H}_4-\underset{\underset{\text{CH}_3}{|}}{\text{OCHOCH}_2\text{CH}_2\text{OCH}_2\text{CH}_2\text{OR'}}$

R	R'	Avg. rating with chemical placed	
		Below	Above
p-CH$_3$	-C$_2$H$_5$	3.8	4.0
p-CH(CH$_3$)$_2$	-C$_2$H$_5$	2.4	4.0
p-Cl	-C$_2$H$_5$	4.0	4.0
m-Cl	-C$_2$H$_5$	3.8	2.6
3,4-OCH$_2$O- (sesamex)	-C$_2$H$_5$	1.6	2.6
3,4-OCH$_2$O-	-CH$_3$	2.0	2.6
3,4-OCH$_2$O-	-C$_3$H$_7$	2.0	2.0
F.M.E. (Std)[a]	-C$_3$H$_7$	3.2[a]	3.2[a]
Control (acetone)		0.0	0.0

[a]Farnesyl methyl ether applied at a conc. of 12.5 µg/pupa.

its higher homolog (no. 15 of Table 13) were the most active among the (methylenedioxy)phenyl compounds, and of those with other aryl substituents, 3,4-dichloro and m- and p-chloro (no. 1, 8, and 6 of Table 15, respectively) rated best among the non-methylenedioxy compounds.

Active JH compounds were further sought among phenyl terpenoid ethers, some being related to the aromatic epoxygeranyl ethers found active by Bowers (11). The twelve general structures shown in Table 18 were varied by changes in the aromatic substituents (17); compounds were tested as synthesized and are undoubtedly isomeric mixtures. The table gives the JH activities of the compounds in tests against the large milkweed bug, yellow mealworm, and the fall armyworm.

About half of the compounds in Table 18 are the olefin

TABLE 17

Juvenile hormone activity rating [a] of the 14 most active
test chemicals of Tables 13 and 15 applied topically
(0.1 to 10 µg in 1 µl of acetone) to <u>Tenebrio</u> pupae.

No. [b]	µg/µl / pupa	Avg rating	No. [b]	µg/µl / pupa	Avg. rating
15.(13)	10	4.0	3.(15)	10	4.0
	1	2.9		1	2.2
	0.1	2.3		0.1	1.4
14.(13)	10	4.0	2.(15)	10	4.0
	1	3.4		1	3.6
	0.1	2.1		0.1	1.2
13.(13)	10	4.0	9.(15)	10	3.3
	1	2.7		1	1.1
	0.1	0.8		0.1	1.0
1.(15)	10	4.0	4.(15)	10	4.0
	1	3.6		1	3.0
	0.1	2.4		0.1	0.6
8.(15)	10	4.0	5.(15)	10	4.0
	1	2.9		1	1.6
	0.1	2.2		0.1	0.4
6.(15)	10	4.0	11.(15)	10	3.2
	1	2.4		1	2.2
	0.1	1.8		0.1	0.2
10.(15)	10	4.0	29.(15)	Std. 6.25	4.0
	1	2.6			
	0.1	1.6	30.(15)	Control	0.0
7.(15)	10	4.0			
	1	3.2			
	0.1	1.4			

[a] See Bioassay Methods for description of rating system.
[b] See Tables 13 and 15 for chemical structures. Table
no. in parentheses.

TABLE 18

Juvenile hormone activity ratings [a] of phenyl terpenoid ethers in tests against the large milkweed bug, yellow mealworm, and fall armyworm.

I

No.	X	Large milkweed bug μg/nymph					Yellow mealworm μg/pupa					Fall armyworm ppm
		10	1.0	0.1	0.01	0.001	10	1.0	0.1	0.01	0.001	
1.	3,4-OCH$_2$O-	3.0	2.8	0.2			4.0	4.0	2.0	0.5		>50
2.	3,4-di-Cl	1.0					1.4					50
3.	3,4-di-CH$_3$	3.0	2.7	0.2			2.8	1.8				
4.	m-Cl	3.0	1.5				2.0					>50
5.	p-Cl	3.0	0.3				3.2	2.0	0.8			>50
6.	m-OCH$_3$	3.0	3.0	2.2	1.0		3.0	0.4	0.6	0.2		>50
7.	p-OCH$_3$	0.0					3.6	1.4				>50
8.	m-NO$_2$	0.0					0.2					>50
9.	p-NO$_2$	3.0	3.0	0.0			3.0	2.0	0.2			>50
10.	H	0.0					0.0					>50
11.	m-CH$_3$	0.0					2.0					>50

Structure II

No.	X	Values
12.	p-CH₃	0.0 — 4.0 3.0 1.2 0.0 — >50
13.	p-CH(CH₃)₂	0.4 — 4.0 1.4 — >50
14.	p-C(CH₃)₃	0.0 — 3.0 0.7 — >50
15.	3,4-OCH₂O-	3.0 0.3 — 3.0 1.8 — 4.0 4.0 2.4 — >10
16.	3,4-di-Cl	3.0 3.0 — 3.0 — 3.0 2.0 0.0 — >50
17.	3,4-di-CH₃	3.0 0.0 — 3.0 0.0 — >50
18.	m-Cl	3.0 3.0 — 2.3 2.0 0.0 — 2.6 3.8 1.6 — >50
19.	p-Cl	3.0 3.0 — 1.6 — 4.0 3.0 0.2 — 50
20.	m-OCH₃	3.0 3.0 — 1.6 — 4.0 — >50
21.	p-OCH₃	1.8 0.6 — 4.0 3.6 0.8 0.2 — >50
22.	p-SCH₃	2.7 0.6 — 4.0 3.8 1.0 — >50
23.	m-NO₂	3.0 1.0 — 0.0 — >50
24.	p-NO₂	3.0 3.0 — 3.0 1.4 — 3.0 2.2 0.8 — >50
25.	H	2.7 0.0 — 0.5 0.8 — >50
26.	m-CH₃	1.0 — 3.0 — >50
27.	p-CH₃	1.8 — 4.0 4.0 3.0 0.8 — 50

TABLE 18 (cont'd.)

No.	X	Large milkweed bug μg/nymph					Yellow mealworm μg/pupa					Fall armyworm ppm
		10	1.0	0.1	0.01	0.001	10	1.0	0.1	0.01	0.001	
28.	p-C$_2$H$_5$	3.0	1.8	1.4			4.0	4.0	4.0	4.0	2.0	
29.	p-CH(CH$_3$)$_2$	2.2					4.0	4.0	4.0	1.6	0.8	50
30.	p-C(CH$_3$)$_3$	3.0	0.0				4.0	4.0	1.2			>50

III

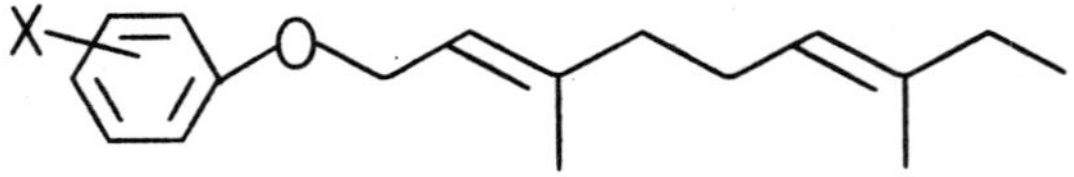

No.	X	Large milkweed bug μg/nymph					Yellow mealworm μg/pupa					Fall armyworm ppm
		10	1.0	0.1	0.01	0.001	10	1.0	0.1	0.01	0.001	
31.	3,4-OCH$_2$O-	3.0	0.0				4.0	3.2	1.0			0.1
32.	3,4-di-Cl	3.0	3.0	0.7			2.0	0.0				>50
33.	3,4-di-CH$_3$	1.2					2.0					>50
34.	3-CH$_3$,4-SCH$_3$	0.7					1.5					>50
35.	o-Cl	0.0					0.0					>50
36.	m-Cl	3.0	2.2	0.0			3.0					>50
37.	p-Cl	3.0	0.0				3.6					>10
38.	p-Br	3.0	0.0				4.0	1.6				>50

No.	Substituent							
39.	$o\text{-}OCH_3$	2.0			0.2			>50
40.	$m\text{-}OCH_3$	0.2			3.0	2.0		>50
41.	$p\text{-}OCH_3$	3.0	1.3		3.0	0.0		1.0
42.	$p\text{-}SCH_3$	3.0			4.0	3.4	0.6	>50
43.	$o\text{-}COCH_3$	2.8			0.0			>50
44.	$m\text{-}COCH_3$	0.0			1.0			>50
45.	$p\text{-}COCH_3$	3.0	1.6		3.8	3.0	0.2	>50
46.	$m\text{-}COC_2H_5$	0.0	2.8	0.0	0.0			>50
47.	$p\text{-}COC_2H_5$	3.0	3.0	0.0	0.0			>50
48.	$p\text{-}COCH_3$	3.0		1.0	0.0			>50
49.	$o\text{-}NO_2$	0.0			0.0			>50
50.	$m\text{-}NO_2$	2.0	0.3		0.0			>50
51.	$p\text{-}NO_2$	3.0	3.0		2.7	0.8		>50
52.	H	0.5			1.3			>50
53.	$o\text{-}CH_3$	2.0			2.0			>50
54.	$m\text{-}CH_3$	0.2			3.0			>50
55.	$p\text{-}CH_3$	0.0			4.0	1.0		1.0
56.	$m\text{-}C_2H_5$	3.0	0.0		3.0			

TABLE 18 (cont'd.)

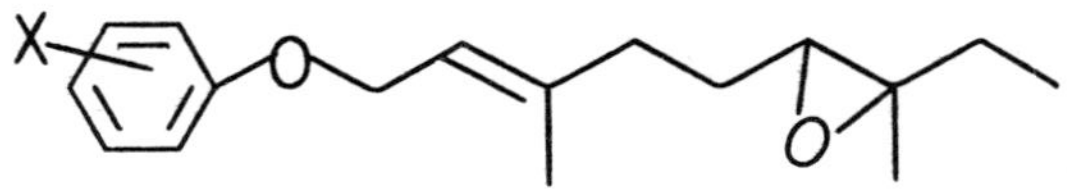

No.	X	Large milkweed bug μg/nymph					Yellow mealworm μg/pupa					Fall armyworm ppm
		10	1.0	0.1	0.01	0.001	10	1.0	0.1	0.01	0.001	
57.	p-C₂H₅	2.2					4.0	3.6	0.5			>50
58.	p-CH(CH₃)₂	0.0					3.8	2.4	0.0			>50
59.	p-C(CH₃)₃	0.0					3.5	2.0	0.0			>50
60.	3,4-OCH₂O-	3.0	0.3				4.0	4.0	4.0	0.6		>0.1
61.	3,4-di-Cl	3.0	3.0	3.0	2.2	0.2	4.0	2.8	0.6			>50
62.	3,4-di-CH₃	3.0	0.4				3.0	0.6				>50
63.	o-Cl	3.0	0.0				2.0					>50
64.	m-Cl	3.0	3.0				3.0	0.4				>50
65.	p-Cl	3.0	2.7	1.7	0.2		4.0	3.4	1.8			>10
66.	p-Br	3.0	3.0	1.7			4.0	4.0	2.0			50
67.	o-OCH₃	3.0	0.2	1.7			0.8					>50

IV

No.	R											
68.	m-OCH$_3$			2.0	0.0			4.0	3.5	0.8			1.0
69.	p-OCH$_3$			0.0	0.0			4.0	4.0	1.4			0.1
70.	p-SCH$_3$			3.0	0.5			4.0	3.8	1.2			>50
71.	o-COCH$_3$				1.2		0.0		0.0				
72.	m-COCH$_3$				1.6		0.2						>50
73.	p-COCH$_3$		3.0	2.0	0.0			4.0	4.0	2.8	0.5		>0.1
74.	p-COCH$_3$	3.0	3.0	2.0	0.0		3.0						50
75.	m-COC$_2$H$_5$				2.0		0.3						>50
76.	p-COC$_2$H$_5$	3.0	2.6	2.0	0.4		0.6						>50
77.	o-NO$_2$		3.0	2.0	0.0		0.2						>50
78.	m-NO$_2$			2.8	1.0		1.0						>50
79.	p-NO$_2$	3.0	3.0	3.0	1.0		3.0		3.0	2.8	0.4		>50
80.	H		3.0	3.0	0.0			4.0	4.0	0.4			>50
81.	o-CH$_3$		3.0	2.8	0.3			3.0	3.0	1.4			>50
82.	m-CH$_3$			2.0	0.2			3.8	3.0	0.0			>50
83.	p-CH$_3$				2.5			4.0	4.0	2.8	1.7		>50
84.	m-C$_2$H$_5$		3.0	2.7	0.0			4.0	2.0				
85.	p-C$_2$H$_5$			3.0	0.7			4.0	4.0	3.6	3.0	0.5	>1.0

287

TABLE 18 (cont'd.)

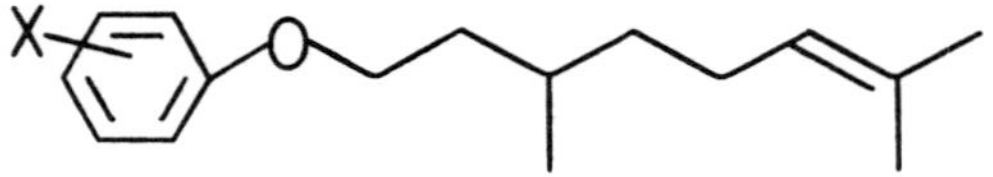

No.	X	Large milkweed bug μg/nymph					Yellow mealworm μg/pupa					Fall armyworm ppm
		10	1.0	0.1	0.01	0.001	10	1.0	0.1	0.01	0.001	
86.	p-CH(CH₃)₂	2.2					4.0	4.0	4.0	2.4	0.5	>50
87.	p-C(CH₃)₃	1.7					4.0	4.0	3.0	0.2		>50

V

No.	X	10	1.0	0.1	0.01	0.001	10	1.0	0.1	0.01	0.001	ppm
88.	3,4-OCH₂O-	3.0	3.0	0.0			4.0	2.6	0.0			>50
89.	3,4-di-Cl	3.0	3.0	0.2			1.7					>50
90.	3,4-di-CH₃	1.6					0.4					>50
91.	m-Cl	3.0	3.0	0.0			0.0					>50
92.	p-Cl	3.0	0.0				4.0	3.0	1.0			>50
93.	p-Br	0.0					0.0					50
94.	m-OCH₃	3.0	0.0				1.8					>50

288

No.	R							
95.	p-OCH$_3$	2.0	1.7		3.0	0.2		>50
96.	p-SCH$_3$	2.4	2.0	0.2	4.0	2.8	0.4	>50
97.	m-CCH$_3$ (=O)	0.0	0.0		0.2			>50
98.	p-CCH$_3$ (=O)	3.0	1.0		4.0	1.3		>50
99.	m-COC$_2$H$_5$ (=O)	0.0	0.0		0.2			>50
100.	p-COC$_2$H$_5$ (=O)	3.0	1.0		0.2			>50
101.	m-NO$_2$	1.2			0.6			>50
102.	p-NO$_2$	3.0	3.0	0.0	2.0			>50
103.	H	3.0	0.0		0.0			>50
104.	m-CH$_3$	0.0			0.4			>50
105.	p-CH$_3$	0.2			1.0			>50
106.	m-C$_2$H$_5$	3.0	0.7		1.6			>50
107.	p-C$_2$H$_5$	1.6			4.0	3.5	1.0	>50

289

TABLE 18 (cont'd.)

VI

No.	X	Large milkweed bug μg/nymph					Yellow mealworm μg/pupa					Fall armyworm ppm
		10	1.0	0.1	0.01	0.001	10	1.0	0.1	0.01	0.001	
108.	p-CH(CH₃)₂	3.0	0.0				3.0	0.0				>50
109.	p-C(CH₃)₃	0.8					2.0					>50
110.	3,4-OCH₂O-	3.0	2.0	0.0			4.0	2.6	0.0			>50
111.	3,4-di-Cl	3.0	3.0	3.0	2.4	1.5	3.0	0.0				>50
112.	3,4-di-CH₃	3.0	2.0	0.8			3.0	0.2				>10
113.	m-Cl	3.0	3.0	3.0	3.0	0.2	0.6					>50
114.	p-Cl	3.0	3.0	3.0	1.2		4.0	3.5	1.2			>50
115.	p-Br	3.0	3.0	2.0			4.0	4.0	1.5			>50
116.	m-OCH₃	3.0	3.0	2.0			3.0	0.0				>50
117.	p-OCH₃	2.8	0.4				4.0	0.5				>50
118.	m-CCH₃, O	3.0	0.8				0.2					>50

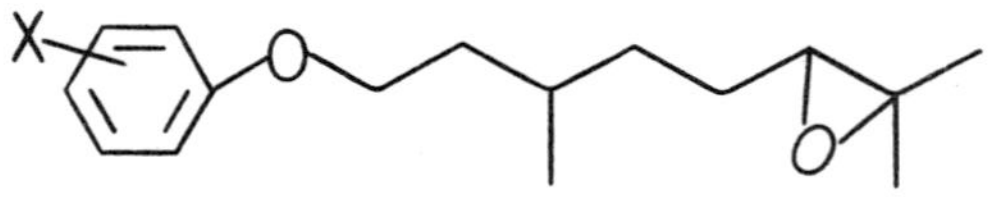

No.	R									
119.	p-OCH₃	3.0	2.0	2.0		3.0	2.7	0.0		>50
120.	m-COC₂H₅	3.0	3.0	1.8		0.2				>50
121.	m-NO₂	3.0	3.0	0.0		0.4				>50
122.	p-NO₂	3.0	3.0	3.0	2.0 0.0	2.6	1.6			>50
123.	H	3.0	1.8	1.0		1.2				>50
124.	m-CH₃	3.0	1.2			3.0	0.0			>50
125.	p-CH₃	2.0	0.2			4.0	1.2			>50
126.	m-C₂H₅	3.0	2.8	2.0		4.0	0.2			50
127.	p-C₂H₅	3.0	2.0	0.0		4.0	4.0	3.0	0.8	>50
128.	p-CH(CH₃)₂	2.0				4.0	2.6	0.4		50
129.	p-C(CH₃)₃	2.8	0.8			3.0	2.5	0.0		

291

TABLE 18 (cont'd.)

No.	X	Large milkweed bug μg/nymph					Yellow meal worm μg/pupa					Fall armyworm ppm
		10	1.0	0.1	0.01	0.001	10	1.0	0.1	0.01	0.001	
	VII											
130.	3,4-OCH₂O-	0.8					3.0	3.0	0.4			
131.	p-Cl	2.0					3.0	0.2				
132.	p-NO₂	1.8					2.0					
133.	p-C₂H₅	0.0					3.5	2.0	1.2			
	VIII											
134.	3,4-OCH₂O-	0.2					3.0	1.3	0.0			
135.	p-Cl	0.5					3.0	**3.0**	0.0			
136.	p-SCH₃	0.0					3.8	3.0	0.0			
137.	p-NO₂	1.6	0.0				2.0	0.0				

138. p-C$_2$H$_5$ 0.7   4.0   4.0   4.0   2.2   0.2

IX

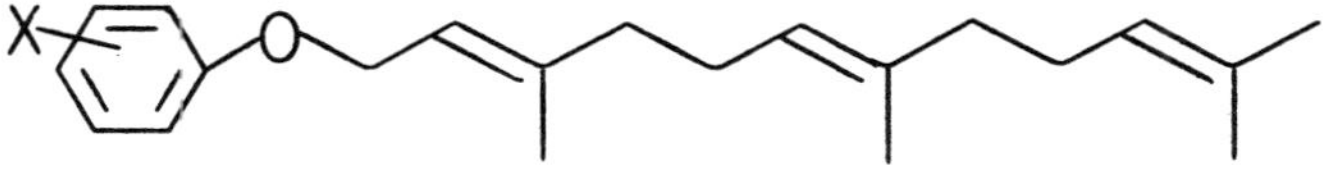

No.	X				
139.	3,4-OCH$_2$O-	2.0	0.0	4.0	3.0	0.2
140.	3,4-di-Cl	1.8		0.2		
141.	m-Cl	0.0		0.0		
142.	p-Cl	0.0		1.5		
143.	p-NO$_2$	1.3		4.0	2.0	
144.	p-CH$_3$	2.0	0.0	1.0		
145.	m-C$_2$H$_5$	0.0		0.6		
146.	p-C$_2$H$_5$	0.8		3.0	0.0	
147.	p-CH(CH$_3$)$_2$	0.0		0.4		

293

TABLE 18 (cont'd.)

No.	X	Large milkweed bug μg/nymph					Yellow mealworm μg/pupa					Fall armyworm ppm
		10	1.0	0.1	0.01	0.001	10	1.0	0.1	0.01	0.001	
148.	3,4-OCH$_2$O-	3.0	0.6				4.0	3.0	1.8			
149.	3,4-di-Cl	3.0	2.0	0.0				1.8				
150.	m-Cl	3.0	0.0					1.2				
151.	p-Cl	2.4	0.0				3.0	1.5				
152.	p-NO$_2$	3.0	2.0	0.0			4.0	1.4				
153.	p-CH$_3$	0.4					3.0	0.6				
154.	m-C$_2$H$_5$	1.0						0.5				
155.	p-C$_2$H$_5$	1.7					4.0	3.0	2.0			
156.	p-CH(CH$_3$)$_2$	0.2					3.0	1.0				

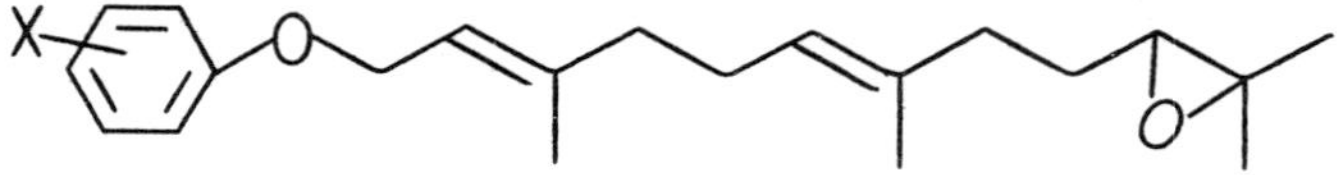

294

XI

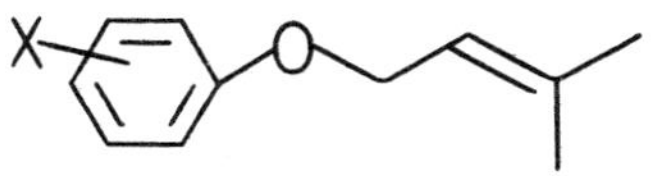

157.	3,4-OCH$_2$O–	3.0	0.0
158.	3,4-di-Cl	1.4	0.0
159.	m-Cl	0.0	0.0
160.	p-CH(CH$_3$)$_2$	0.0	0.0

XII

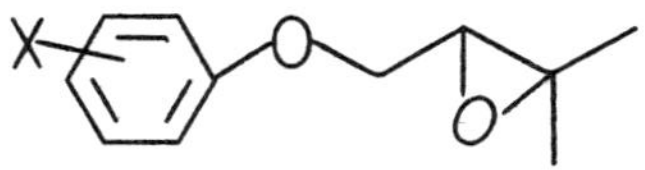

161.	3,4-OCH$_2$O–	3.0	0.2	1.0
162.	3,4-di-Cl	0.0		0.0
163.	m-Cl	0.2		0.0
164.	p-CH(CH$_3$)$_2$	2.2		0.0

ᵃSee Bioassay Methods for description of rating system.

295

precursors of the epoxy structures (epoxy group on double bond most distal from aromatic ring). The best epoxy compounds were generally more active than their olefin precursors, often markedly so. However, some of the precursors did exhibit appreciable activity, a result that suggests that the insects may epoxidize the compound. Despite its lesser activity in these tests, the olefin precursor might perform better than its epoxy analog in the field if the stability of the olefin greatly exceeded that of its epoxy analog. (Epoxides are known to be labile, especially to acid.)

Several features of the data in Table 18 are noteworthy. There is great disparity in the JH activity of compounds against the large milkweed bug and the yellow mealworm. Among the more active compounds, compounds highly active against the large milkweed bug are low in activity against the mealworm, and vice versa. The difference tends to be much less with compounds of low or intermediate activity.

Compounds found active against the fall armyworm were most often active against the yellow mealworm; however, the degree of activity of a given compound against these two species is often very different. Part of this divergence may result from the difference in the mode of administration, i.e. oral vs. topical.

Of the twelve structural types in Table 18 the most active compounds were those with epoxygeranyl (II), "epoxyethylgeranyl"* (IV), and epoxycitronellyl (VI) sidechains. Against the large milkweed bug, the most active of these contained 3,4-dichloro, m-chloro, and p-nitro as their aromatic substituents; furthermore compounds with these substituents rated high in each of the three series (structures II, IV, VI). The best three compounds, 3,4-dichlorophenyl 6,7-epoxycitronellyl ether (no. 111), m-

---

*Ethylgeranyl refers to 3,7-dimethyl-2,6-nonadienyl and epoxyethylgeranyl to 6,7-epoxy-3,7-dimethyl-2-nonenyl. The term ethylgeranyl, used previously by others, **shows** relationship to other terpenoids, but is deceptive.

chlorophenyl 6,7-epoxycitronellyl ether (no. 113), and p-nitrophenyl 6,7-epoxyethylgeranyl ether (no. 79), gave ratings of 2.4, 3.0, and 3.0, respectively, at 0.01 µg/insect. Against Tenebrio, the best compounds had the epoxygeranyl (II) and the "epoxyethylgeranyl" (IV) side chains; aromatic substituents of the most active compounds were 3,4-methylenedioxy, p-methyl, p-ethyl, and p-isopropyl. The most active compound, p-ethylphenyl 6,7-epoxygeranyl ether (no. 28), rated 4.0 at 0.01 µg/insect and 2.0 at 0.001 µg/insect.* Against the fall armyworm eight compounds with the ethylgeranyl (III) and "epoxyethylgeranyl" (IV) side chains had activity ratings below the 10-ppm level. (Only structures I through VI were tested against the fall armyworm.) The best compounds, which gave a 50% reduction in adult emergence at 0.1 ppm in the diet, are p-methoxyphenyl 6,7-epoxyethylgeranyl ether (no. 69), p-acetoxyphenyl 6,7-epoxyethylgeranyl ether (no. 73) and 3,4-(methylenedioxy)phenyl ethylgeranyl ether (no. 31).

Results of tests on the stable fly and the boll weevil are given in Table 19; only compounds with structures I-IV of Table 18 were tested. Compounds with the epoxygeranyl side chain were generally the most active against the stable fly. The best compounds, which caused 100% inhibition of adult eclosion at 0.1 µg/pupa, are 3,4-(methylenedioxy)phenyl 6,7-epoxygeranyl ether (no. 15), m-methoxyphenyl 6,7-epoxygeranyl ether (no. 20), and 3,4-(methylenedioxy)phenyl 6,7-epoxyethylgeranyl ether (no. 60). Interestingly, some of the compounds depressed or eliminated egg hatch without exerting much JH action. Of the compounds tested against the boll weevil, 3,4-(methylenedioxy)-phenyl 6,7-epoxygeranyl ether (no. 15) was best; it caused 100% juvenilization at 10 µg/pupa.

A review of the results of testing the extensive series of compounds listed in Tables 18 and 19 against the five insect species is impressive in the diversity of compounds turning up as most effective for the different species. These JH-active compounds appear therefore to be much more selective (or specific) in their attack than insecticides, which generally are effective against many insect species.

---

*Pallos et al. (18) previously described the synthesis and excellent morphogenetic activity of compound 28 and related analogs. See also chapter 13.

TABLE 19

Juvenile hormone activity ratings [a] of mixed ethers in tests against the stable fly and boll weevil

No. [b]	Stable fly						Boll weevil	
	% inhibition of adult eclosion					% egg hatch [c]	Activity	juvenilized %
	μg/pupa							10 μg/pupa
	10	1	0.1	0.01	0.001			
1.	100	100	9	0		95 (0.1)	+	
2.	30					98	−	
4.	53					d	−	
5.	14					96	−	
6.	74	0	0	0		98 (1.0)	−	
7.	0						+	
8.	19					73	−	
9.	13					98	−	
10.	8					98	−	
11.	18					86	−	
12.	53					90	−	
13.	0						−	
14.	12						−	
15.	100	100	100	57	4	80 (0.01)	++	100
16.	0					98	−	
18.	21					d	−	
19.	66					d	+	
20.	100	100	100	44	16	80 (0.01)	+	5

298

30

- + I + I I + + ++ + I II I I I I I I I I + I I + I + I I I I

Compound						%	(conc)
2J	16						
23	4						
24	25						
25	29						
26	84	66	12	8		98	
27	100	100	46	4		60	
29	100	92	48	12		d	
30	12				0	45	(0.01)
31	100	100	76	9		45	(0.1)
32	40					87	(0.1)
33	63					91	
34	0	0	4	4		93	(0.1)
35	54					98	
36	33	4	16	4		86	(1.0)
37	28					98	
38	22					d	
39	5					95	(1.0)
40	20					98	
41	13					98	
42	9					98	
43	32					98	
44	85	0	0	0	0	6	
45	14					98	
46	40					98	
47	17					98	(1.0)
48	42					98	
49	17					98	
50	35					85	
51	5					98	

TABLE 19 (cont'd.)

	Stable fly						Boll weevil	
	% inhibition of adult eclosion							
	μg/pupa							% juvenilized
No. [b]	10	1	0.1	0.01	0.001	% egg [c] hatch	Activity	10/μg/pupa
52.	15					86	–	
53.	36					98	–	
54.	35					60	–	
55.	28					98	–	
58.	53					d	–	
59.	0					98	–	
60.	100	100	100	40		85 (0.01)	++	10
61.	43					d	–	
62.	40					98	–	
63.	36					d	–	
64.	100	4	8	17		98	+	
65.	20						+	10
66.	22						–	
67.	0					90	+	
68.	13					43	–	
69.	100	100	40	0		90	–	
71.	8					98	–	
72.	20					98	–	
73.	53					98	‡‡	
74.	10					98	‡‡	
75.	0					98	–	

76.	4				56	++	10
77.	14				98	−	
78.	25				70	−	
79.	10				98	−	
80.	4				95		
81.	100	8	4	20	98 (1.0)	−	
82.	36				d	−	
83.	100	74	17	17	83 (1.0)	−	
86.	13				d	++	10
87.	9					+	10

a See Bioassay Methods for description of rating system.

b See Table 18 for chemical structure.

c At a concn. of 10 μg/pupa except where noted in parenthesis.

d No eggs.

References

1. H. Röller, K. H. Dahm, C. C. Sweely, and B. M. Trost, Angew. Chem. 79, 190 (1967).
2. B. H. Braun, M. Jacobson, M. Schwarz, P. E. Sonnet, N. Wakabayashi, and R. M. Waters, J. Econ. Entomol. 61, 866 (1968).
3. M. Schwarz, B. H. Braun, M. W. Law, P. E. Sonnet, N. Wakabayashi, R. M. Waters, and M. Jacobson, Ann. Entomol. Soc. Am. 62, 668 (1969).
4. N. Wakabayashi, P. E. Sonnet, and M. W. Law, J. Med. Chem. 12, 911 (1969).
5. V. B. Wigglesworth, J. Insect Physiol. 15, 73 (1969).
6. P. E. Sonnet, B. H. Braun, M. W. Law, M. Schwarz, N. Wakabayashi, R. M. Waters, and M. Jacobson, Ann. Entomol. Soc. Am. 62, 667 (1969).
7. M. Schwarz, P. E. Sonnet, and N. Wakabayashi, Science 167, 191 (1970).
8. M. Schwarz, R. E. Redfern, R. M. Waters, N. Wakabayashi, and P. E. Sonnet, Life Sci. 10, Part II, 1125 (1971).
9. M. Schwarz, N. Wakabayashi, P. E. Sonnet, and R. E. Redfern, J. Econ. Entomol. 63, 1858 (1970).
10. P. E. Sonnet, R. E. Redfern, M. Schwarz, N. Wakabayashi, and R. M. Waters, J. Econ. Entomol. 64, 1378 (1971).
11. W. S. Bowers, Science 164, 323 (1969).
12. P. E. Sonnet, R. M. Waters, R. E. Redfern, M. Schwarz, and N. Wakabayashi, J. Agr. Food Chem. 20, 65 (1972).
13. W. S. Bowers, Science 161, 895 (1968).
14. M. Beroza, J. Agr. Food Chem. 4, 49 (1956).
15. R. E. Redfern, T. P. McGovern, and M. Beroza, J. Econ. Entomol. 63, 540 (1970).
16. T. P. McGovern, R. E. Redfern, and M. Beroza, J. Econ. Entomol. 64, 238 (1971).
17. R. E. Redfern, T. P. McGovern, R. Sarmiento, and M. Beroza, J. Econ. Entomol. 64, 374 (1971).
18. F. M. Pallos, J. J. Menn, P. E. Letchworth, and J. B. Miaullis, Nature 232, 486 (1971).

SYNTHESIS AND ACTIVITY OF
JUVENILE HORMONE ANALOGS

Ferenc M. Pallos
Western Research Center
Stauffer Chemical Company
Richmond, California 94804

Julius J. Menn
Agricultural Research Center
Stauffer Chemical Company
Mountain View, California 94040

Abstract

Several series of terpenoid derivatives were synthesized and bioassayed for juvenile hormone activity in
Tenebrio molitor, Culex pipiens q. and several other insect
species. Among these, certain aromatic ethers of geraniol
and their epoxides showed potent juvenoid activity.
Structure activity studies revealed that para-substituted
phenyl geranyl ether epoxides, and specifically 1-(4'-
ethylphenoxy)-6,7-epoxy-3,7-dimethyl-2-octene, consistently
displayed the highest order of morphogenetic activity in
the tests which are described.

Introduction

In a prophetic statement, Carroll Williams wrote 15
years ago that, "It seems likely that the (juvenile)
hormone, when identified and synthesized, will prove to be
an effective insecticide" (1).

This prophesy has now come close to reality and has
given major impetus to the initiation of a new technology
in the control and management of insects.

A recent review (2) lists 172 references on the
subject of the juvenile hormone (J.H.) of insects and

juvenile hormone analogs (J.H.A.). The reader is also referred to several chapters in this book and to other recently published, noteworthy reviews on this subject (3, 4,5,6).

It has recently become apparent that terpene derivatives other than farnesol possess significant juvenoid activity. Bowers (7) obtained excellent antimetamorphic activity with certain aromatic terpenoid ethers when bioassayed on the yellow mealworm, Tenebrio molitor L., and the milkweed bug, Oncopeltus fasciatus (Dallas). Some of these compounds showed a much higher order of morphogenetic activity than the major, natural J.H. of Cecropia silk moth.

The discovery by Bowers that certain geraniol derivatives display a high order of J.H.-type activity suggested to us that further chemical modifications in this class of terpene derivatives may result in other highly active compounds.

Methods, Results and Discussion

Initially, we synthesized a number of 6,7-epoxy-geranyl methyl substituted acrylates (8).

The relation of chemical structure, in this group of compounds, to morphogenetic activity in the yellow mealworm and mosquito larvae (Culex pipiens quinquefasciatus, Say), and ovicidal action in milkweed bug eggs, is shown in Table 1.

The testing procedures used are as follows: Test compounds are topically applied in acetone (1 µl) to the abdomens of yellow mealworm pupae less than 24 hr old. Treated pupae are incubated for seven days at 28°C. Abnormal developmental effects considered in the assay include: retention of urogomphi, gin traps, pupal cuticle, and formation of adult-larval intermediates (9). Ten late fourth instar (prepupal) mosquito larvae are placed in 100 ml water containing the test compounds in graded concentrations. The treated larvae are maintained at 24°C and held until all the control mosquitoes have emerged as adults. Percent adult emergence of treated larvae is recorded and

TABLE 1

Morphogenetic and Ovicidal Activity
of Certain Geranyl Ester Epoxides

Code	R	ED_{50} [a]		
		T. molitor μg/pupa	C. pipiens q. ppm/10 larvae	O. fasciatus ppm/egg cluster
1~		10	>1	>1000
2~		5	>1	>1000
3~		5	0.1	>1000

[a] Effective dose resulting in abnormal development or failure to hatch of 50% of treated test organisms.

ED_{50} values are established.

Ovicidal effects are assayed on freshly oviposited milkweed bug egg clusters (50-75 eggs per cluster) by dipping for two seconds in a two ml acetone solution of the test compounds. Treated eggs are held in containers provided with water and milkweed seeds, maintained, and observed for egg hatch and nymphal development.

Esters 1, 2, and 3 (Table 1) show marginal morphogenetic activity on T. molitor and C. pipiens q. Only compound 3 showed partial inhibition of normal adult hatch at 0.1 ppm. Essentially, no abnormalities were observed in the development and hatching of milkweed bug eggs treated with 1000 ppm of the test compounds (1, 2, and 3). Riddiford (10) found that topical application of as little as 0.25 µg J.H. to milkweed bug eggs prior to blastokinesis resulted in significant delayed metamorphic effects resulting in production of abnormal adultoids and reduction in metamorphosis to normal adults. However, Riddiford (10) observed normal hatching of treated eggs.

The marginal biological activity of these simple geranyl esters suggested to us the feasibility of further synthesis of related, relatively uncomplicated, aromatic geranyl derivatives of the type reported by Bowers (7).

These compounds were synthesized from geranyl bromide by treatment with m-chloroperbenzoic acid to form the epoxide, which is reacted with appropriate phenols by refluxing in acetone in the presence of anhydrous potassium carbonate to form the final products. Geranyl bromide was used directly in the ether synthesis of the unepoxidized compounds. Structures were confirmed by infrared, nuclear magnetic resonance and mass spectral data (9).

Unsubstituted phenyl compounds 4 and 5 show marginal activity in the yellow mealworm assay, as shown in Table 2. However, substitution of halogens on the aromatic ring strongly enhances morphogenetic activity (Table 3). Para substitution of chlorine results in higher activity than meta substitution (6 and 8). This relationship is even more pronounced in the case of the respective epoxidized forms 7 and 9. Furthermore, compound 9 is 100-fold more

306

TABLE 2

Morphogenetic Activity of
Unsubstituted Phenyl Geranyl Ethers

Code	Structure	ED_{50}[a] T. molitor μg/pupa
4	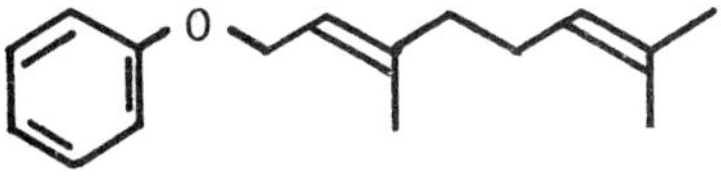	30
5	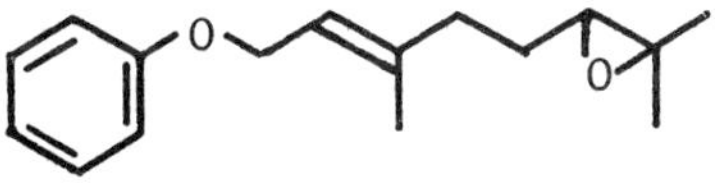	5

[a]Effective dose resulting in abnormal development
of 50% of treated pupae.

TABLE 3

Morphogenetic Activity of Chloro Phenyl
Geranyl Ethers on T. molitor Pupae

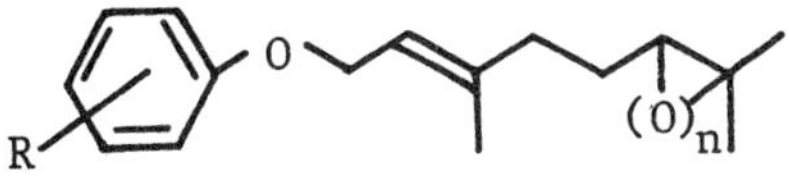

		ED_{50}[a] (μg/pupa)		Ratio $\dfrac{n=0}{n=1}$
Code	R	n=0	n=1	
6	m-Cl	60		6
7	m-Cl		10.0	
8	p-Cl	1		10
9	p-Cl		0.1	

[a]Effective dose resulting in abnormal development
of 50% of treated pupae.

active than the epoxidized m-Cl structure, compound 7.

In the halogenated series, p-substitution of bulkier bromo and iodo groups results in further enhancement of morphogenetic activity, as shown in Table 4.

Para substitution of methoxy (12) and thiomethyl (13) groups on the phenyl ring (Table 5) results in juvenoids which retain morphogenetic activity on T. molitor in the range shown by the previous compounds (Tables 3 and 4). Furthermore, compounds 12 and 13 significantly inhibit normal hatching of mosquito pupae in the range of 0.03 - 0.003 ppm. This order of activity is substantially higher than that shown by geranyl ester epoxides (Table 1).

The effect of p-alkyl substitution on activity is shown in Table 6. Relatively poor activity in the T. molitor assay is shown by compound 14 containing a bulky t-butyl group. This is somewhat unexpected, since moving from p-chloro (9) to p-Br (10), increases activity 2-fold; and moving from p-CH₃O (12) to p-CH₃S (13) substitution, we observe a 5-fold increase in morphogenetic activity on T. molitor. Reduction in branching and length of alkyl chain improves activity through the ethyl substituent (18) and then decreases with the methyl group. Compound 18 is exceptionally active in the T. molitor assay (9), and in inhibiting normal adult hatch of mosquito larvae (Table 6). Regression analysis for a series of para-substituted geranyl phenyl ethers supports the empirical findings that compound 18 shows the strongest morphogenetic activity (11).

It appears that a moderately sized substituent in the para-position is required for morphogenetic activity. It is also possible that the para-ethyl substituent renders the juvenoid more refractory to rapid metabolic degradation in susceptible insects, thus optimizing transport to the site of action. However, this hypothesis awaits experimental proof.

The structure activity relationship of size of the alkyl substituent vis-a-vis mosquito activity is similar to the pattern established for T. molitor. Peak activity is reached with para-ethyl (18) and decreases with the

TABLE 4

Morphogenetic Activity of Bromo-
Iodophenyl Geranyl Ethers on T. molitor

Code	Structure	ED_{50}[a] (µg/pupa)
10	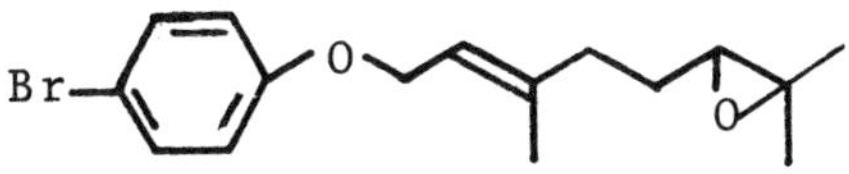 Br—⬡—O~~~epoxide	0.05
11	I—⬡—O~~~epoxide	0.05

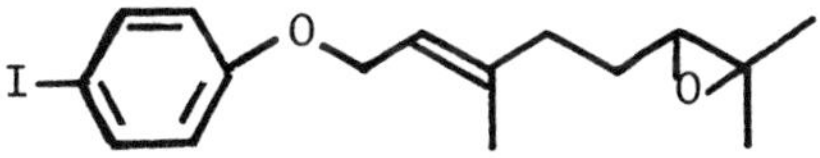

[a]Effective dose resulting in abnormal development
of 50% of treated pupae.

TABLE 5

Morphogenetic Activity of Alkoxy
and Thioalkyl Substituted Phenyl Geranyl Ethers

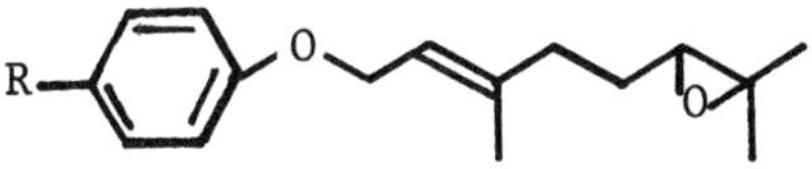

R—⬡—O~~~epoxide

		ED_{50}[a]	
Code	R	T. molitor µg/pupa	C. pipiens q. ppm/10 larvae
12	p-CH$_3$O–	0.1	0.003
13	p-CH$_3$S–	0.02	0.03

[a]Effective dose resulting in abnormal development
or failure to emerge of 50% of treated insects.

TABLE 6

Morphogenetic Activity
of Alkylphenyl Geranyl Ethers

Code	R	ED$_{50}$[a] T. molitor µg/pupa	ED$_{50}$[a] C. pipiens q. ppm/10 larvae
14	t-C$_4$H$_9$	0.2	0.002
15	sec-C$_4$H$_9$	0.1	0.001
16	n-C$_3$H$_7$	0.2	0.02
17	i-C$_3$H$_7$	0.01	0.0003
18	C$_2$H$_5$	0.0025	0.0001
19	CH$_3$	0.05	0.01
20	Cecropia Hormone[b]	3.0	0.2

[a]Effective dose resulting in abnormal development of 50% of treated insects.

[b]Methyl cis-10-epoxy-7-ethyl-3,11-dimethyl-trans, trans-2,6-tridecadienoate. Included for comparison. Kindly provided by W. S. Bowers, USDA, Beltsville, Md.

shorter methyl (19) substituent.

In our standardized assay on T. molitor pupae, the dl Cecropia J.H. (20) is 1000-fold less active than juvenoid 18. Conversely, Williams (12) found that compound 18 proved to be highly active in the Polyphemus pupal assay, being only about an order of magnitude less active than the synthetic dl Cecropia J.H. However, compound 18 was significantly less active topically per unit live weight of Oncopeltus and Pyrrhocoris newly molted fifth stage larvae. These graded responses to the juvenoid (18) indicate a considerable degree of selectivity, a property which could be usefully exploited in the field.

The importance of proper ring configuration with the p-ethyl compound (18) is shown in Table 7. Comparing compounds 21 and 22, we note a 50-fold increase in activity by moving the ethyl substituent from the meta to the para position. Even a more striking increase in activity is obtained with the corresponding epoxidized structures (23 and 18), where a 400-fold increase in activity is noted. Moving from the unepoxidized meta (21) to the epoxidized para compound (18), we observe a 2000-fold increase in activity.

The effect of geometric isomerism across the 2,3 double bond is shown in Table 8. We observe here that the trans isomer (18) is 12-fold more active than the cis form (24).

Thus, it appears that in the series of compounds discussed here, highest morphogenetic activity is realized with compound 18.

Compound 18 was further tested on a representative stored product pest, the confused flour beetle, Tribolium confusum du Val, to demonstrate the feasibility of pest population management in stored products by means of hormonal action. Twenty adult beetles were placed in glass bottles containing 100 g flour. The compound was thoroughly premixed with the flour in concentrations ranging from 0.01 to 1000 ppm. Untreated flour was used as a control. Results of these tests are reported in Table 9.

TABLE 7

Effect of Ring Configuration
on Activity of Ethyl Phenyl Geranyl Ether

Code	R	ED_{50}[a] $\underline{T. \text{ molitor}}$ ($\mu g/pupa$)		Ratio m/p
		n=0	n=1	
21	m-C_2H_5	5.0	–	
22	p-C_2H_5	0.1	–	50
23	m-C_2H_5	–	1.0	2000
18	p-C_2H_5	–	0.0025	400

[a]Effective dose resulting in abnormal development
of 50% of treated pupae.

TABLE 8

Effect of Geometric Isomerism
on Activity of p-Ethyl Phenyl Geranyl Ether Epoxide

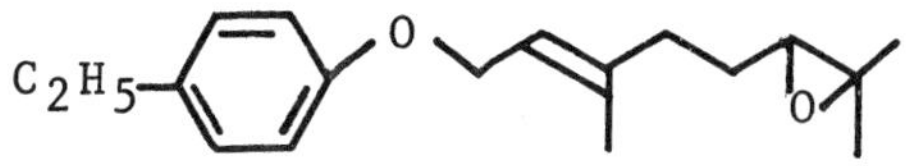

Code	Isomer	ED_{50}[a] T. molitor (μg/pupa)	Ratio cis/trans
24	cis	0.03	
18	trans	0.0025	12

[a]Effective dose resulting in abnormal development
of 50% of treated pupae.

313

TABLE 9

Effect of Compound 18 on <u>Tribolium confusum</u>
Populations Grown in Treated Flour[a]

Life Stages Present 120 Days After Treatment	Concentration in Flour (ppm)						
	0	.01	.1	1	10	100	1000
Adults: No. Alive	600	286	180	57	20	20	19
No. Dead	6	264	120	93	0[b]	0	1
Pupae	+++	+++	+++	+++	+++	+	0
Larvae	+++	+++	+++	+++	+++	+	+
Supernumerary Larvae	0	0	0	+	+++	+++	++
Adult-Pupal Intermediates	0	0	0	0	+	++	0

[a]From Pallos <u>et al</u>. Nature (1971).

[b]0 = none, + = few, ++ = moderate, +++ = many

TABLE 10

Acute Toxicity Evaluation of
a Geranyl Phenyl Ether (18).

Species and Sex	Application	Observation Period (Days)	LD_{50} (mg/kg)[a]
Rat ♀	Oral	30	>4640
Rabbit	Dermal	14	>4640
Mouse ♂	Oral	21	>3690
Mosquito fish	in Water	5	>10 ppm

[a]Unless otherwise indicated

Adult development of T. confusum was completely
arrested when exposed to flour treated at 10 ppm and
higher. Premature death of adults was observed even at the
lowest test concentration (0.01 ppm). Survival of the
original 20 adults at the highest test concentration (1000
ppm) eliminated the possibility of direct toxicity of the
compound to the test insects (9).

These preliminary results indicate the possible potential of controlling stored product insects with compounds
demonstrating J.H. activity. The foregoing data indicate
also that the ethyl compound exerts its morphogenetic
action by contact and/or ingestion.

Some of the compounds discussed here are currently
undergoing extensive testing in other laboratories. Preliminary data indicate that certain members of this series
markedly influence morphogenetic and gonadotropic development in a number of economically important insect species
including: mosquitoes, cotton boll weevil, Indian meal
moth, stable flies, aphids, alfalfa weevil, tobacco budworm, and others. When evaluated by standard testing
procedures, compound 18 proved to be essentially non-toxic
to rats, mice, rabbits and mosquito fish, Gambusia affinis
(Table 10). These results appear to be in accord with
those reported for the natural Cecropia J.H. (13).

The data reported here on a novel group of synthetic
geranyl phenyl ethers suggest that these juvenoids offer
challenging possibilities for new approaches to insect
population management.

Acknowledgments

We thank P. E. Letchworth, J. B. Miaullis and H. Lee
for biological testing, J. Chan for the cis isomer of
compound 18, K. Tseng for NMR work, and F. X. Kamienski for
mammalian toxicity data.

References

1. C. M. Williams, The Juvenile Hormone of Insects,
Nature 178, 212 (1956).

2. K. Slama, Insect Juvenile Hormone Analogs, <u>Annual Review</u> <u>of</u> <u>Biochemistry</u> <u>40</u>, 1079 (1971), E. E. Snell, Ed., Academic Press, New York, London.

3. J. B. Siddall, Chemical Aspects of Hormonal Interactions in "Chemical Ecology" (E. Sondheimer and J. B. Simeone, Eds.), p. 281, Academic Press, New York, London, (1970).

4. C. M. Williams, Hormonal Interactions Between Plants and Insects in "Chemical Ecology" (E. Sondheimer and J. B. Simeone, Eds.), p. 103, Academic Press, New York, London, (1970).

5. W. S. Bowers, Juvenile Hormones in "Naturally Occuring Insecticides" (M. Jacobson and D. G. Crosby, Eds.), p. 307, Marcel Dekker, Inc., New York, (1971).

6. YU. S. Tsizin and A. A. Drabkina, The Juvenile Hormone of Insects and Its Analogs, <u>Russ.</u> <u>Chem.</u> <u>Revs.</u> <u>39</u>, 496 (1970).

7. W. S. Bowers, Juvenile Hormone: Activity of Aromatic Terpenoid Ethers, <u>Science</u> <u>164</u>, 323 (1969).

8. H. Lee, J. J. Menn, and F. M. Pallos, Insecticidal 6,7-epoxy-geranyl β,β-di-methylacrylate. Ger. Offen. 2,023,791, <u>Chem.</u> <u>Absts.</u> 74, 316 (1971).

9. F. M. Pallos, J. J. Menn, P. E. Letchworth, J. B. Miaullis, Synthetic Mimics of Insect Juvenile Hormone, <u>Nature</u> <u>232</u>, 486 (1971). F. M. Pallos, H. Lee, and J. J. Menn, Insecticidal Phenylgeranyl-ethers and epoxides, Stauffer Chem. Co., Belgian Patent 734,904 (1969).

10. L. M. Riddiford, Prevention of Metamorphosis by Exposure of Insect Eggs to Juvenile Hormone Analogs, <u>Science</u> <u>167</u>, 287 (1970).

11. D. R. Baker, Personal Communications, Stauffer Chem. Co., Western Research Center, (1969).

12. C. M. Williams, Personal Communication, (1970).

13. J. B. Siddall and M. Slade, Absence of Acute Oral Toxicity of <u>Hyalophora</u> <u>cecropia</u> Juvenile Hormone in Mice, <u>Nature</u> <u>New</u> <u>Biology</u> <u>229</u>, 158 (1971).

CECROPIA JUVENILE HORMONE
HARBINGER OF A NEW AGE IN PEST CONTROL

Andre S. Meyer

Department of Biology, Case Western Reserve University Cleveland, Ohio 44106

Early Experiments

The existence of insect juvenile hormone (JH) was quite well established by the early forties. Sometimes while thinking about the hormone, I wonder how JH might have fared with a less captivating name than that given by Wigglesworth (*cf.* 1954); if, let us say, his Greek term "neotenin" might have prevailed...In any event, the JH field got a stimulating boost in 1956 by Williams' discovery of the Cecropia elixir. Were it not for his immediate and forceful advocacy of the insecticidal potentialities of JH fifteen years ago, the symposium might not have come to fruition at this time.

By 1961, in collaboration with our colleagues Profs. H. A. Schneiderman and L. I. Gilbert who were in charge of the onerous bioassay chores, we succeeded in securing our first greatly enriched (5×10^4) Cecropia JH preparation (Fig. 1). At that time no adequate physicochemical methods existed for monitoring the course of purification of the Cecropia oil, and we had to rely primarily on the results of bioassays. By this criterion the preparation appeared to be pure, since its *specific* activity had remained constant through three purification steps. We had, however, reason to be skeptical (concomitantly unexplained losses of recovered activity were experienced), and indeed mass spectral analysis indicated the presence of butyl phthalate and other solvent residues in the sample. Nonetheless the preparation's molecular ion (M^+) with the largest mass (m/e 294) was derived from a JH molecule, and it has since become evident that the preparation was approximately 15% pure.

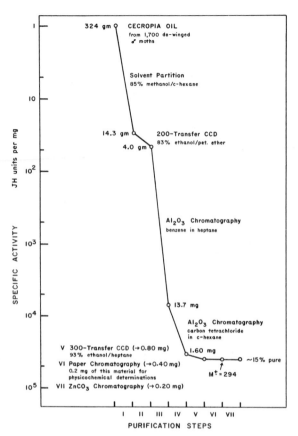

Fig. 1 Schematic representation of the purification sequence of the first batch of Cecropia oil. (One JH unit corresponds to the activity elicited by 3 ng of pure JH.)

In the same year, a series of experiments suggested that more than a single compound might contribute to the JH activity of the Cecropia extract. When samples of the crude oil or the above enriched preparation were subjected to 300-transfer countercurrent distributions (CCD) and the resulting bands comprising the hormone activity were assayed (Fig. 2), it was invariably noticed that the most polar segment of the band was significantly more active than expected. This finding could be interpreted by assuming the presence of a second, slightly more polar compound in these materials. Therefore we commented that "if the JH should not be a single compound, a possible active

318

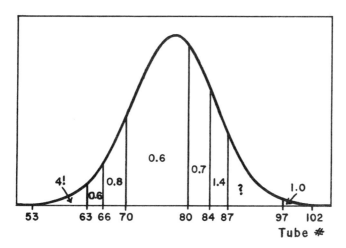

Fig. 2   Distribution curve of Cecropia oil. Washed
oil was processed in a 93% aqueous ethanol—heptane system
(300 transfers, ratio of volumes of upper to lower phase
1:2). Values in the segments of the curve represent the
bioactivities per 1% of theoretical solute content (calcd.
0.7 JH units).

companion substance would have very similar physicochemical
properties" (Meyer and Ax, 1965a).

Because our goal of a pure preparation apparently
eluded us the first time around, we proceeded to elaborate
a different purification sequence. In addition, to analyze
purified fractions, we availed ourselves of the then novel
gas—liquid chromatography (GLC) and, most opportunely, the
crucial ultrasensitive spectrometric techniques were being
improved from year to year. By the end of 1963 we had
obtained a second JH preparation (725 μg) that was six
times more active (3×10^5 JH units per mg) than the first
one; its purity was estimated by a GLC analysis to be at
least 90% (Meyer et al., 1965). The preparation was separated into two active components by micropreparative GLC.
Both compounds possessed specific activities of the same
order of magnitude as had the preparation. The predominant
Compound B was responsible for about 4/5 and the less abundant constituent, Compound E, for 1/5 of the endocrine

activity of the extract.   Unfortunately, external circumstances prevented us from performing spectrometric measurements of the preparation, and this essential task had to be
deferred.   A chronicle of these early experiments has been
presented at last year's International Symposium on JHs in
Basle (Meyer, 1971).

The Two Cecropia JHs

In 1967, Röller *et al.* reported in a short communication the structure of one Cecropia JH (I).   At that time,
we had again isolated the two active compounds, both in
pure form (Fig. 3) as judged by a specially designed (Meyer
and Knapp, 1970) ultrasensitive. GLC system.   We were subsequently able to demonstrate that (a) the main Compound B

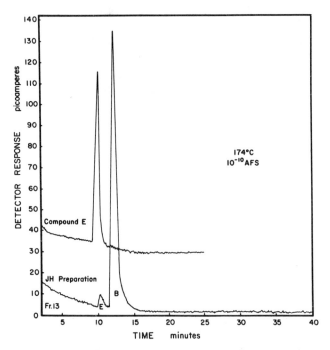

Fig. 3 Gas chromatograms of a fraction of the pure JH
preparation (72 ng) and of the isolated Compound E (44 ng).
Carbowax column (180 × 0.3 cm) was under a carrier flow of
60 ml of argon per minute.

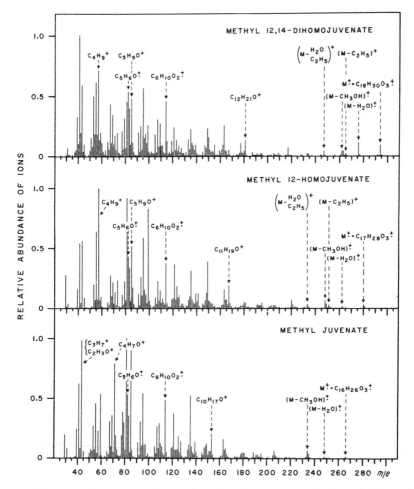

Fig. 4 Mass spectra of natural compounds I and II and of synthetic compound (±)-III (the latter two are low-resolution spectra). Elemental compositions were determined by high-resolution mass spectrometry and have been indicated in the diagrams for a number of selected ions; the abundance of these ions amounts to 75% or more of that represented by the particular bar.

All the mass spectral measurements mentioned in this paper were done at the Mass Spectrometry Facility for Biomedical Research at MIT through the courtesy of its director, Prof. K. Biemann.

321

was identical with the reported structure (I) and (b) Compound E (II) was a lower homolog of that structure, the ethyl branch at C-7 of the molecule being replaced by a methyl group (Meyer et al., 1968). The evidence has been described in detail (Meyer et al., 1970); here I can only summarily list the data.

The homology of the two hormone molecules was readily revealed by their mass spectra (Fig. 4). (The third spectrum in Fig. 4 is that of the next lower homolog, methyl 10,11-epoxy-trans,trans-farnesate (III), originally prepared by van Tamelen et al. in 1963 and shown to have morphogenetic activity by Bowers et al. in 1965.) The proton nuclear magnetic resonance (NMR) spectrum of Compound E with its characteristic resonance at δ 1.63 ppm (from the tetramethylsilane reference) clarified the position of the methylene group in question (Fig. 5). Moreover, the infrared spectra were in accord with the structural deductions (Fig. 6). Finally, the result of a hydrogenation experiment, in which the tetrahydro (IV, V) and hexahydro (VI) products were isolated, also corroborated the proposed structures. Stereoselective synthesis of (±)-II by Johnson et al. (1969) confirmed the structure of Compound E and made additional material available for testing. In Table 1 our final purification sequence for obtaining a pure JH preparation from Cecropia oil is recorded (Meyer et al., 1970).

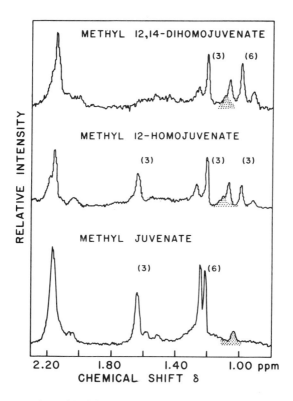

Fig. 5 High-field segments of proton NMR spectra of ∿50 µg each of natural compound I and II and of synthetic compound (±)-III in ∿30 µl of carbon tetrachloride. Values in parentheses are relative peak areas in round figures; stippled zones are due to solvent impurities.

To unambiguously distinguish the two Cecropia JHs, we proposed the juvenate nomenclature (see Glossary, Table 2). This notation seems to us preferable to the C_{18}—C_{17} terminology for the two JHs, because it is more versatile and, moreover, some of the investigators in this research area tend to disregard the common methyl ester grouping and have called the hormones C_{17}—C_{16} compounds. In this context it should once more be pointed out that the expression "analog" has a well-established structural connotation and should therefore not be applied to substances that can be

323

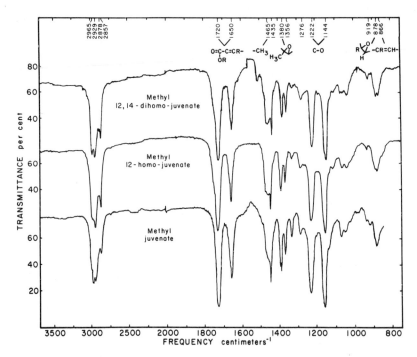

Fig. 6 High-resolution infrared spectra of ∿50 μg each of natural compounds I and II and of synthetic compound (±)-III in ∿3 μl of carbon tetrachloride.

compared only by their similar biological effects.

It is likely that the JHs of most Lepidoptera are structurally identical with those of the Cecropia silk moth. We arrived at this view some time ago, after lipoid extracts from five species belonging to four different lepidopteran families (*Hyalophora cecropia, Samia cynthia ricini, Prodenia eridania, Bombyx mori,* and *Galleria mellonella*) were compared by efficient alumina column chromatography (Meyer and Ax, 1965b). More recently, Dahm and Röller (1970) demonstrated by a GLC technique that *H. gloveri* produces the same two JHs as does the *H. cecropia* moth.

TABLE 1

Purification Sequence of Cecropia Oil (Fourth Batch)

Purification Steps	Active Fraction g	Estimated Bioactivity kilo-unit	Specific Bioactivity k-unit/g
Ether extract	9.93×10^2	1100	1.1×10^0
I. Molecular distillation	5.34×10^1	1000	1.9×10^1
II. Base washing	2.37×10^0	920	3.9×10^2
III. Alumina chromatography	8.20×10^{-2}	880	1.1×10^4
IV. Silica gel chromatography	5.10×10^{-3}	840	1.6×10^5
V. Alumina chromatography	2.50×10^{-3}	830	3.3×10^5

TABLE 2

Glossary of Terms in Usage for JHs and Other Morphogenetic Substances

Abstruse	Correct	Recommended
The JH or Cecropia JH	Cecropia C_{18}-JH or JH-1	Methyl 12,14-dihomojuvenate or Methyl 7',11'-dihomojuvenate (I)
Methyl JH or C_{16}-JH	Cecropia C_{17}-JH or JH-2	Methyl 12-homojuvenate or Methyl 11'-homojuvenate (II)
Synthetic JH	Methyl 10,11-epoxy-t,t-farnesate	Methyl juvenate (III)
Epoxy C_{17} ethyl ester		Ethyl 12,14-dihomojuvenate
Position isomer of Cecropia C_{17}-JH		Methyl 14-homojuvenate
t,t,t C_{17} methyl ester JH isomer		Methyl 12,14-dihomo-$trans$-10-juvenate
C_{17} methyl ester		Methyl 12,14-dihomo-$trans$,$trans$-cis-farnesate
Synthetic JH mixture	Law et $al.$'s (JH) mixture	Hydrochlorination product according to Law et $al.$
Analog (activity)	Bio-analog or Juvenoid	(Hormono)mimetic or Morphogenetic compound Analog (structure)

Biological Activity of Natural
versus Racemic Hormone

Many syntheses of the *racemic* hormones have been described in recent years. Originally (Dahm *et al.*, 1967) the biological activities of these substances were found to be equal to those of the natural hormones. This raised the question of whether the latter are racemic products instead of single enantiomers. In our *Galleria* assay the synthetic racemic substances, kindly provided by Prof. W. S. Johnson, showed in repeated testing a trend toward lower bioactivity (Meyer *et al.*, 1970); but it was not possible to distinguish their potencies with certainty from those of the natural hormones, because the assay did not perform at its best during that season. A fair comparison of homogeneous natural and racemic synthetic methyl 12-homojuvenate (II) is illustrated in Fig. 7. Two dosages of the natural hormone gave responses double those elicited by the synthetic ester, whereas the third point of the test series was low (*cf*. Meyer, 1971). A more rigorous distinction was achieved by Prof. V. B. Wigglesworth (private communication,

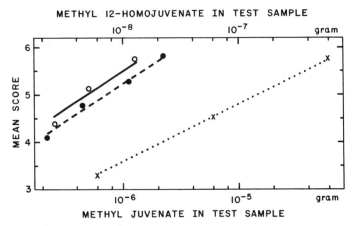

Fig. 7 *Galleria* wax test of homogeneous natural (o) and racemic synthetic (•) methyl 12-homojuvenate (II), as well as of synthetic methyl ($\pm$)-juvenate (III) (×); activities 3.1×10^5, 2.0×10^5, and $\sim 1.5 \times 10^2$ JH units per mg, respectively. About 1/125 of a test sample was applied onto the wound area of a single waxmoth pupa.

November 1970) in his topical *Rhodnius* assay (1969); the natural methyl 12,14-dihomojuvenate (I) proved to be about twice as potent as the synthetic racemic product (Table 3).

TABLE 3

Bioactivity of JHs in *Rhodnius* Assay by Wigglesworth

Methyl Ester	Estimated Dose	Source of Material
12,14-dihomojuvenate (cont. 9% of 12-homojuv.)	15 ng	Meyer *et al.*, 1968
(±)-12,14-dihomojuvenate	30 ng	Johnson *et al.*, 1968
(±)-12-homojuvenate	45 ng	Johnson *et al.*, 1969

JH was diluted in 10,000 parts of peanut oil, and the dose that elicited a score of 10 (*cf.* Wigglesworth, 1969) was determined.

A very recent report by Loew and Johnson (1971), who synthesized the *optically active form* of I in an enantiomeric purity of at least 90%, again suggests that only the natural enantiomer has substantial hormonal activity (tests reported for *Galleria* and *Tenebrio*).

For comparison purposes we have compiled in Table 4

TABLE 4

Relative Doses of Various Synthetic Compounds
in Topical Morphogenetic Assays

Methyl Juvenate		*Galleria*[a]	*Tenebrio*	*Rhodnius*[c]
12,14-dihomo	(±)-I	1	1[b]	1
12-homo	(±)-II	1	4[b]	1.5[†]
Parent compound	(±)-III	10^3	(20)	40[*]
Farnesyl methyl ether		10^5	(3×10^2)	4 (!)
Trans,trans-farnesol		10^6	(3×10^4)	400
Dodecyl methyl ether		10^5	(3×10^4)	$>10^3$

[a]Meyer *et al.*, 1965, 1970; Schneiderman *et al.*, 1965.
[b]Johnson, Krishnakumaran *et al.*, 1969.
[c]Wigglesworth, 1969; *ethyl ester. [†]*cf.* Table 3.
()From various reports, including Bowers *et al.*, 1965.

the relative doses of a number of synthetic substances in three commonly used test insects; as can be seen, the morphogenetic effectiveness of the compounds varies considerably from species to species. (Our biological studies have been recently reviewed; Meyer, 1971.)

Absolute Configuration

The first definite proof that the Cecropia JHs are *not* racemic was our demonstration of their optical activity. A fraction of our pure preparation (*cf.* Table 1) exhibited a plain positive dispersion curve (Fig. 8); $[M]_D^{28}$ ∿+20.5°.

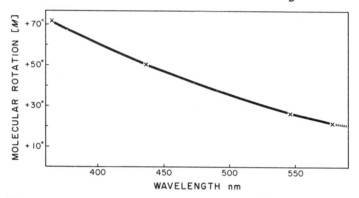

Fig. 8 Optical rotatory dispersion curve of a pure JH preparation (I:II = 9:1) in chloroform at 28°C (*c* 0.1214%; $[M]$ ±12°).

The molecular rotation allowed us to compute the absolute configurations (10*R*,11*S*) of the hormone molecules, but there was some question as to the reliability of the assignment (Meyer and Hanzmann, 1970). Hence we were anxious to substantiate it by a chemical route. The fact that the principal carbon chain of the structures is *cis* oriented at the oxirane, implies *R* configuration on one of the carbon atoms of the epoxide and *S* configuration on the other. The immediate task therefore was to determine the absolute configuration of one of these vicinal chiral centers. I am going to present this study, omitting any discussion of details (see Meyer *et al.*, 1971).

At first it seemed fairly remote that we would be able to deduce the desired stereochemical information from the limited amounts of isolated natural hormone; but a thorough review of Horeau's method strengthened our belief that this procedure, when drastically reduced in scale, might be practicable after all. Fortunately we had a modern photo-electric polarimeter at our disposal, on which optical rotations at select wavelengths could be reliably measured in the millidegree range. Horeau reported his method in 1961, and since then the configurations of numerous opti-cally active secondary alcohols have been successfully elu-cidated (cƒ. Balavoine, Horeau et al., 1970). Esterifica-tion of such a chiral hydroxyl group with an excess of racemic α-phenylbutyric anhydride takes an asymmetric course permitting the deduction of the correct configura-tion. For instance, an alcohol with R configuration reacts preferentially with the enantiomer of the anhydride that has R-(—) configuration, giving rise in the reaction mix-ture to an acid fraction with positive rotation that can be readily analyzed.

To take advantage of this diagnostic reaction, the hormone first had to be converted to its vic-diol by hydra-tion of the epoxide function. It is known that in aqueous acid unsymmetrically alkyl-substituted oxiranes usually undergo attack almost exclusively at the more substituted carbon atom. For the interpretation of our experiment with methyl 12,14-dihomojuvenate (I), it was essential to ascer-tain the course of the particular reaction. Thus the acid-catalyzed hydrolysis was conducted in oxygen-18 labeled water, making it possible to assess by mass spectrometry the entry of the molecule of water into the two chiral hydroxyl groups of the glycol product isolated by silica gel chromatography. It was found with a sample of syn-thetic (±)-I, kindly provided by Dr. J. B. Siddall, that hydration indeed proceeded as predicted and that at least 94% of the incorporated labeled oxygen atoms were present in the tertiary hydroxyl group of the diol (VII). Hence the bonding around C-10 of the hormone (I) remains largely unaltered on hydration. Accordingly, what can be learned about the configuration at this center by an apposite reac-tion of the glycol (VII), is equally valid for the struc-ture of the hormone. It is of little import, as far as such a reaction is concerned, that the 10,11-threo epimer of VII was not the sole product of the epoxide hydration and that as well nearly 30% of *erythro* epimer (*cis* opening!) were formed.

Some 0.8 mg of the glycol mixture (VII) were available for acylation with a large excess of α-phenylbutyric anhydride. The reaction took place with an efficiency of about 80%. The phenylbutyric acid recovered from the reaction mixture was dextrorotatory (Table 5). Consequently, the chiral center C-10 of VII has R configuration. The optical yield of the particular experiment amounted to 11%. Inasmuch as the stereochemical relationship between the hormone and its glycol VII had been established, we concluded that the structure of methyl 12,14-dihomojuvenate is methyl (E,E)-(10R,11S)-(+)-10,11-epoxy-7-ethyl-3,11-dimethyl-2,6-tridecadienoate (I). By analogy, methyl 12-homojuvenate,

the less abundant hormone, presumably has the corresponding 3,7,11-trimethyldienoate structure (II).

TABLE 5

Optical Rotatory Dispersion Measurement of
the Recovered α-Phenylbutyric Acid from
the 2.5-μmol Acylation Experiment

λ nm	$α^a$ milli- degree	$[M_{exp}]^b$ degree	$[M]^c$ degree	Observed Optical Yield^d %	Optical Yield, Actual^e %
365	+14	+47.0	+469	10.0	
436	+7	+23.5	+280	8.4	
546	+4	+13.4	+154	8.7	
578	+3.5	+11.8	+135	8.7	
sign: positive			mean:	9.0	11.2
			(S.E.)	±0.7	±1.2

[a]Observed rotation (± 3 millidegrees) of acid fraction of
reaction mixture diluted in methanol to 840 mm^3 and measured in a 1.000-dm tube at 29°C.
[b]Observed rotation expressed per 1 mol of reacting glycol
and dilution of acid fraction to 100 cm^3.
[c]Interpolated molecular rotation of pure enantiomeric
α-phenylbutyric acid in methanol (c 0.58 %) at 27°C.
[d]Quotient $[M_{exp}]/[M]$.
[e]Corrected for esterification efficiency of 80 ± 2%.

Very recently, Faulkner and Peterson (1971), starting
with a precursor of known absolute configuration ((S)-(+)-
2,2-dimethoxy-3-methyl-pentan-3-ol), synthesized the optically active form of I in a stereochemical purity of about
75% and an enantiomeric purity of maximally 85%. It was
gratifying to note that, on the basis of our published
rotation value, these authors arrived at the same configuration assignment as was deduced from our analytical study.
The same conclusion was apparently also drawn from as yet
unpublished circular dichroism measurements of the glycol
derivative from the synthetic hormone (I) of Loew and
Johnson (1971) mentioned earlier.

ANDRE S. MEYER

The Prospects for "Third-Generation"
Pest Control Agents

We can start by asking the question: Where do we
stand, now that all the details of the Cecropia JH structure have been ascertained? We are all familiar with the
divergent opinions concerning JH as an insecticide.
Because JH is a natural substance, some contend, the hormone can be expected to be inoffensive ecologically, and
insects should find it hard to evolve a resistance or
insensitivity to their own secretory product. Other peo-
ple, however, reason that the unspecific nature of JH could
cause more harm than good and, moreover, that prolongation
of the voracious larval state of a pest is not exactly a
desirable goal. These simplistic views all contain a ker-
nel of truth. Obviously, the use of JH *per se* can be con-
templated for only very restricted purposes, and then the
hormone likely will have to be applied in considerably
higher than biological concentrations. Insofar as a variety of structures exert JH-like activity, one wonders
whether the frequently postulated natural JHs of insects
other than Lepidoptera will all possess a juvenate structure. The JH mimics, which can be tailored for greater
specificity, are unnatural substances and thus may be subject to all the vagaries of the more conventional chemical
pesticides.
But such arguments and speculations pale, if we consider the great impact that the timely research in the JH
field has brought about. Morphogenetic screening procedures have become standard in many laboratories. The
search for various types of chemical insect control agents
is gaining in breadth and depth. It also has been recognized that their effective application will require a great
deal of perspicacity. The demonstration by Siddall and
Slade (1971) that the hormone is devoid of any acute toxicity in mice is reassuring, though admittedly the time when
laboratory tests can assure the safety of the hormone to
man and his environment is still some years off. Our
appreciation goes to those who have embarked on the
involved studies to provide us with this and other basic
information. The imino analog of ($\pm$)-I was found in the
Polyphemus moth to enhance the morphogenetic activity of
the epoxy hormone, probably by interfering with its

332

deactivation (Riddiford *et al.*, 1971). Many of the JH-like substances are epoxides and thus belong to the class of alkylating agents. Recent experiments with a strain of inbred mice have indicated that carcinogenic aliphatic epoxides may lose their fearful attribute by some slight alteration of their chemical structure (van Duuren *et al.*, 1967), which is an encouraging result.

Yet how little is known to date biochemically about insect development, including endocrinology, or the effects of morphogenetic agents upon the crucial regulatory events in the life of an insect. Here lies a fertile field for further research, and I believe that it is most opportune and very much in the realm of feasibility to go ahead with thorough investigations of the development and behavior of some of the most important pests for crop and man. Undeniably, this is demanding work, and quick and spectacular answers can hardly be expected. But once we find out more about the critical control processes that make our adversaries tick, the problem of contending with them sensibly should become easier. Furthermore, a better understanding of the biosynthesis of JH or of its mode of action should permit the rational design of metabolic inhibitors.

As in other fields of human endeavor, it is the powerful scientific technology that has brought to an end the *laissez-faire* era in pest control. From here on, pest control agents will be meticulously scrutinized for their potential hazards to the vulnerable biosphere of our planet and to all innocuous creatures that populate it. It will not always be easy to strike a judicious balance between tangible short-range benefits and possible long-range risks. More than ever the research scientist is called upon to help resolve this dichotomy of which we have become so acutely aware. Given the broad concept of "third-generation" pesticides, the researcher can draw upon the revolutionary advances made in biochemistry and molecular biology and is in a good position to extend them to the creation of new control agents that satisfy demands with respect to enhanced specificity, innoxious biodegradability and negligible toxicity for non-target organisms. For certain, up to now scarcely the surface of the many options has been scratched.

Looking beyond, no one can predict what place the various kinds of new chemical (or for that matter any other) control agents are going to hold in a future integrated control scheme, all the more as insects inevitably will adapt to some of the new tools and stratagems that human ingenuity is bound to devise. While this evolutionary contest promises to produce some fascinating drama, it does not seem probable that man will lightly forfeit his upper hand in this perennial struggle. Around the corner, however, loom other, more insidious ecological disasters, posing a host of entirely new and enormous problems with which, alas, mankind is psychologically and philosophically less attuned to cope. Therefore let us hope that in our long-established area we shall rise to the challenge in setting an enlightened example of how to stem and contain the perils that threaten our very survival.

References

Balavoine, G., A. Horeau, J-P. Jaquet, and H. Kagan, *Bull. Soc. Chim. France*, 1910 (1970).

Bowers, W. S., M. J. Thompson, and E. C. Uebel, *Life Sciences 4*, 2323 (1965).

Dahm, K. H., and H. Röller, *Life Sciences 9* [II], 1397 (1970).

Dahm, K. H., B. M. Trost, and H. Röller, *J. Amer. Chem. Soc. 89*, 5292 (1967).

Faulkner, D. J., and M. P. Petersen, *J. Amer. Chem. Soc. 93*, 3766 (1971).

Johnson, W. S., T.-t. Li, D. J. Faulkner, and S. F. Campbell, *J. Amer. Chem. Soc. 90*, 6225 (1968).

Johnson, W. F., S. F. Campbell, A. Krishnakumaran, and A. S. Meyer, *Proc. Nat. Acad. Sci. U.S.A. 62*, 1005 (1969).

Loew, P., and W. S. Johnson, *J. Amer. Chem. Soc. 93*, 3765 (1971).

Meyer, A. S., *Bull. Soc. Entomol. Suisse 44*, 37 (1971).

Meyer, A. S., and H. A. Ax, *Anal. Biochem. 11*, 290 (1965a).

Meyer, A. S., and H. A. Ax, *J. Insect Physiol. 11*, 695 (1965b).

Meyer, A. S., and E. Hanzmann, *Biochem. Biophys. Res. Comm. 41*, 891 (1970).

Meyer, A. S., and J. Z. Knapp, *Anal. Biochem. 33*, 429 (1970).

Meyer, A. S., H. A. Schneiderman, and L. I. Gilbert, *Nature 206*, 272 (1965).

Meyer, A. S., H. A. Schneiderman, E. Hanzmann, and
  J. H. Ko, *Proc. Nat. Acad. Sci. U.S.A.* **60**, 853 (1968).
Meyer, A. S., E. Hanzmann, H. A. Schneiderman,
  L. I. Gilbert, and M. Boyette, *Arch. Biochem. Biophys.*
  137, 190 (1970).
Meyer, A. S., E. Hanzmann, and R. Murphy, *Proc. Nat. Acad.*
  Sci. U.S.A. *68*, 2312 (1971).
Riddiford, L. M., A. M. Ajami, E. J. Corey, H. Yamamoto,
  and J. E. Anderson, *J. Amer. Chem. Soc.* *93*, 1815 (1971).
Röller, H., K. H. Dahm, C. C. Sweeley, and B. M. Trost,
  Angew. Chem. Int. Ed. Engl. *6*, 179 (1967).
Schneiderman, H. A., A. Krishnakumaran, V. G. Kulkarni, and
  L. Friedman, *J. Insect Physiol.* **11**, 1641 (1965).
Siddall, J. B., and M. Slade, *Nature New Biol.* **229**, 158
  (1971).
van Duuren, B. L., L. Langseth, B. M. Goldschmidt, and
  L. Orris, *J. Nat. Cancer Inst.* *39*, 1217 (1967).
van Tamelen, E. E., A. Storni, E. J. Hessler, and
  M. Schwartz, *J. Amer. Chem. Soc.* *85*, 3295 (1963).
Wigglesworth, V. B., *Physiology of Insect Metamorphosis*
  (Cambridge University Press, Cambridge, England, 1954)
  p. 56.
Wigglesworth, V. B., *J. Insect Physiol.* *15*, 73 (1969).
Williams, C. M., *Nature 178*, 212 (1956).

SUBJECT INDEX

A

Acarina, lack of response to insect juvenile hormone analogs, 89
Acetals, juvenile hormone activity, 278 (T), 279 (T), 280 (T), 281 (T)
Alfalfa weevil, field tests with juvenile hormone mimics, 129-131
Anoplura, effects of insect juvenile hormone analogs, 90
Anthonomus grandis, 122, 137
compounds with juvenile hormone activity against, 249ff.
bioassay, 252-253
Aphis gossypii, 122, 137
compounds with juvenile hormone activity against, 249ff.
bioassay, 253-254
Arthropods, effect of insect hormones on non-insect, 21-22
Aryl citronellyl carbamates, 249
Aryl terpenoid compounds, 249
juvenile hormone activity, 259 (T), 260 (T), 261 (T)
structure and, 263 (T)

B

Bioassay
of insect juvenile hormone analogs, assay of vapor effects, 83-84
food treatment, 83
injection tests, 81
objectives, 78-80
pupal wax test, 80-81
scoring, 84-86

graded, 84-85
quantal, 85-86
specific target organisms and effects, 86-90
spray applications, 84
substrate treatment, 82-83
systemic application, 83
technology, 80-84
topical application, 81-82
Bovicola bovis, 133, 137
compounds with juvenile hormone activity against, 249ff.
bioassay, 252
Bowers compounds, *see also* Juvenile hormone(s), synthetic mimics
activity in laboratory tests, 151 (T)
structure, 145 (T)
toxicity, 147 (T)

C

Cecropia juvenile hormone(s)
absolute configuration, 232-233, 328-331
activity, of geometrical isomers, 227 (T)
isolation and structure, 220-222
metabolism by insects, 155-174
by *Hyalophora cecropia*, 165-166, 170-174
by *Manduca sexta*, 158-165, 170-174
by mice 174-175
by *Sarcophaga bullata*, 167-169, 170-174
by *Schistocerca vaga*, 166-167, 170-174
number of, 320ff.

337